"Few authors understand what makes a true crime book stand out like a beacon from the mass of prosaically gruesome re-telling of police reports. Ron Franscell does! *The Darkest Night* explores the true story of this unholy sacrifice of youth and misplaced trust in a gripping, throat-tightening way. It is an almost-hypnotic read, hard to look away from. This is a very, very, good book—a gem for readers who look for the whole story, written by a good writer."

New York Times be
Stranger Beside Me and *Gre*

"In an elegant and powerful voice normally seen only in fiction, Ron Franscell captures the sights, sounds, and smells of this Wyoming saga and masterfully gets inside the emotional marrow of its participants. I highly recommend this engaging book."

—VINCENT BUGLIOSI
New York Times best-selling author of *Helter Skelter*

"Heartbreaking . . . the girls' last terrifying moments are delivered with such vivid texture that they are almost too painful to read. The technique and execution is not unlike Truman Capote's *In Cold Blood*. And just when your heart is broken by this terrible tragedy, Franscell adds a coda that will further disturb your peaceful sleep."

—*Chicago Sun-Times*

"A chilling account of one of this country's more brutal crimes."

—*San Antonio Express-News*

"A 'must' for any lending library strong in true crime exposés."

—*Midwest Book Review*

"Ron Franscell's breathless *The Darkest Night* [is] a true-crime tale that grabs readers on the first page and doesn't let go until long after the final word. . . . Thanks to Franscell's daily journalism experience, his polished, yet conversational writing style appeals to the Everyman . . . Franscell delivers a crackling story of lives and innocence lost."

—*Rocky Mountain News*

DELIVERED FROM EVIL

DELIVERED FROM
EVIL

TRUE STORIES OF ORDINARY PEOPLE WHO FACED MONSTROUS MASS KILLERS AND SURVIVED

RON FRANSCELL

Text © 2011 by Ron Franscell

First published in the USA in 2011 by
Fair Winds Press, a member of
Quayside Publishing Group
100 Cummings Center
Suite 406-L
Beverly, MA 01915-6101
www.fairwindspress.com

15 14 13 12 11   1 2 3 4 5

ISBN-13: 978-1-59233-440-7
ISBN-10: 1-59233-440-7

Library of Congress Cataloging-in-Publication Data
Franscell, Ron, 1957-
  Delivered from evil : true stories of ordinary people who faced monstrous mass killers and survived / Ron Franscell.
    p. cm.
  Includes bibliographical references and index.
  ISBN-13: 978-1-59233-440-7
  ISBN-10: 1-59233-440-7
  1. Mass murder—United States—Case studies. 2. Serial murders—United States—Case studies. 3. Victims of violent crimes—United States—Biography. I. Title.
  HV6529.F73 2011
  364.152'34092273—dc22

                                                                                10028368

Cover and book design: Peter Long
Book layout: Sheila Hart Design, Inc.
Cover image: © Bettmann/CORBIS. A women hides behind a statue from Charles Whitman's bullets.

Printed and bound in China

In memory of
Charles Cohen
(1937–2009)

He opened his heart to a stranger
and revealed why
these stories must be told

CONTENTS

INTRODUCTION

THE SHADOWLANDS BETWEEN

EMMA WOLF WAS ONLY EIGHT MONTHS OLD on April 22, 1920, when an angry neighbor murdered her father, mother, five sisters, and the chore boy on the family farm in Turtle Lake, North Dakota.

The berserk killer left little Emma in her crib, where she lay for two days until the slaughter was discovered.

Within days, the Wolfs' neighbors set to the bleak task of burying the family. Before the eight caskets were lowered side by side into the prairie earth on a windswept hill, the good people of Turtle Lake posed behind them for a grim photograph. One of the womenfolk held little Emma—and standing among the mourners was the killer.

Weeks later, the killer—a nearby farmer infuriated by the Wolfs' wandering dogs—was identified, and he quickly confessed. A jury sent him to prison for the rest of his life, which wasn't long; he died behind bars in 1925.

For the rest of her life, Emma was known by the locals simply as "the girl who lived." As a young woman, she worked in a local mercantile where strangers would sometimes come just to gawk at her. She was a living reminder to people of the horror they were trying not to talk about. Not because they wanted to forget, but because they didn't want anyone else to know.

Even now, more than ninety years later, the curious still drive past the old farmhouse or the cemetery and whisper about it.

Emma had already died when I found her son Curtis, a hospital chaplain who lives today in Turtle Lake and still owns the family farm where the horror happened. He says Emma grew up never trusting anyone, never feeling love. After the murders, she was put in the care of an aunt and uncle with their own big family. Later, she was adopted by a family of strangers in Bismarck, who forestalled her threats to run away by locking her in a closet. She was eventually returned to her aging and ailing aunt and uncle, who handed her off to a local store owner, who made her work in his mercantile business. She eventually married and had three children—and for the first time in her life felt love.

Emma died at age eighty-four in 2003, and she almost never spoke of her family's mass murder or her survival.

But the ethereal Emma's vapors encircle each of the ten survivors in this book. They are all connected, even if each is unique. They speak for Emma—and so many others—when they speak about forgiveness, persistence, and mourning. We might hear Emma's voice when they talk about the strange calculus of grief and hope. We get a glimpse into Emma's heart as these survivors try to articulate the role of God, luck, or fate in one deadly moment.

What they all understand about life, deep down in their wounded hearts, might just be the key to prevailing over not just the ghosts of killers, but all of life's great sorrows.

BABY EMMA WOLF, HER BLANKET MARKED WITH AN "X," IS HELD BY A NEIGHBOR AT THE FUNERAL OF HER FAMILY AND THEIR CHORE BOY, WHO WERE SLAUGHTERED BY AN ANGRY NEIGHBOR IN 1920 IN NORTH DAKOTA. STANDING AMONG THE UNSUSPECTING MOURNERS IS THE KILLER, HENRY LAYER, FAR LEFT, AN "X" ABOVE HIS HEAD. FOR THE REST OF HER LIFE, EMMA WOLF WAS KNOWN AS "THE GIRL WHO LIVED."
Courtesy of Thanatos Archives

We know plenty about mass murderers and serial killers, but we have not yet developed any science that can foil a murderous rampage that is hatched inside a maniac's head and leaves no trail until too late.

And that means we will continue to have victims and survivors, about whom we can predict even less. They are the rest of us.

Worse, most of us can't even name the victims who've gone before. Oh, we know the names and crimes of Charlie Starkweather, James Huberty, Dylan Klebold, Richard Speck, Charles Whitman, George Hennard, Charles Manson, and Nidal Malik Hasan. But who among us can identify Merle Collison, Lauren Townsend, Debra Ann Gray, Thomas Ashton, or Amy Krueger—just a few of the people they killed? Alive or dead, victims become mere cameo players in these real-life horror shows, a fact that only compounds the tragedy.

I spent more than a year with the survivors you will read about in these pages, and a few truths rise from the tumult of memories, documents, and interviews. For one, time erodes feeling and creates indifference. Society is condemned to be shocked, to grow complacent, then to forget . . . then to be shocked all over again.

Is it not fascinating that one of America's deadliest public rampages—a madman's 1927 school bombing in Bath, Michigan, that killed forty-five people, mostly children—is all but forgotten in the twenty-first century? That every generation since then has been stained by a mass murder that invariably is labeled as the deadliest (Howard Unruh in 1949, Charles Whitman in 1966, James Huberty in 1984, Seung-Hui Cho in 2007), even though none equals the horrifying death toll in Bath? It's either because our memories fail us or because every generation wants its own monsters.

Another truth is that forgiveness is more difficult than we can imagine. Most of these survivors understand that without forgiveness, they rot from the inside out—and the people they can't forgive don't care. These survivors don't excuse the behavior of monsters nor deny their own pain, but rather have revoked permission for their monsters or their feelings to darken the rest of their lives. They don't make nice with their would-be killers, but instead they move beyond them. It is more about unburdening than absolution.

All of these survivors feel some debt to the dead. They are aware that to squander this gifted life would be to betray what the victims lost. If the dead trust the living to preserve their memory, the living must trust the dead to help us know who we can be. They give us a past so we can have a future.

No magical formula exists for their inclusion in this book. Fortunately, true survivors of mass murders and serial killings are few. I sought people who were not mere witnesses to a monstrous crime, but who had been directly in the line of fire, so to speak. To harvest their perspective and wisdom, it was important that some time had passed, so the survivors' "second life" would at least be well begun, and the process of contemplating their interrupted lives had simmered.

So these ten stories explore the moments when the survivors and killers crossed paths, but they also examine how the survivor has coped with the trauma and its ripple effects over the years. Each story is as much about surviving life after such tragedies as it is about the tragedies themselves.

In short, these ten people all have embraced the gift of a second life that not everyone received on one tragic day. It is a treasure to them, misbegotten but secured by blood.

This book is about the capacity of the human spirit to triumph over monsters. Distilling it into words and putting it between the covers of a book seems somehow inadequate. I'm not sure these chapters can tell the complete story of what happened to these people, or what is happening still, or can explain what it feels to owe a debt to the dead.

Yet they are a beginning.

CHAPTER 1

THEY'RE ALL DEAD

CHARLES COHEN AND THE INSANE SPREE KILLER HOWARD UNRUH

THE PAST IS GONE ON RIVER ROAD, as if maybe it never happened. Today, where it passes through the Cramer Hill neighborhood, River Road is just another street in the bleak city of Camden, New Jersey. On one side of the narrow, uneven pavement, the old café was long ago boarded up, and nobody even bothers to paint over the gang graffiti anymore. The apartment house is now a shabby Chinese takeout place. Its rolling doors, like little garages, are padlocked shut, and it's no longer possible to see shadows through the windows. A bit of tattered crime scene tape flutters in the gutter outside what was once the American Stores grocery, now a market where Spanish-language signs in the window push disposable cell phones that can call Latin America, and promise to accept welfare vouchers.

Back then, this was an intimate little stage, a short block with only five buildings on one side and three one-story stores on the other—hardly the scene for the momentous tragedy that was played out here.

And now, sixty-plus years on, some of the most feeble buildings built before the First World War have been yanked out like rotten teeth, leaving seedy gaps. The haunted barbershop was one of those buildings. A few years ago, on the empty lot where it had sat, three kids accidentally locked themselves in the trunk of an abandoned car and suffocated. It was big news, but even the local paper failed to mention the horror that had happened on that same spot fifty-six years before. Memories are short.

Almost nobody here remembers what happened back in '49—certainly not the toothless junkie panhandling for his next fix on the corner at Thirty-Second. He doesn't give a shit that he is standing on the exact spot where a man died on an autumn morning. The fact that nobody remembers . . . well, it's as if he never existed at all. It's all just a figment of the fractured memory of Cramer Hill.

The gray, stuccoed hulk on the corner behind the junkie is the old drugstore. For a long time, you could still see the bullet pockmarks in the plaster walls, but no more. Now it's a cheap *zapatería*—a shoe shop—where the Latina clerk speaks only broken English. She rents the place, but the landlord has locked the doors leading to the second floor, hiding its secrets. Nobody is allowed up there.

Ah, but the clerk's son knows, even though he can't possibly remember. The kid, maybe a second grader, points to the bolted door and says one word: *fantasmas.*

Ghosts.

ON SEPTEMBER 6, 1949, TWELVE-YEAR-OLD CHARLES COHEN WAS EAGERLY AWAITING THE START OF JUNIOR HIGH SCHOOL, WHERE HE HOPED TO PLAY IN THE BAND. BUT THE MORNING BEFORE SCHOOL WAS TO START, HIS WORLD WAS SHATTERED.

Courtesy of the Cohen Family

"HE'S GOT A GUN!"

The last day of summer vacation dawned warm under a pallid sky, but no twelve-year-old boy could have been sunnier than Charles Cohen. His trumpet was polished, his trousers pressed, his shoes shined. Tomorrow, he would begin seventh grade at Camden's stately Veterans Memorial Middle School, and he could hardly wait. Next to his upcoming bar mitzvah, seventh grade felt to him like the next natural step to becoming a man.

Charles lived with his parents and grandmother in a three-bedroom apartment over his father's River Road drugstore. After breakfast, his father, Maurice, and mother, Rose, opened the shop, as always, at nine o'clock sharp, while Charles got ready for the twenty-minute bus ride to Philadelphia with his grandmother Minnie, who'd promised to buy him new school clothes for his first day, maybe a new suit for the High Holy Days.

Maurice Cohen, the son of Polish and Russian immigrants, was just forty. He had worked for a chain of drugstores after he graduated from Temple University's pharmacy school, but he dreamed of being his own boss. His father, a Russian immigrant who wasn't rich, invested in his son's dream in 1936 at the height of the Great Depression. Now, thirteen years later, Maurice

wasn't just a successful druggist, but an essential part of Cramer Hill. If anybody needed a prescription in the middle of the night, he knew "Doc" would roll out of bed and compound it for him.

Rose was his unofficial nurse. The couple had met right after pharmacy school in Philly and married after a whirlwind courtship. Also the daughter of Russian émigrés, she helped around the shop, handing over penny candy and scooping ice cream at the store's six-chair soda fountain. Now they'd been married twenty years, partners in every way.

This Tuesday morning, the day after the Labor Day holiday, was already bustling. Most Tuesdays, Maurice's widowed mother, Minnie, spent the morning with her sister Rose, but today she was taking Charles to the city. She watched the clock so they wouldn't miss the next bus across the Delaware River.

The Cohens had no car, but not because Maurice was old-fashioned. Oh, they had one of those newfangled television sets—Charles especially loved *Howdy Doody* and the *Kraft Television Theatre*—and the drugstore had pay phones that everybody in the neighborhood used because not everyone could afford a phone in 1949. Sure, the druggist had refused to put pinball machines or jukeboxes in the store, but only because he felt a drugstore was no place for gambling or wasting lunch money. No, it was just that Maurice, a kindly sort, feared he might hurt somebody in an automobile.

Besides, cars were always breaking down—a source of endless entertainment for kids on River Road. Invariably, some salesman's Ford would stall on the street, and he'd get out in a blue cloud of marvelous profanity, throw open the hood, and tinker in the greasy guts until it started again.

So that morning, when Charles heard backfires on the street, he ran to his grandmother's bedroom window overlooking the intersection of River Road and Thirty-Second, where the only stoplight for blocks usually confounded even the best drivers.

While Minnie made her bed, Charles pushed the screen out and looked down. Odd, he thought, there were no cars in the intersection.

All he saw was Junior, the odd fellow who lived next door, walking in front of the store. Since coming home from the war, Junior had lived with his mother and didn't work. He always walked around in a jacket, tie, and combat boots, carrying a Bible and blurting out gospel passages to anybody whom he passed, but people had stopped taking him seriously. Today, looking tidy as always in a light brown suit, white shirt, and a striped bow tie, he seemed to have more purpose in his step. His thin lips were tight, his face intent. And he wasn't carrying his Bible.

THE CHILDREN OF RUSSIAN AND POLISH ÉMIGRÉS, A YOUNG MAURICE AND ROSE COHEN EMBRACE IN THIS FAMILY PHOTO. THEY TOOK EVERY THURSDAY OFF FROM THEIR CRAMER HILL DRUGSTORE JUST TO SPEND TIME TOGETHER, OFTEN RELAXING AN HOUR AWAY IN ATLANTIC CITY WITH THEIR SON CHARLES AND DREAMING OF SOMEDAY RETIRING THERE. Courtesy of the Cohen Family

He had a gun.

As Charles watched, Junior walked right up to Mr. Hutton, his father's insurance man, who'd just emerged from the drugstore's front door. They spoke a few words that Charles couldn't hear, then Junior raised his lanky arm and fired his gun into Mr. Hutton. Then again . . . and again.

The insurance man crumpled on the sidewalk as Junior then calmly walked through the front door of the Cohens' drugstore.

"Junior's got a gun!" Charles yelled. He heard his mother scream.

Minnie was stunned until she heard Rose running up the stairs from the store.

"Hide, Charles, hide!" Rose screamed. "Mama, run away, run away!"

As Charles scampered to his little room at the back of the house, Rose shoved him in his closet.

"Don't make a sound!" she ordered him before she hid in her own closet down the hall. But he could still hear his grandmother frantically dialing the police on the phone next to her bed.

> **Howard Unruh didn't just hold grudges.**
> **For twenty-nine years, he nourished and**
> **cultivated them like black orchids.**

"He's got a gun!" she shrieked into the receiver. "He's got a gun!"

Charles covered his ears, but he heard a few rapid gunshots outside, then the sound of heavy footsteps coming up the stairs. His grandmother was still screaming into the phone, her fingers clattering the cradle as if the line were dead, trying desperately to connect to someone, anyone . . .

Then a shot. And silence.

Charles sucked in his breath and closed his eyes. He tried to make himself invisible in the dark at the back of his suffocating little closet as he heard the heavy footsteps coming down the hall.

Three more shots rang out, then after a few seconds, a fourth.

Before he could hear the footsteps fading away down the stairs, Charles fell into a terrified unconsciousness.

When he awoke minutes later, his whole world had changed.

AVENGING GRIEVANCES

Howard Unruh didn't just hold grudges. For twenty-nine years, he nourished and cultivated them like black orchids. He was a collector of wounds.

Since he had come home from the war, he'd heard his neighbors talking about him. Sometimes behind his back, sometimes to his face. At the bus stop. In the dinette. On the street. He was a mama's boy, they said. He was a queer, they said. He was a gangster because he carried a gun, they said. "See that guy?" they'd say when he walked past. "You can get him to stay all night with you."

The lying tailor told somebody that he saw Unruh going down on some guy in an alley. The shoemaker threw his trash in the Unruh yard. The barber dug his new cellar and purposely piled the dirt so that the rain flooded his poor mother's basement.

That kid who sold the Christmas trees—Sorg was his name—plugged his lights into an outlet in the basement and stole Unruh's electricity. Sure, he offered to pay for it, but he never came around with money. He was a thief.

And the druggist, Cohen, was the worst. Cohen and his whole family. They talked about Howard in their house. He could hear them through the walls. The Jew and his wife shortchanged people and kept the money. His son played that damn trumpet and the radio too loud and then made it louder if anybody complained. And Cohen's wife. She bawled out Unruh in public for leaving her damn gate open because stray dogs got in the yard they shared and scattered the trash around. She said she could see by his eyes he wasn't right. That's why he built the new gate in the back—so they couldn't embarrass him anymore by scolding him where everyone could hear.

They were wrong about him. All of them. Unruh didn't smoke, curse, drink, or run with loose women. He loved the sad, somber music of Brahms and Wagner—which they ridiculed, so he played it loud. He believed in God and loved his mother, and they hated him for it.

All of them. All of them were tearing him down, destroying his character, planning to gang up on him, to make him use his guns. They were building their shops too close, changing their money like the sinners they were . . . He could see them, all of them, as they walked past, and he knew that they were talking about him.

For more than two years, Unruh kept lists of his grievances and secretly plotted to kill his enemies. He made pages of notes, recording what they said about him:

C—   *See that guy? He's letting his mother support him.*
M—   *Hay fever. Hope it gets him good.*
M—   *Wish he would drop dead in his tracks.*
CH—   *Loud noises — loud horn blowing for our benefit.*
L—   *Retaliated.*
M—   *You dirty bum. I wish you were dead.*
L—   *Let's give him a lot of noise when his mother's asleep.*
CH—   *Wanted to create trouble for me.*

Then Unruh began to imagine how he would even the score. He bought a machete to decapitate the Cohens. He bought a fountain pen that dispensed tear gas to protect himself in case he was jumped. He started collecting guns, and he built a shooting gallery in his basement and made his own bullets so he could kill the others.

The brooding Unruh kept other lists, too. For three years in the war, as his unit rolled from Italy to Germany, he wrote down every Nazi he had killed, with details of where and how he'd done it.

And he kept a secret list of the men he met on his clandestine nocturnal trips to the city.

The broken gate was the final straw.

After supper on Labor Day, Unruh took the bus to Philadelphia. At about 7:30, he bought a forty-cent ticket to the Family Movie Theater on Market Street, an all-night grind house and popular gay hangout after the war. A double feature was playing: the low-budget murder mystery *I Cheated the Law* and *The Lady Gambles*, the latter starring Barbara Stanwyck in a lurid morality play about obsessive gambling.

But Unruh wasn't there for the movies. He didn't even know their titles. Whatever happened inside the dark theater, he sat through two showings of both films and left almost seven hours later, at 2:20 a.m., to catch a bus back to Camden. At 3 a.m., he got off the bus at Cramer Hill and walked to the alley behind his mother's apartment, where he could use the new gate and nobody would know he'd been out. But the gate was broken.

It enraged him. The gate was his independence, and they destroyed it to spite him. The time had come to settle his grievances once and for all.

RETRIBUTION

Unruh left a note on the kitchen table for his mother to wake him at eight and locked himself in his bedroom at the back of the apartment. He took the Luger and two spare clips from its wooden case. He laid out thirty-three bullets—plenty to do what needed to be done—and went to bed.

But Unruh couldn't sleep. He lay awake, their mocking faces flashing in his head, every insult catalogued, every indignity remembered. His fury wouldn't allow him to rest.

So he made another list: the ten people he must kill in the morning. Cohen . . . Cohen's wife . . . Cohen's mother . . . Pilarchik, the shoemaker . . . Hoover, the barber . . . Zegrino, the tailor . . . the tailor's son . . . the man in the apartment next to the tailor . . . Latela, the dinette owner . . . the kid named Sorg.

Then he chose the moment his retribution would begin. Nine-thirty. Their stores would all be open and he could walk right in. The money changers and rumormongers would die.

List made, plans laid, so finally, Howard Unruh could sleep.

His mother called him at 8 a.m. on the dot. He shaved, brushed his wavy hair, and dressed in his best suit. He ate a breakfast of Post Toasties, milk, sugar, and fried eggs, but his mind was elsewhere. When he finished, he went down to his basement target range and reached up into the rafters where he'd hidden a length of lead pipe. He'd planned to lure the kid Sorg down here someday and bludgeon him with it. Now he needed it for something else.

Back upstairs, he stood by the old console radio in the living room and called his mother from her ironing. First, she saw the empty look in his eyes. Then she saw the pipe in his hand.

"Howie!" she cried. "Howie, what's wrong?"

He said nothing. He didn't even seem to know her.

"You're frightening me!" she said.

Suddenly, Unruh raised the pipe over his head, ready to crush her skull with it. His mother cowered, whimpering.

"Why would you do that, Howard? Why?"

In the moment he hesitated, she backed away slowly, then ran out the back door toward a friend's apartment across the street. When the friend tried to calm her down, all she could say was, "Howard doesn't love me anymore."

Killing his mother had not been part of his plan, and Unruh didn't even know why it had crossed his mind. But he had no such doubt about what came next.

He shoved thirty-three bullets into his coat pocket and racked the first cartridge into the Luger's chamber. The day of reckoning, a warm and slightly overcast Tuesday, was about to begin.

Howard Unruh shoved thirty-three bullets into his coat pocket and racked the first cartridge into the Luger's chamber. The day of reckoning, a warm and slightly overcast Tuesday, was about to begin.

The shoemaker was first. Twenty-seven-year-old John Pilarchik, who had served four years as an Army medic in the Pacific without a scratch, was working behind his counter and didn't even look up until Unruh was standing in front of him. Without saying a word, Unruh aimed the gun at Pilarchik and pulled the trigger. The gut-shot cobbler looked stunned as he staggered back and fell to the floor. Unruh stood over him and shot him once in the head just to be sure.

Then Unruh went next door to the barbershop, where six-year-old Orris Smith was sitting on an ornate carousel horse, having his hair cut by barber Clark Hoover for his first day in first grade. When Hoover saw Unruh come in the door with a gun, he dodged around the hobbyhorse, but Unruh shot the

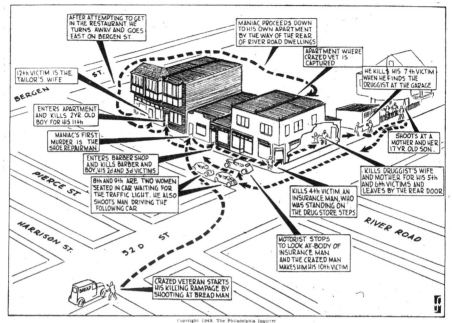

Inside the diagram:

AFTER ATTEMPTING TO GET IN THE RESTAURANT. HE TURNS AWAY AND GOES EAST ON BERGEN ST.

MANIAC PROCEEDS DOWN TO HIS OWN APARTMENT BY THE WAY OF THE REAR OF RIVER ROAD DWELLINGS

APARTMENT WHERE CRAZED VET IS CAPTURED

HE KILLS HIS 7th VICTIM WHEN HE FINDS THE DRUGGIST AT THE GARAGE

12th VICTIM IS THE TAILOR'S WIFE

BERGEN ST.

ENTERS APARTMENT AND KILLS 2YR. OLD BOY FOR HIS 11th

MANIAC'S FIRST MURDER IS THE SHOE REPAIRMAN

ENTERS BARBER SHOP AND KILLS BARBER AND BOY, HIS 2d AND 3d VICTIMS

8th AND 9th ARE TWO WOMEN SEATED IN CAR WAITING FOR THE TRAFFIC LIGHT. HE ALSO SHOOTS MAN DRIVING THE FOLLOWING CAR

PIERCE ST.

HARRISON ST.

32 D ST.

SHOOTS AT A MOTHER AND HER 17 YR. OLD SON.

KILLS DRUGGIST'S WIFE AND MOTHER FOR HIS 5th AND 6th VICTIMS AND LEAVES BY THE REAR DOOR

KILLS 4th VICTIM, AN INSURANCE MAN, WHO WAS STANDING ON THE DRUG STORE STEPS

RIVER ROAD

MOTORIST STOPS TO LOOK AT BODY OF INSURANCE MAN AND THE CRAZED MAN MAKES HIM HIS 10th VICTIM

CRAZED VETERAN STARTS HIS KILLING RAMPAGE BY SHOOTING AT BREAD MAN

BREAD

Copyright 1949. The Philadelphia Inquirer

DIAGRAM OF ROUTE USED BY MANIAC KILLER IN HIS DEATH-DEALING RAMPAGE

little boy in the head while his mother watched in horror, then chased down the barber and killed him, too, with one shot behind the ear.

From there, he went to the drugstore, where the insurance man, James Hutton, forty-five, was just coming out.

"Excuse me, sir," Unruh said, seeming not to recognize the man from whom he himself had bought a policy.

Hutton was dumbfounded, frozen in his tracks.

If Hutton couldn't choose whether to live or die, Unruh would decide for him. He shot him point-blank in the heart. Indecision killed the insurance man. Later, Unruh would tell police, "That man didn't act fast enough. He didn't get out of my way."

The shot that killed Hutton startled Maurice and Rose Cohen, who bolted from their shop floor. Maurice sprinted out the back while Rose ran upstairs screaming at Charles to hide—and Unruh followed.

Maurice was shot in the back as he fled and died in the gutter near his own garage. In the Cohens' second-floor apartment, Unruh heard Rose whimpering in her bedroom closet and fired three shots through the door, wounding her. He then opened the door and fired a single shot into her head.

Hearing Minnie trying to call police, Unruh went into her room and shot her in the face. She fell across her bed, the phone receiver still in her hand.

Skipping Charles's bedroom, Unruh went back downstairs and paused to reload one of his clips, intent on raising his body count out on the street, where he strolled mechanically, looking for victims.

He killed a passing motorist, twenty-four-year-old TV repairman Alvin Day, who had slowed down to watch Unruh as he walked toward the tailor's shop. Unruh casually stepped in front of the car and shot Day through the windshield.

In his deadly hunt for the tailor, Tom Zegrino, Unruh spied the curtains moving in the window of a ground-floor apartment next door. He fired through the glass, killing a two-year-old boy who'd been trying to see the commotion outside.

Nobody was in the tailor shop except the tailor's new wife, Helga. They'd been married only one month, and she was working in the back. She screamed, "Oh no, no!" when she saw Unruh with a gun. He shot her.

For reasons he couldn't explain later, Unruh went back to the American Stores grocery, the little market across from the drugstore. He bore no grudges against the grocer but remembered he'd once quarreled with a clerk over his change. However, word of his rampage had already swept like wildfire through the street, and six people had locked themselves safely inside. So a frustrated Unruh turned to see two women and a child in a coupe at the stoplight on River Road. He walked up and shot them all.

In twelve minutes, Howard Unruh had fired thirty-three shots. Thirteen people were dead or dying, and three were wounded.

Leaving them all to die, he walked boldly down the middle of the street, popping gunfire at anybody or anything that moved. He fired several shots at some young men standing near the tap house and at the driver of a parked bread truck. Cramer Hill was mayhem. Up and down the street, people were screaming and shouting, "Crazy man!" One shopkeeper even shot back.

On his final stop, Unruh broke into a home behind his apartment, beyond his broken gate, and wounded a mother and her teenage son. He would have killed them—and many more, he told police later—but he ran out of bullets.

In twelve minutes, Howard Unruh had fired thirty-three shots. Thirteen people were dead or dying, and three were wounded. Three of the dead were children.

"WHY ARE YOU KILLING PEOPLE?"

He was done, and he was pleased. He returned to his mother's apartment, walked upstairs to his room, and laid the Luger on his writing desk. He crawled into his rumpled bed and pulled the sheet over his face.

He wanted to sleep but couldn't. A commotion arose in the backyard. Somebody was yelling. Unruh got out of his bed and looked out the window. Armed cops were everywhere, standing on the Cohens' garage, hunkering behind the hedges, dashing around like blue cockroaches when the light is switched on. Some fired their pistols and tommy guns up at the building, while others trampled his mother's morning glories and asters. And they were all hollering at Unruh.

He backed into the hallway, away from the window. His plan didn't provide for this. He wasn't sure what to do.

Then the phone rang. Unruh picked it up.

"This Howard?" a man on the other end asked.

"Yes, this is Howard," he answered. "What's the last name of the party you want?"

"Unruh."

"Who are you? What do you want?"

"I'm a friend," the voice said. In fact, it was Phil Buxton, assistant city editor of the *Camden Evening Courier*. After the first police calls came in, he'd looked up Unruh's number—Camden 4-2490W—in the phone book. He was astounded when Unruh actually answered, and even more astounded that he could hear gunfire in the background.

"I want to know what they're doing to you down there," Buxton asked.

Unruh thought a moment and replied calmly.

"They haven't done anything to me—yet. I'm doing plenty to them."

Buxton asked how many people Unruh had killed.

"I don't know. I haven't counted 'em, but it looks like a pretty good score."

"Why are you killing people?"

"I don't know," Unruh said, his voice flat. "I can't answer that yet. I'm too busy now."

The dogged Buxton didn't want to lose the connection.

"Howard! Howard! Listen to me," he pleaded. "I want to talk to you."

"I'll have to talk to you later," Unruh said as he hung up. "A couple of friends are coming to get me."

At that moment, glass shattered. Police lobbed a tear-gas canister through Unruh's bedroom window, but it was a dud. Soon, another canister came in, and the room filled with acrid smoke as the cops fired their guns at the broken window.

Unruh thought about shooting back, but he had no quarrel with the cops. He wasn't mad at them. All he could do was shout to them above the din that he wanted to give up, explain it all to them, and get whatever was coming to him.

Then the shooting stopped.

"Unruh, you comin' out?" a sergeant yelled from the yard.

The torn white curtains at the shattered window rustled and the long-limbed Unruh appeared to the police below.

"Okay," he shouted. "I give up. I'm coming down."

"Where's that gun?" the cop hollered.

"It's on my desk, up here in the room," Unruh told him. "I'm coming down."

Within seconds, a coughing Unruh appeared at the back door, his hands held high. While cops patted him down and cuffed him, angry onlookers cried out. "Lynch him!" they said. "Hang him now!"

But Unruh remained impassive. He surrendered as serenely as he had killed.

"What's the matter with you?" one of the angry cops asked him. "You a psycho?"

Unruh looked at the cop, his burned, dark eyes empty.

"I'm no psycho," he said. "I have a good mind."

Amid the chaos of the siege, a little boy's voice sounded out.

"Help us!" he cried from a second-floor window in the building next to Unruh's apartment. "He's killing everybody!"

Even as cops prepared to smoke out the killer barely twenty feet away, the child crawled out onto a first-floor roof.

It was Charles Cohen.

He'd emerged from his closet to find his mother's bloody body on the floor, and his father's corpse lay in the street just below him. A cop rushed up to the Cohens' living quarters to pull Charles to safety, as Unruh hid in the apartment next door.

The cop scooped Charles up and took him to a waiting police car.

"You watch," he said. "I'm going to be a hero, kid."

From that moment, Charles Cohen never spoke about the tragedy on Cramer Hill again that morning. He wanted to forget. He wanted the world to forget.

But there came two moments when he could remain silent no longer.

The first time was when he told his new bride, on their wedding night, the dark secret he carried.

And the next time was when the world—which hadn't forgotten, but hadn't exactly remembered, either—appeared ready to forgive Howard Unruh.

COMING UNDONE

Even before all the bodies had been counted and collected, Howard Barton Unruh sat expressionless in a Camden detective's office.

Less than ninety minutes before, he was murdering his neighbors in a brief but methodical "walk of death," as the newspapers and radio broadcasts would soon call it. Now, here sat a tall, lean, detached young man in a white shirt and bow tie, his hands in his lap as if he were in church. He was cooperative and polite to the officers, even thanked them for doing their job. His pale face betrayed neither worry nor remorse. Behind his wire-rimmed glasses, he looked almost too fragile to be a mass murderer.

But he was a murderer, and he confessed it readily.

"I deserve everything I get," he told them, "so I will tell you everything I did and tell you the truth."

For more than two hours, detectives pieced together the puzzle of Howard Unruh, a man who'd never gotten a jaywalking ticket, much less shown homicidal tendencies.

Under questioning by District Attorney Mitchell Cohen (no relation to the druggist), Unruh described in scrupulous detail how he hated his neighbors, how they'd plotted against him, and how he'd been planning to kill them all for more than two years. He meticulously recounted how he gathered his ammunition, laid out his gun, left a note to be awakened at 8 o'clock sharp, ate his cereal and eggs, and then killed as many people as he could.

He unemotionally described the murders, one after the other. He narrated each death as if it were no more hideous than finding a dead sparrow on the sidewalk. He'd spilled more blood than any single killer in living memory, but to hear him tell the story, it was no more dramatic than a morning walk in the park.

None of it made any sense.

Howard Barton Unruh was born January 20, 1921, in Haddonfield, a Camden suburb. A younger brother was born four years later.

But their parents separated when Howard was ten. The boys went with their mother to Camden, where she worked for a soap factory, while their father lived and worked on a dredge in the Delaware River.

Howard grew up solitary, preferring always to be alone. He played with his train sets, read voraciously, and collected stamps. He never brought friends home, and he seldom made trouble.

> **Unruh's pale face betrayed neither worry nor remorse. Behind his wire-rimmed glasses, he looked almost too fragile to be a mass murderer.**

In school, Unruh appeared to be studious, but he was an average student. He never had a girlfriend, never went to a dance, and avoided most social activities. Except church. He took to carrying a Bible with him everywhere, faithfully attending Sunday services and Monday Bible classes at St. Paul's Lutheran Church.

After graduating from Woodrow Wilson High School in 1939, he worked as a pressroom helper at a publishing company, then briefly as a sheet-metal worker at the Philadelphia Navy Yard until he enlisted in the Army in 1942.

Unruh was stationed stateside until his self-propelled field artillery unit landed in Naples, Italy, in 1944. He served as a tank gunner in battles across Italy, France, Belgium, Austria, and Germany, winning two battle stars and sharpshooter ribbons, and taking meticulous notes about the Germans he killed along the way.

Every day, he wrote to his mother. Sometimes, his letters posed deep theological questions that troubled him; other times, they discussed military matters as if his mother had technical expertise.

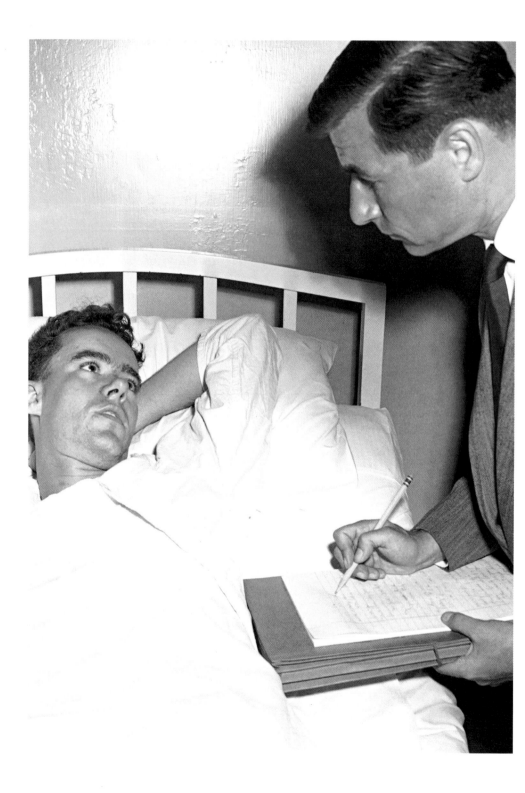

In November 1945, he was honorably discharged and came home to his mother's flat in Camden. His family noticed a distinct difference in him, as if he had retreated into a shell. He rarely spoke about the war. He threw out his stamp collection and started to collect guns. He built a target range in his basement, stacking newspapers against the far wall to absorb the bullets he often reloaded himself. Neighbors often heard the *pop-pop-pop* of his cellar gunfire, but they thought young Unruh must have been hammering on a carpentry project.

His church fixed him up with a young woman and subtly encouraged them to marry. But after a while, Unruh broke it off, promising the girl it would be "a mistake" to marry him.

One day in 1947, Unruh spotted a German Luger in a shop window. When he inquired, the clerk told him he needed a permit from the Camden police before he could buy it. Dutifully, he got the permit a few days later and paid $37.50 for the gun—the same gun he used to kill his neighbors two years later.

Unruh took a few odd jobs after the war, but he never worked for very long. Hoping to study pharmacy at Temple University, Unruh used the GI Bill to pay for some college prep classes and even enrolled at Temple, where his nemesis and later victim Maurice Cohen had graduated, but he quit after three months. He sold some of his train sets for pocket money and never worked again.

Nothing about Howard Unruh's first twenty-eight years screamed bloody murder. Sure, he was a little eccentric. Maybe a loner. Maybe a loony. But a cold-blooded killer? What made Howard Unruh come undone?

JUSTIFYING MURDER

While Unruh was being interrogated, detectives scoured his mother's apartment for clues to his state of mind. They found more than they could have imagined.

They found his basement shooting gallery and bullet-making equipment easily enough. They also found his cache of war souvenirs, from bayonets and pistols to ashtrays made from artillery shells. They found the machete he planned to use to cut off the Cohens' heads.

There were many books—some about gun collecting, others about sexual science.

In his bedroom, detectives discovered the notebook containing sketchy details of his dalliances.

CAMDEN COUNTY DISTRICT ATTORNEY MITCHELL COHEN, RIGHT, INTERROGATED CONFESSED GUNMAN HOWARD UNRUH FOR TWO HOURS AFTER THE SHOOTING UNTIL HE REALIZED UNRUH HAD BEEN SLIGHTLY WOUNDED IN THE BUTTOCKS. AFTER UNRUH WAS TREATED AT A LOCAL HOSPITAL, COHEN CONTINUED HIS QUESTIONING AT UNRUH'S BEDSIDE. Associated Press

Some of the men were listed only by first names, some simply as "a man." Some names were followed by the words "a car." Beside each name was a date, and sometimes there were several names on the same date. He'd make such notations every night for weeks at a time.

And beside Unruh's bed, they found his Bible, lying open to chapter twenty-four of St. Matthew, the chapter in which Christ predicts the destruction of the temple and all the catastrophes to come. "The lord of that servant shall come in a day when he looketh not for him, and in an hour that he is not aware of," it said. "And shall cut him asunder, and appoint him his portion with the hypocrites: there shall be weeping and gnashing of teeth."

The interrogation of Howard Unruh might have continued longer if DA Cohen hadn't seen blood puddling under Unruh's chair. When they examined him, they found he'd been shot in the buttocks with a small-caliber bullet. He was rushed to the hospital, the same hospital where his victims had been taken, but doctors determined that removing the small bullet would do more damage than the bullet itself had done. For the rest of his life, he carried the slug in his butt.

Within sixteen hours of his arrest, Unruh was taken to the New Jersey State Hospital at Trenton to be further evaluated. Through weeks of interviews, psychiatrists noted that Unruh "rarely spoke spontaneously" and was "at all times entirely free from anxiety or guilt." He spoke in a monotone "with a marked degree of emotional flattening." He never showed any emotion, even when the most delicate subjects were discussed—until asked about his attack on his mother, when he appeared to be guilty and fearful.

Some findings were surprising, if not lurid. Unruh had an unnaturally close relationship with his mother, though there was no evidence that it was sexual. He'd made sexual advances toward his brother as a youngster, but they were rebuffed. He started having sex with men during the service and continued after the war, and he struggled mightily with guilt over his behavior.

More to the point of his killings, there was little evidence that the insults Unruh imagined had ever really happened or, if they did, were as meaningful as he made them out to be. Maybe his neighbors *were* talking about him, but psychiatrists believed many of the insults Unruh "heard" were in his imagination. Either way, he was unable to laugh off a practical joke or a friendly jab and walk away; his paranoia simply wouldn't let him.

And although his family disagreed, several psychiatrists found no link between Unruh's war experiences and his ultimate unraveling. Unruh wasn't psychologically right before the war, they said, and while combat certainly didn't help, his slow decay was set in motion long before he ever fired a shot in anger.

A month after the shootings, the hospital's staff declared Unruh to be suffering from a case of paranoid and catatonic schizophrenia that was slowly getting worse. In short, Howard Barton Unruh was insane, even if he understood his actions were wrong, and he would only get worse as time passed.

"He knew what he was doing," the psychiatrists concluded, "but seemed to be operating from an automatic compulsion to continue shooting and killing until his ammunition was exhausted. . . .

"His narcissism is such that at all times he has felt justified in the killings of the particular people whose murders he plotted from the beginning. [He] has always acknowledged that it was wrongful and has usually stated that he should die in the electric chair. He has shown himself totally unable to identify emotionally with the victims of his crime or to sense in any way the reactions directed against him by the survivors."

Howard Unruh would never stand trial on thirteen counts of murder. He would never face the electric chair. He wouldn't even face his accusers in a court of law.

Instead, DA Cohen announced that Unruh would be committed to the New Jersey State Hospital at Trenton where "he and the community will be protected from injury or danger should there be a recurrence of his homicidal impulses."

For some, that wasn't enough. A judge ordered Howard's estranged father, Samuel, to pay the state of New Jersey $15 a month for his son's care at the asylum.

And just in case Howard Unruh should ever be "cured," the indictments against him would stand for decades.

A SUITCASE OF MEMORIES

While the world fascinated itself with the enigmatic and diseased mind of Howard Unruh, it overlooked young Charles Cohen.

Death had rubbed a callus on the heart of postwar America. A million Americans were killed or wounded in the war. Everyone else was simply lucky.

Thus it was with Charles. He'd lost his entire family to a madman's fury, but because he suffered no physical wounds, he was "lucky." So the wise men of science gathered 'round the maniac and sent the lucky little boy home.

Suddenly an orphan, he was briefly taken by the police to the station, where he was told to wait for a relative to claim him. While Charles sat there in shock, cops brought Unruh in for booking, and their eyes met for an incalculable moment. Then the killer was gone.

At that moment, Charles had not considered the awful truth. He'd seen his mother lying in a pool of blood, but believed his father and grandmother were still alive. It was an aunt who finally told him bluntly, "They're all dead."

The pain was sudden and incalculable. Charles had loved his parents deeply, and they had loved him. They took him everywhere. With them, he felt like a little man, trusted to run errands into Philadelphia even before he was ten. They placed their faith in him, and he felt it.

But the morning after his parents and grandmother were slain, Charles awoke in a strange bed in a strange new world. He'd left with only an old brown suitcase of clothes and a few other possessions. He pushed the sudden loneliness, bewilderment, and, in time, the anger deeper, where nobody would see. He didn't want to disappoint all the people who marveled at his luck.

The three caskets of Maurice, Rose, and Minnie Cohen were buried side by side at Philadelphia's Roosevelt Memorial Park a few days after the killings. Charles was there to watch them be lowered into the ground. He didn't remember too much about that day, but he promised himself that when he stopped crying, he would live the life they expected for him. He would grow up the best he could, marry, work hard, and have children of his own.

Having relatives to care for him, Charles lived with several aunts and uncles after the shootings. But they were building their own families, and he always felt like an outsider, always extra. Their homes weren't his home, and he began to feel as though they weren't even his family. He was a child of the dead.

In the blue-collar world of the fifties, only crazies sought mental help. Therapy was electroshock and lobotomies. A sudden death in the family, even three, certainly didn't prompt anyone to suggest counseling, especially for a Jewish orphan kid who was, after all, lucky to be alive. Sad wasn't the same as crazy.

In the luckiest stroke of all, Charles and his older brother—in the military at the time of the tragedy—shared the money from the sale of their parents' drugstore, enabling Charles to pay the rent that some of his relatives took from him and, when the time came, to pay for his own bar mitzvah, too.

Some of the money paid his tuition at a private military academy where nobody knew just how lucky Charles was. For the first time since the shootings, he felt as if he had a family. He was happy there until his classmates began to whisper about who Charles really was, so he left.

The suitcase that once contained the remnants of his life was now filling with odd clippings, photographs, and mementos of that day. Initially, *Life* magazine and others had come around to do stories, but as time passed, Howard Unruh was forgotten, except as a macabre measuring-stick. "Starkweather Three Short of Worst Killing Spree" said one 1958 headline. "Mass Murder of Chicago Nurses Recalls Unruh" said another in 1966. And finally in that same deadly summer "Texas Tower Sniper Kills Fourteen in Worst Shooting Ever."

Days went into days, and Charles kept pushing the memories deeper inside himself. A word, a sound, even the slant of the light could trigger a flashback in which he relived the whole sickening episode. He smiled when people told him how well he was doing, but inside, he knew he was barely holding it together. In time, those people just believed he had overcome his loss. Lucky for him, they didn't know.

Days went into days, and Charles kept pushing the memories deeper inside himself. A word, a sound, even the slant of the light could trigger a flashback in which he relived the whole sickening episode.

He hadn't conquered his pain. It still lived inside Charles like some black creature he kept locked up in the darkest recesses of his mind. Outwardly, he grew to be jovial, even silly at times. He had a knack for making people laugh. But despite the superficial light, black things writhed in him, seldom on display but always a shadow behind his dark eyes.

EVERY YEAR SINCE 1981,
THE STATUS OF INSANE MASS
MURDERER HOWARD UNRUH
(SHOWN HERE IN 1998) AT THE
TRENTON STATE HOSPITAL
WAS REVIEWED BY THE
COURTS, WHICH KEPT HIM
INSTITUTIONALIZED UNDER
MAXIMUM SECURITY ALMOST
UNTIL THE END OF HIS LIFE
SIXTY YEARS AFTER HIS 1949
CAMDEN, NEW JERSEY,
SHOOTING SPREE.
Associated Press

Almost from the start, Charles had yearned to rebuild his lost family.

In 1958, he married Marian Schwartz, a young woman who had admired Charles from afar since she was a teenager. On their wedding night, he sat on the edge of their hotel bed and told her the whole story of that heartbreaking September day and everything after. He told her he only wanted to live a normal life, but he couldn't be at peace until Howard Unruh was dead.

It never came up again.

He became a linen salesman, and he was good at it. His customers liked him; he made them laugh.

Charles and Marian had three daughters. Growing up, the girls never knew what horrors their father had survived or still haunted him. He never spoke of Howard Unruh or the day everyone died, fearing he might pass some of the toxic darkness to them.

But they sensed something. They knew their father never gave cut flowers because they always died. He forbade them from having pets because they, too, died. He worried about them incessantly, even more than other girls' fathers. When they asked about their grandparents, they were told they died in an accident. One night, one of his young daughters wept as she watched Jackie Gleason's film portrayal of Gigot, the gentle but mute janitor obsessed with strangers' funerals. She saw her father in him, but she didn't know why.

Charles Cohen finally had the family he so desperately wanted. He lived in his own house, not someone else's. His children were happy. The hidden wounds inflicted by Howard Unruh had remained secret.

But like some horror-show monster, Unruh wouldn't die until he had loosed all of Charles's pent-up emotions one last time.

LETTING LOOSE THE DARKNESS

A month after the shootings on Cramer Hill, without a single competency hearing, Howard Unruh was committed to the New Jersey State Hospital's Vroom Building, a special hellhole for the criminally insane. Its concrete walls were surrounded by razor wire, its every window blocked by steel bars. The clangor of bars and insanity bouncing off the cold walls was deafening. Even on the brightest days, Vroom was gloomy.

Unruh, or Patient No. 47,077, was locked in cell eleven. Paint flaked from the Spartan cubicle's walls, which defined Unruh's new world: a steel cot with a thin, soiled mattress, a toilet, a sink, and a footlocker for whatever possessions Unruh might prize enough to keep in an asylum.

His mother visited faithfully every three weeks, but Unruh grew steadily more insane. He believed the television was spying on his thoughts. For decades, his days were spent mostly listening to the voices in his head, walking in endless circles in a small, fenced-in grassy area outside, and discussing the Oedipus complex, the unwelcome thoughts in his brain, and all the other inmates who were talking about him behind his back and plotting to hurt him. Dutifully, Unruh voted in every election, although his ballots were routinely thrown out until 2009, when New Jersey banned its insane citizens from voting.

At first, he read many books, especially those about science and astronomy, but he began to suspect that all books were contaminated, so he refused to touch them.

In 1954, twenty-three insane criminals rioted for two hours in the Vroom Building's dining hall, taking a guard prisoner and setting fire to the furniture. Howard Unruh simply sat and watched.

With the advent of antipsychotic drugs such as Thorazine, Unruh's delusions and hallucinations were tamed. Unruh grew exceedingly competent by legal standards. In articulate, handwritten letters in 1965, he asked a judge to dismiss the thirteen murder indictments against him—still standing after fourteen years—and transfer him to a safer, more comfortable Veterans Administration hospital. The request was denied.

Then in 1979, the fifty-eight-year-old Unruh asked to be transferred to a minimum-security state psychiatric hospital, closer to his sickly, eighty-two-year-old mother, but citizens in that town rose up in protest. Unruh was, after all, still a confessed mass murderer.

A sympathetic public defender, James Klein, came to Unruh's rescue. The mad killer's only chance to escape the dark, medieval Vroom Building was to have all the murder indictments dismissed, effectively making him (in the law's eyes) just another mental patient entitled to a life outside what was, in effect, a maximum-security prison.

"I think if we don't transfer him he'll die shortly," the New Jersey State Hospital's administrator said behind closed doors in 1979. "If we don't transfer him before his mother expires then he will go downhill very rapidly. I think the environment, coupled with the fact that there's a great distance between him and his mother, exacerbates this slow physical deterioration."

So, in 1980, a state judge ruled that Unruh's constitutional right to a speedy trial had been violated and threw out the murder indictments. The Camden County prosecutor's office immediately appealed, setting up a hearing that would determine whether Unruh was well enough to live in a less restrictive, more humane environment.

With the rap of a gavel, Charles Cohen's carefully buried secrets were about to be exhumed, thirty-one years after he had laid them to rest.

Charles could not stand by silently and let his parents' killer win a moment's comfort without a fight. It frightened him that the murder charges had been dropped, opening the door to increasing freedom for a madman . . . maybe even to eventually letting him go free.

It was a waking nightmare, and every horrific memory came flooding back. A lifetime of grief unreeled in living color.

His only hope was to speak out, to let loose the darkness inside him—not to hide in a closet but to fight with every fiber of his being. Thirty-two silent years had passed, but now he was going to speak in a desperate attempt to keep the killer Howard Unruh where he belonged until he died: behind bars.

Before Unruh's hearing, Charles sat his children down and told them the whole harrowing story. Then he picked up the phone and called a reporter.

CATHARSIS

In the courtroom, Charles saw Unruh for the first time since they'd crossed paths in the Camden police station on September 6, 1949, less than an hour after Charles's parents and grandmother were slaughtered.

Now Unruh was a stooped, shambling old man. His belly hung low and his hair had gone white, but his dark eyes were still empty. He was sixty-one, but looked much older. He sat, pasty-faced and sedated, at his lawyer's table, more pathetic than sinister.

Charles trembled. He was a tinderbox of rage, hate, and fear, awaiting only the spark that would set the flame that would consume him. From where he sat, it appeared the world now pitied the monster and had forgotten his victims. He felt every possible feeling of hate a human can have for another human. He didn't just want to hurt Unruh; he wanted him to suffer.

The hearing began with psychiatrists who had studied Unruh. They painted a portrait of a submissive, compliant patient who was heavily medicated and not a significant threat to himself or fellow inmates. A 1980 psychiatric report noted he was "suffering from a malignant, progressively deteriorating schizo-phrenic illness . . . over the years, his mental condition has deteriorated greatly. His physical condition has also deteriorated, and he has aged far beyond what would be expected merely by the number of years that have passed."

The same report also noted Unruh's unsettling response when he was asked if he could ever commit such a crime again.

"I hope not" is all he said.

When Unruh himself was called to testify, as he stood up, his ill-fitting, state-issued pants dropped to his knees, revealing his long, old-fashioned boxer shorts. The gallery was momentarily sorry for the oblivious old man, who simply pulled his trousers up and proceeded to the witness stand.

Speaking in a quiet, raspy voice, Unruh slowly and tersely answered questions from his lawyer, James Klein, just as he'd answered the prosecutor's questions thirty-two years before.

"Do you believe you are suffering from a mental illness?" Klein asked.

"I was."

"How about today?"

"I don't think so."

Charles watched Unruh's face intently. It was vacant of any emotion.

"What are your goals ultimately? What would you like to see happen to yourself?" the lawyer asked.

"I would like to be transferred to a civil ward at Ancora [another state hospital], then receive treatment to prepare me for the street," Unruh replied.

"You think you need some preparation before you go to the street?"

"I don't, but the doctors do."

The prospect of Howard Unruh roaming the streets again chilled Charles, who sat with Marian in the back of the courtroom, his every muscle tensed. Unruh wanted to be closer to his ailing mother, whose companionship he'd enjoyed for more than sixty years. Charles seethed. When he wanted to visit his mother, he had to go to a cemetery.

After fifteen minutes, Klein rested, and the prosecution had no questions. But the judge asked the question everyone wanted to hear.

"Mr. Unruh, do you have the feeling that you want to hurt anybody?"

"Not anymore."

"How long ago was it that you stopped having those feelings, if you did have them?"

"Ever since I was sent to the Vroom Building."

Ten minutes later, the judge ruled. Howard Unruh, he said, remained a threat to himself and the public, and more freedom was likely only to mean more risk to innocent people.

Charles Cohen had gotten his way this round, but the fight was far from over.

For the rest of his natural life, Howard Unruh was entitled to a similar hearing once a year. Every year, a judge would determine whether the killer was entitled to a more comfortable life.

> **"I was only twelve years old,"**
> **Charles Cohen told one reporter.**
> **"I was a kid. I listened to my mother.**
> **She yelled 'Hide, Charles, hide!'**
> **That's what I did. I hid in the closet."**

So Charles Cohen became a zealot. His story came pouring out in great torrents. He spoke to every newspaper, TV, and radio reporter who would listen. He began to speak into a portable tape recorder, as he planned to write a book about the massacre and its aftermath. He wanted everyone to see how this one man, Unruh, had outlived all the families he destroyed in his berserk, twelve-minute rampage. Charles wanted the world to understand what he'd lost. He wanted other survivors to be able to get past it, even if he hadn't. He wanted Unruh to never enjoy a moment of freedom beyond the dark, noisy walls of the Vroom Building.

But most of all, he wanted his parents to be proud of him. If he said nothing, the dead could never forgive him. He must live with purpose so there would be a purpose in their deaths.

The only place he never spoke was the courtroom. Throughout Unruh's many hearings, no judge, jury, or lawyer ever asked Charles to speak for the dead.

"I was only twelve years old," he told one reporter. "I was a kid. I listened to my mother. She yelled 'Hide, Charles, hide!' That's what I did. I hid in the closet.

"Thing is, I'm still in there."

He talked about the suitcase full of ghosts he kept in the attic, too.

He told another reporter about his fantasy of a phone call delivering the news that Howard Unruh was dead. He'd give his statement of condolences to the surviving families of Unruh's victims, piss on his grave, then bury the suitcase once and for all. His ghosts would be exorcised.

Unruh remained confined to the high-security Vroom Building for the criminally insane at Trenton Psychiatric Hospital until 1993, when he was transferred across the grounds to less restrictive wards in a geriatric unit. And every year, Charles Cohen sat through another hearing, ready to speak for the dead.

And every time some other lunatic cut loose with a gun—Nebraska, Austin, New Orleans, San Ysidro, Killeen, Atlanta, Littleton, Red Lake, Montreal, Virginia Tech, Binghamton, and all the places whose names and streets would be forever stained by mass murderers—the ghosts of Cramer Hill came back to life for Charles. He knew there'd be people who would live with the horror for the rest of their lives and never know what to do.

Headlines called him "the father of mass murder," but Unruh had not been the first American mass murderer, or even the most prolific. But he stood out, albeit for mysterious reasons.

His body count was nowhere near records set in earlier mass murders, such as the all-but-forgotten 1927 school bombing in Bath, Michigan, in which forty-five people—mostly children—died. But the most shocking American mass murders have never been purely about the number of deaths.

Unruh's crime has echoed for decades because nobody could possibly have predicted his explosion, which happened in a place that seemed all too familiar to most people—in this case, an ordinary neighborhood. For the rest of the twentieth century and beyond, the shocking combination of unexpected horror in a "safe" place would happen again and again in restaurants, schools, public parks, and small businesses.

But Unruh also fascinated America, in part, because he lived. There was no suicide, no fatal shootout with cops, no electric chair, not even emotional death by remorse. He was different because he survived.

Charles Cohen survived, too. He sometimes walked past the old drugstore, but he never went inside. He visited his parents' graves on the Hebrew date of their deaths, always leaving a stone as a sign that he'd come.

He continued to pursue a book about his experience, making notes and amassing a stack of audiotapes on which he would secretly record his memories and reflections. He often stopped the tape when the ghosts overwhelmed him, such as describing visiting his parents' graves before seeing Unruh in court.

"This is my catharsis; this is my coming out and discussing what, why, and how," he said plaintively on one of the tapes.

"I want to be able to tell people that no matter how shitty things get in life and how depressed you may feel and how bad things may seem to you, sometimes it is better to talk about it and get it out. Either talk to the right person or find your time to talk to the world. . . ."

> **"I want to be able to tell people that no matter how shitty things get in life and how depressed you may feel and how bad things may seem to you, sometimes it is better to talk about it and get it out. Either talk to the right person or find your time to talk to the world. . . ."**

Where Charles had once kept secrets out of fear that his pain might poison his children, he now hoped his old secrets could bind them into the family he had always dreamed of rebuilding.

"The reason I am doing this is to keep Howard Unruh in a maximum security situation for the rest of his life. But perhaps that's not really the reason. Maybe I now have to talk about it. I have to lay it all out. I have to look at it myself. Perhaps I can live whatever life I have left—and I hope I have a long life with my family—and we can enjoy whatever time it is even with a better quality than we have at this point because I am sure that my holding back [has] kept a lot of feelings inward that perhaps could have made it easier on everyone else."

Sadly, Charles Cohen died unexpectedly on Friday, September 4, 2009, after a massive stroke at his summer home in Ventnor City, New Jersey. He was seventy-two. Jewish funeral customs require that the dead be buried as soon as the day after death, except on Saturdays, the Jewish Sabbath. Thus, some say it was God's intent, others mere coincidence, that Charles was buried on Sunday, September 6, 2009—the sixtieth anniversary of Howard Unruh's deadly rampage.

Howard Unruh outlived Charles by only six weeks. Unruh died of old age in a state nursing home on October 19, 2009, after spending the last sixty years of his life in an insane asylum. He was eighty-eight. His lawyer said he remained lucid up to his last few days, but he never talked about the Cramer Hill massacre except to say that he was sorry children had died.

The killer was secretly buried in an unmarked grave beside his mother in Whiting, New Jersey, after a private funeral attended by only two relatives and a pastor. A few days later, a cemetery worker planted a small American flag in the fresh dirt, just as he did for all departed soldiers.

Charles Cohen's suitcase, the repository of a life diverted by a madman, was never buried. It is safe in his daughters' hands.

CHAPTER 2

"TODAY IS GONNA BE VISUAL"

BRENT DOONAN AND THE ATLANTA DAY-TRADER SPREE

ATLANTA WAS BURNING. A suffocating heat wave had engulfed the city and simmered near 100°F (38°C) for days. The dead air, curdled humidity, and sunlight caroming like a white-hot blade off the modern high-rises made a killer hot spell even hotter.

People were dying elsewhere, but in Atlanta's elegant, air-conditioned Buckhead district, there was at least some comfort in the electric coolness of the upscale shops, chic clubs, and posh offices, separated from the deadly dangers outside by a barrier of reflective glass and steel.

But walls and windows couldn't protect All-Tech Investment Group from storms in the stock market, and today was a bearish day. The NASDAQ was tanking; losses were mounting. The heat was rising on Wall Street, too.

So Brent Doonan, the twenty-three-year-old co-owner of All-Tech, wasn't surprised to see his friend, a day trader named Mark Barton, push through the trading floor's glass doors a little before 3 p.m. He was dressed in a comfortable red polo shirt, khaki shorts, and tennis shoes and was sweating. He was carrying a small duffel bag. Maybe he was here to pay a $30,000 shortfall in his account, Brent hoped. In any event, he was glad to see his buoyant, laid-back friend who drifted through life unfazed by the fact that on any given day he might win or lose ten thousand bucks gambling on the stock market.

Barton motioned to Brent, who was making a sales pitch to a potential new day trader behind the glass walls of All-Tech's conference room. Brent waved back but couldn't walk away from a potential new customer.

Barton paced outside the room for a few minutes, making small talk with other traders, even offering them sodas from a nearby refrigerator. But he couldn't wait. He impatiently rapped his knuckles on the window. Brent apologized to his trainee and motioned the excited Barton in.

"Hey, Brent, I need to talk to you. It's important," Barton said with a peculiar little smile. "Can I have a minute?"

Brent looked at his watch.

"Yes, Mark," he said. "In just a minute."

Barton smiled big and left.

While Brent looked for a stopping point with his new client, Barton chatted up some of his old buddies on the trading floor. Somebody noticed spatters of red on his hands, forearms, and collar, and they reckoned he must have been painting. Someone else wondered why Barton casually closed the office blinds before he went back to the conference room and interrupted Brent.

"Brent, come here quick," he said, an odd look on his face. "Really, you're gonna love this!"

So Brent excused himself and led Barton to All-Tech's main office, where Brent's partner, Scott Manspeaker, and administrative assistant Kathy Van Camp were working. Barton closed the door behind them, the same quirky smile still on his face. Brent turned to face Barton, who was standing just a couple feet away, suddenly breathing hard. The smile faded and Barton fixed a vacant glare on Brent.

"What's up?" Brent asked.

Barton's voice was suddenly ominous.

"Today is gonna be visual."

DARK SECRETS

All-Tech opened in 1997, a child of the blossoming Internet's perfect marriage to the dot-com boom. Its business plan was simple: provide the training, workspace, and technology so that adventurous investors could buy and sell stocks online throughout the day, banking on big profits in the minutes— sometimes seconds—that they owned them. The advent of personal computers, high-speed phone lines, and the Internet had destroyed the conventional wisdom that investors should ride out swells and troughs in the market by holding securities for long periods. Now anyone sitting at a well-connected computer could instantly buy and sell thousands of dollars worth of securities with a single mouse click.

In less time than it would take Buckhead baristas to make a double-shot cappuccino, daring day traders could make themselves rich—or lose a fortune. Dot-com stocks commonly catapulted 500 percent in a single day. It was the Wild West on a new frontier, where frothy dreamers, gamblers, and quick-draw artists all sought their fortunes in a lawless landscape. All they needed was a fast computer and a sense of adventure. And day-trading firms like Brent Doonan's All-Tech snagged a piece of the action by charging commissions on all transactions and fees for using their broadband connections and state-of-the-art computers.

For Brent, launching All-Tech had been a nerve-racking investment. The former All-American athlete and high school honor student from the Kansas heartland had a degree in finance from Indiana University and was working for a Big Six accounting firm in Chicago when his sister's boyfriend, Scott

FOR ALL OUTWARD APPEARANCES, MARK BARTON WAS A DEVOTED FAMILY MAN, BUT AFTER HIS DEADLY 1999 RAMPAGE IN ATLANTA, A MUCH DARKER PORTRAIT OF A CONTROLLING, OBSESSIVE, AND ANGRY MAN EMERGED. HE'S SHOWN HERE WITH HIS WIFE LEIGH ANN, HIS DAUGHTER MYCHELLE, AND HIS SON MATTHEW.

Getty Images

Manspeaker, pitched the idea of opening a day-trading firm. Carefully weighing the risks and rewards, Brent wrestled with the idea for months. Barely out of college, he felt it all seemed bigger than him, but he eventually embraced the idea enough to take out a daunting quarter-million-dollar business loan and move to Atlanta, where he and Manspeaker felt they could make the most money.

Despite his youth, Brent was a driven competitor, mature beyond his years. He hated losing, and he'd do whatever it took to succeed. Very quickly, he was working seventy-hour weeks, and the money started to roll in.

Among Brent's first and most enthusiastic customers was Mark O. Barton, a gregarious, fortysomething family man who lived in a manicured, middle-class neighborhood, went to church every Sunday, led his son's Cub Scout troop, and appeared to skate through life with an imperturbable wit. Even at 6 feet, 4 inches and 250 pounds (2 meters and 113 kilograms), he appeared to be a gentle, if occasionally puckish, soul. A bright but socially invisible student, he held a college degree in chemistry and claimed to be working on a revolutionary new soap formula that would soon make him rich.

Barton traded with zeal. Where other day traders were cautious, Barton was aggressive. In 1998 and 1999, as the stock market was piling up unprecedented gains, his buddies called him "the Rocket" because his high-rolling successes launched him into wild celebrations. Wagering up to a quarter million dollars per session, Barton once scored a $106,000 profit in a single day.

The affable Barton seemed to always be smiling, even on his inevitable bad days. Brent grew to like him and enjoyed having him around. The usually sunny Barton was good for business.

But Barton's smile hid dark secrets.

GETTING AWAY WITH MURDER

Barton had been a bright public school student, especially in chemistry and math, but he was also a misfit. He had no friends in school, much less girl-friends. He rebelled against his disciplinarian father by elaborately planning petty crimes and ingenious getaways, increasingly convinced he was a criminal mastermind, a natural schemer who was smarter than the average thug—until he got caught burglarizing a local drugstore at age fourteen.

Fascinated by chemistry, Barton began to experiment with homemade drugs. One frightening overdose landed him in the hospital, and a counselor said he withdrew further. He began to fear demons coming through the floor and had other delusions, so he was treated with antipsychotic drugs. At one point, Barton completely lost his ability to read, shaved his head, and plunged briefly into a strange religious fanaticism that isolated him even more.

Though he was a National Merit Scholarship semifinalist, Barton drifted after high school. Dropping out of Clemson University after only a semester, he eventually enrolled at the University of South Carolina, where he majored in chemistry—and began making and selling methamphetamine. He was arrested again for another drugstore break-in, but given probation.

After graduating in 1979, he married a college classmate, Debra Spivey, and took a series of dead-end jobs until he was hired as a chemist at a small Texarkana, Texas, chemical dealer. He eventually became the company's operations manager, but in 1990 when his behavior became intolerably erratic and malicious, he was fired.

A week after the firing, someone broke into the company's office and stole confidential formulas and financial data before completely disabling the office computers. After Barton was arrested and charged with the crime, he cut a deal with his former employer that let him go free if he returned the stolen material and left Texas forever. He was never prosecuted. His first ingenious getaway.

Barton fled to Georgia with his wife, Debra, and their toddler son, Matthew. He got a job as a chemical salesman. But soon after his daughter Mychelle was born in 1991, his marriage was in trouble. His affair with a young receptionist named Leigh Ann Lang had started three days after he met her. They flirted openly at work and were inseparable at after-hours parties with their colleagues.

The quarrels began. Debra accused her husband of infidelity and he denied it—even as he was secretly buying a $600,000 life insurance policy on his wife. More ominously, in June 1993, Barton told some of his mistress's friends that he loved her more than he'd ever loved anyone, and that by October he'd be able to marry Leigh Ann. Was a divorce from Debra imminent?

On Labor Day weekend in 1993, Debra and her mother left Mark home with the kids and rented a small trailer at an Alabama campground. On Sunday, police found their viciously hacked corpses in the trailer, both virtually unrecognizable. The killer had literally split Debra's skull in half with a small ax and battered her face with almost twenty more blows, splattering blood, flesh, and brains on the walls and curtains. Her mother had also been bludgeoned about ten times. Some cash was missing, but the sheer brutality suggested to cops this wasn't a simple robbery gone bad.

There was more: Before fleeing, the enraged killer vomited on the floor and in the toilet, a sign that the intruder was ultimately sickened by what he'd done—more evidence that he was known to his victims.

One witness told police he'd seen a man fitting Barton's description at the campground, and investigators later found traces of blood in Barton's car and splashed on his kitchen wall and sink, as if someone had washed blood from his hands. Barton refused to take a polygraph test about his whereabouts that night, and even before his dead wife was buried, he told relatives he intended to marry his mistress Leigh Ann, who was still married at the time.

But forensics failed to find any conclusive link between the stains and the murder, and a series of other errors doomed the investigation from the start. Yes, cops found blood on the ignition switch and a seat belt of Barton's Ford Taurus. Barton couldn't explain how it got there; instead, he brazenly challenged investigators: "If there is a ton of blood in my car, why aren't you arresting me? Why am I not in handcuffs?"

Ultimately, no one would ever be charged, and the suspicious insurance company reluctantly settled Barton's insurance claim for $450,000—insisting that $150,000 be set aside in trust funds for the children.

A week later, Leigh Ann moved in with Barton and his kids.

> **Barton's behavior went quickly from weir to worse. He killed his eight-year-old daughter's kitten, then took her to search for her "lost" pet.**

And within a few weeks of the murder, Debra and her mother were finally buried after a small, private funeral. During the services, Barton sat in the last pew, expressionless. When the ceremony ended, he hurried out the doors ahead of the other mourners, skipping the burial. Outside, Leigh Ann was waiting in her Mustang convertible, the stereo blaring.

Barton jumped in and they sped away in a cloud of Georgia suspicion. His second ingenious getaway.

Barton and Leigh Ann left their jobs together a year after the murder and married in 1995, but it wasn't a peaceful union. They often bickered, and Leigh Ann would usually move out for a few days before they would reunite and begin the whole sordid cycle again.

In 1994, Barton's three-year-old daughter, Mychelle, told her babysitter that her father had sexually molested her. No charges were ever filed, but Barton was ordered to undergo mental evaluations in which a court-appointed psychologist described him as "certainly capable" of murder.

From there, the Bartons' miserable cycle of dysfunction only continued to spiral out of control. Leigh Ann would move out, then move back in. Barton ordered his wife not to answer the phone when he wasn't home and exerted strict control over everything she did. She grew distant and cold, sometimes taking the children away from him for days. His get-rich-quick day-trading was burning through Debra's insurance money at a startling rate. Barton sometimes won big, but he'd usually lose it all within a few days. When the insurance money was gone, he sold the family furniture in yard sales to feed his habit. But to the outside world, he continued to behave as if the losses made no difference at all.

In October 1998, Leigh Ann left, supposedly for good. He became obsessed with his computer. One of his online profiles listed his hobbies as guns and day-trading, and his favorite quote was Dirty Harry's taunting, "Go ahead, make my day." Barton's behavior went quickly from weird to worse. He killed his eight-year-old daughter's kitten, then took her to search for her "lost" pet. Meanwhile, his obsession with day-trading grew more desperate.

Like so many times before, Leigh Ann relented. Only twenty-seven, she allowed Barton, now forty-four, to move into her two-bedroom apartment in the Atlanta suburb of Stockbridge because she missed the children.

But it was already too late. Mark Barton had lost control. He visited a minister and told him about his night terrors, his addiction to day-trading, and his fear that he'd inherited "mental imbalances" from his authoritarian father. His fragile hold on reality was being overwhelmed by his demons.

Over the next few desperate months, Barton would lose more money he didn't have. In early June, when All-Tech cut him off for an unpaid $30,000 shortfall in his account, he simply walked across the street to Momentum Securities, another day-trading outfit, and plunked down a fresh $87,500 to start trading again. When he lost it, he borrowed another $100,000 from Momentum. Within a few weeks, he owed Momentum more than $120,000 and was so deep in the red that his trading was halted on July 27, 1999.

His escape route had been blocked. Too many people were standing between Mark Barton and one last ingenious escape. Brent Doonan was one of them.

"I REALLY WISH I HADN'T KILLED HER"

That night, after a Cub Scout den meeting, Barton and Leigh Ann fought again about money.

So he killed her.

Sometime in the wee hours, he bludgeoned her to death with a hammer as she slept. He wrapped her bloody corpse in a blanket and stuffed it behind some boxes in the bedroom closet so the children wouldn't see her. He placed a note on her body: "I give you my wife, Leigh Ann Barton, my honey, my precious love. Please take care of her. I will love her forever."

The next night, he also bashed in the heads of his son, Matthew, age eleven, and daughter, Mychelle, age eight, as they slept in the next room. To make sure they died, he placed them facedown in a bathtub full of water. Then he dried them off, wrapped their little bodies in comforters and laid them side by side in a bed, a stuffed teddy bear on Mychelle's body and a Game Boy on Matthew's.

Also on each was a handwritten note expressing love for "my son, my buddy, my life" and "my daughter, my sweetheart." With only their still faces showing from the blankets, they appeared to be sleeping.

Just before dawn the next morning, Barton sat at his computer and wrote a chilling confession that hinted at his rage, which, incredibly, was not yet spent:

July 29, 1999, 6.38 a.m.

To Whom It May Concern,

Leigh Ann is in the master bedroom closet under a blanket. I killed her on Tuesday night. I killed Matthew and Mychelle Wednesday night. There may be similarities between these deaths and the death of my first wife, Debra Spivey. However, I deny killing her and her mother. There's no reason for me to lie now. It just seemed like a quiet way to kill and a relatively painless way to die.

There was little pain. All of them were dead in less than five minutes. I hit them with a hammer in their sleep and then put them face down in a bathtub to make sure they did not wake up in pain. To make sure they were dead. I am so sorry. I wish I didn't. Words cannot tell the agony. Why did I?

I have been dying since October. I wake up at night so afraid, so terrified that I couldn't be that afraid while awake. It has taken its toll. I have come to hate this life and this system of things. I have come to have no hope.

I killed the children to exchange them for five minutes of pain for a lifetime of pain. I forced myself to do it to keep them from suffering so much later. No mother, no father, no relatives. The fears of the father are transferred to the son. It was from my father to me and from me to my son. He already had it and now, to be left alone, I had to take him with me.

I killed Leigh Ann because she was one of the main reasons for my demise as I planned to kill the others. I really wish I hadn't killed her now. She really couldn't help it and I love her so much anyway. I know that Jehovah will take care of all of them in the next life. I'm sure the details don't matter. There is no excuse, no good reason. I am sure no one would understand. If they could, I wouldn't want them to. I just write these things to say why.

Please know that I love Leigh Ann, Matthew, and Mychelle with all of my heart. If Jehovah is willing, I would like to see all of them again in the resurrection, to have a second chance. I don't plan to live very much longer, just long enough to kill as many of the people that greedily sought my destruction.

You should kill me if you can.

Mark O. Barton

He printed the letter out on a crisp sheet of his personal stationery, signed it in bold script, and left it on the living room coffee table where somebody would find it. He then packed a duffel bag with four loaded handguns—a black 9 mm Glock, a nickel-plated .45-caliber Colt, an H&R .22, and a cheap .25-caliber Saturday night special—and more than two hundred loose rounds of ammunition. After a quick stop at his lawyer's office to change his will, Mark Barton would be well armed as he finally took aim at his demons.

The sun was just rising, and this day was going to be visual.

"OH GOD, PLEASE DON'T LET ME DIE"

Around 2:30 p.m., Barton strolled into Momentum Securities' third-floor offices at 3500 Piedmont Road, carrying his small duffel bag. The trading floor was packed with traders as he stopped to chat with a secretary. He told her he wanted to wire $200,000 into his account but first wanted to talk to Momentum's branch manager, Justin Hoehn, who was running errands but was expected to return soon.

Barton paced, antsy. For a while, he made small talk with other traders but when Hoehn didn't return after a half hour, he'd waited long enough. He wandered into the office break room, where Momentum's office manager owner, Kevin Dial, was hanging out. For a few awkward moments, they bemoaned the flagging markets, then Barton suddenly wheeled around on Dial.

"It's a bad trading day," he growled, "and it's about to get worse."

He drew the Glock and the Colt from under his shirt, sticking one in Dial's back and the other in his chest. He pulled the triggers simultaneously and blew two gaping holes in both sides of his shocked victim. Dial died instantaneously.

The roar of gunshots froze everyone on the trading floor. His face flecked with blood, Barton was back in control. He alone could decide who lived and who died. As he began shooting at the traders, they scrambled to hide behind desks. For more than ten minutes, he prowled the trading floor, shooting both pistols at anyone who moved. Some tried to run, and he fired with uncanny precision. Some broke windows and threw out papers to get someone's—anyone's—attention. Some barricaded themselves in a small room and dodged bullets when Barton fired through the door. Some tried in vain to dial 911 on their cell phones. Some played dead, even as Barton walked around and fired point-blank into still bodies. Four people lay dead or mortally wounded while seven others slowly bled from their wounds. Not a cop or paramedic was within blocks of the killing floor.

Gun smoke filled the room as Barton calmly reloaded and quietly left the building. He drove his green 1992 Ford Aerostar minivan just a block up busy, six-lane Piedmont Road, where nobody yet knew the horror that was still unfolding.

His next stop: All-Tech.

Brent Doonan was confused. What did Barton mean by "today's gonna be visual"? Barton wasn't going to give a translation. He crossed his arms in front over his chest and drew two pistols from his waistband like some B-movie bandito. He fired point-blank at Brent.

The first slug, a hollow-point .45, entered Brent's gut just beneath his sternum, ripping through his liver, spleen, and diaphragm, and narrowly missing his heart before bursting out his back just two inches from his spine. The second, a smaller 9 mm hollow point, lodged in the meaty party of his right arm.

But Brent only saw a couple bright flashes and heard two muffled pops. No pain as the bullets blasted through him . . . no sense of falling . . . no sound . . . no real grasp of time itself . . . as if he might have missed the moment of his own death, had it come.

But he wasn't dead. Yet. He lay dazed, facedown on the floor, wondering what had just happened.

Pain and awareness seeped through him slowly, as if his body were just waking from a deep sleep. He felt his own warm blood puddling in a slowly widening circle around him and he watched it soaking into the synthetic carpet. *My God, this is real!* He felt like he'd taken a cannonball in the chest, and his gut clenched. *That son of a bitch just shot me!* He saw two spent shell casings on the floor nearby and his head spun as he wondered if this was how he would die, right here, alone on the floor. *Where is Scott? Where is Kathy?*

Three more shots rang out.

The first hit administrative assistant Kathy Van Camp in one temple and exited the other, slicing her facial artery and destroying her eyes. The other two hit Brent's partner Scott Manspeaker in the belly and the wrist, and he slumped to the floor beside his desk, motionless.

Brent played dead, his eyes closed. He couldn't see his friends. *How can I get out of here?* He couldn't reach a phone. He knew he would die if he lay there much longer. *Should I try to help the others?* His mind raced as Barton began shooting other traders on the floor. *Can I try to stop him?* The sound of gunfire was making him sick to his stomach, but it hurt too much to puke.

Meanwhile, Barton was methodically killing Brent's customers and friends with dreadful precision. Despite walls of glass throughout the office, he never broke a single one with an errant shot. He

moved purposefully through the room, shooting one gun and then the other before coolly reloading. One trader tried to run, and Barton shot him once in the back and a second time in the buttocks before he fell; he was dead before he hit the floor. Another just stood frozen in fear until Barton fatally shot him twice.

Blood sprayed on the walls, the windows, the floor. Barton stood so close to many of his victims that he, too, was covered in their blood, but he was calm, even ghoulishly jovial.

"I certainly hope this doesn't ruin your trading day!" Barton hollered as he fired.

The gravely wounded Doonan knew he could never overpower the massive Barton, who outweighed him by eighty pounds and was on a fanatical mission. Instead, he plotted his escape through a conference room door and away from the building to get help. He gathered his waning strength and rose to his feet, holding his stomach wound, blood spilling out of his gut shot through his fingers. Suddenly, Barton was standing in the office doorway, his back to Brent, still spraying the bloodied trading floor with bullets.

What do I do now? Lie back down and play dead? Make a run for it?

"I certainly hope this doesn't ruin your trading day!" Barton hollered as he fired.

The choice was made for him.

At that moment, Brent watched Barton shoot a runner in the back, then raise his gun for an easier shot at a woman who had no place to run. Without thinking, Brent lunged through the door and shoulder-blocked Barton in the back. His shot barely missed the woman, but Barton regained his balance and fired twice at Brent, who was now running toward a new escape. One bullet hit his left arm and the other struck under his left shoulder blade, exploding out through the left side of his chest, but Brent was still on his feet and, inexplicably, Barton didn't pursue him, perhaps thinking Brent—now shot four times—would slink off and die like a wounded animal.

Brent reached the exterior hallway, where gun smoke hung in a fluorescent haze. He pinned one injured arm against the trickling hole in his belly as the other hung slack at his side, useless. He looked back. *Where is Mark?* Rapidly losing strength, he felt his way along the white walls, smearing a bloody trail as he struggled toward the door at the end of the fifty-foot hall, which was suddenly longer than he remembered. The stairwell door might as well have been a mile, a horrifying funhouse illusion in the distance.

He couldn't feel his legs, but Brent fled as fast as his wounds and flagging adrenaline would let him—so briskly that one of his shoes flew off—but time and space were out of sync. A monster lurked somewhere behind him, but he felt trapped in a phantasmic half-speed warp, unable to move quickly enough to save himself. Seconds elongated into hours . . . every inch felt like a thousand miles . . . sanctuary grew more distant as the color drained from the walls, the floor, the blood.

Out of the gray light, another door miraculously appeared. The service elevator. Brent used every ounce of his strength to push through a heavy door into the elevator's small vestibule and began to prod the button in an urgent frenzy. He heard the distant drone of the plodding car somewhere, and he glanced back at the door expecting to see Barton coming to finish him off.

The sluggish elevator continued to hum, unhurried. Brent sunk to his knees and tried in vain to pry the elevator doors open.

"Come on!" he seethed under his breath. "Come on!"

In that moment, death touched him. He felt cold and doomed. *This is it. I'm going to die in this little box and nobody will ever know until it's too late.*

He dragged himself to the big vestibule door again to peek down the hall to see whether he had any time left. A panicked woman was running down the narrow hallway, and Brent began to motion her toward the modest safety of the elevator's tiny, enclosed vestibule.

But then Barton appeared behind her. He chased her and pointed one of his guns at the back of her head.

Brent jumped back in fear. The listless elevator continued its endless whirring, still seemingly a thousand miles away.

Oh God, oh God . . . please don't let me die!

One shot cracked.

And the elevator door opened.

Brent crawled into the elevator and frantically stabbed at all the buttons. After what seemed like a deadly eternity, the doors began to close.

Then the vestibule door opened and Barton leaped inside. Brent saw him between the doors as they slowly slid together, and the killer raised his gun to fire.

The doors met before he pulled the trigger.

PRAYING FOR HELP

The elevator rose slowly with Brent crouched on all fours inside. Blood dripped onto the floor and he could literally feel his life leaking away.

The doors opened. Brent didn't know where he was. He had pushed every button and couldn't focus on the numbers that marked the floor. He rose to his unsteady feet and peeked around the corner at an empty hallway. He was relieved Barton hadn't followed him, but he couldn't dawdle. He was dying. If he could reach one of the nearby offices, he had a chance . . . to get help for the others . . . to call the police . . . to live. He stumbled to a nearby office and collapsed in the doorway, drained and bleeding profusely.

"Help! Help me!" he shouted. "I've been shot!"

Several workers ran to help him while somebody called 911.

"Get me out of the doorway," he begged. "Hide me! He's after me and if he sees me we're all dead!"

The police dispatcher assured the shaken caller that help was already on the way. Tragically, confused first responders believed all the distress calls were for the shootings at Momentum Securities. Although calls were coming from All-Tech's building, too, dispatchers and commanders insisted they were wrong, and more than a half hour passed before it dawned on police that there had been two mass shootings in two different places.

Somebody ran to the break room for a roll of paper towels to stanch the bleeding, while another began to pray over Brent, who was sinking fast. Blood pounded inside him as his heart worked to keep him alive. His skin felt seared, as if he had been pierced by a million white-hot needles, and his breathing grew shallow and painful.

Three people pressed towels to Brent's wounds, while someone stripped his bloody shirt away. Through the fog of pain and delirium, he saw horror splash across their faces as they saw what damage the bullets had done. It was a look that told him he was going to die.

So he said what might have been a prayer—for Mark Barton. He tried to forgive his killer, who might have had a brain tumor, or forgot to take some vital medications, or was possessed by demons or—*for God's sake, stop! Dying people think like this, and I don't want to die!*

Still no paramedics. Fifteen minutes had elapsed.

"Where the heck are they?" he moaned weakly. Despite the compresses, blood continued to pool around him from eight different entrance and exit wounds.

Another woman tending Brent's wounds asked whether he had any medical conditions to worry about, and he said no. "Are you allergic to anything?" she asked. "Yeah," he said. "Bullets."

"We don't know," a woman told him.

"They've got to hurry or I'm not going to make it."

"We know," she said, stroking his forehead. "Calm down. You're going to be just fine."

Mortally wounded, Brent couldn't wait for help that might not be coming. This might be his last chance to talk to his mother and father again.

"Could you please call my father?" he asked one of the women. He gave her the number, and she went back somewhere inside the office.

Another woman tending his wounds asked whether he had any medical conditions to worry about, and he said no.

"Are you allergic to anything?" she asked.

"Yeah," he said. "Bullets."

Bad news, the woman with the phone said. "Your father's out of town."

He whispered his mother's number in her ear, but nobody answered there, either.

He gave her his brother Brian's work number, but Brian was also out of town on business.

I'm going to die surrounded by total strangers, he thought.

Still no medics. Minutes rolled by. Dispatchers assured them help was near.

Then a phone rang. It was Brian. One of the women in the office told him what was happening and he asked to talk to Brent. But the cord was too short and the woman was forced to relay messages between the two brothers, who had been close all their lives but whose voices were now separated by a matter of a few feet.

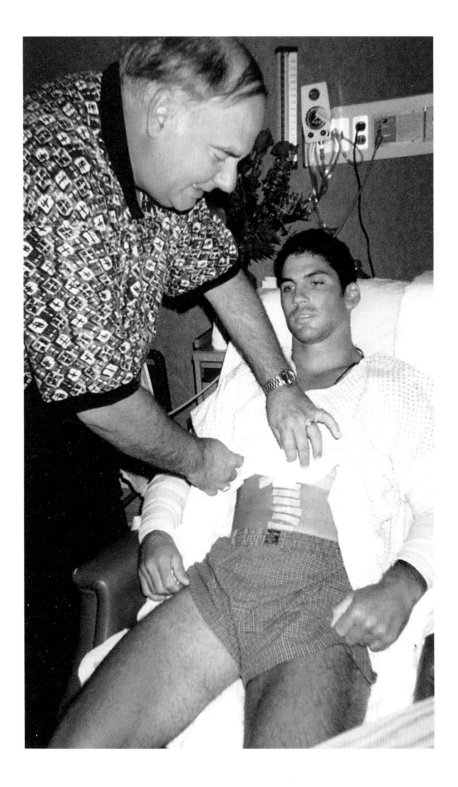

"Brent, you hang on, buddy," the woman spoke for Brian. "Don't give up on me, dammit. Don't you die! Do you hear me?"

Brent whispered his message back to Brian.

"Brian, I love you." His voice began to wither. "Tell Mom and Dad how much I love them, too . . ."

Brent's skin was ashen and he had no discernible pulse. The roll of paper towels was nearly gone and still no ambulance.

"What religion are you?" somebody asked.

"I'm Catholic."

She began to recite the Lord's Prayer and everyone—even Brent—joined her. Then they said a Hail Mary, but Brent's brain was slowly shutting down. The words came out all wrong and everyone knew he was fading.

THE SCOPE OF THE SLAUGHTER

Mark Barton had slipped out of the building unnoticed. He'd simply packed his guns back in his duffel bag and walked out to his minivan in the parking lot—even as police were descending upon the carnage at Momentum across the street. He plopped his bag on the passenger seat and slowly melted away in the traffic on Piedmont.

Forty minutes after he shot Brent Doonan in the belly and launched his assault on All-Tech, Barton was a ghost, and Brent was preparing to die, choking on his own fluids. Still no police. Still no EMTs.

The office workers who had kept Brent alive so far knelt around him in prayer.

"Lord, please take my angel and give him to Brent," one of them said. "He needs all the angels he can get."

In that instant, they said later, they saw a shrouded spirit, maybe an angel, maybe an illusion caused by the suggestion of something divine.

But Brent was still dying. The bullet that tore through his left side had clipped his lung, which was now filling with blood. Each breath became harder, and Brent felt as if he were submerged in a cold lake, breathing through a straw. Every time he breathed out, his own warm blood rose in his mouth and nose.

Suddenly, a startling fifty minutes after Barton's first shot into Brent's gut, paramedics burst into the room. As they hooked up IVs, one of them yelled for a pack of cigarettes. He stripped the plastic wrapping off and used it to seal Brent's wounds because they had run out of proper patches treating the wounded downstairs in the butchery formerly known as All-Tech's trading floor. Down there and elsewhere in the building, they'd found five corpses and at least six wounded.

DAY-TRADING ENTREPRENEUR BRENT DOONAN WAS SHOT FOUR TIMES AND LOST HIS BODY'S ENTIRE BLOOD SUPPLY ON JULY 29, 1999, IN ATLANTA, WHEN HIS FRIEND MARK BARTON COMMITTED THE BLOODIEST WORKPLACE KILLING IN AMERICAN HISTORY. Courtesy of Brent Doonan

Then a tall man crouched between the medics on the office floor and laid his hand across Brent's aching shoulder.

"Son, I'm Dr. Harvey. I'm a trauma surgeon," he said. "Listen to me. If you keep your eyes open you will live. If you close them, you die."

The doc told paramedics Brent's chances were fifty-fifty and that he might not even make it to the ambulance. He'd lost too much blood and was starting to convulse. But they loaded him up, and Brent was finally on his way to the hospital.

For most of his life, Brent had prayed for a happy death. Now he pleaded his case to God that this was not how it should end.

By the time Brent's ambulance was racing to the hospital, police knew who they were hunting. But they had no idea where Mark Barton had gone. Authorities launched one of the largest manhunts in Georgia history, sealing off Atlanta and blocking the state line. His name and face were plastered all over the local news, but Barton remained an elusive phantom. Critical hours passed as the true scope of his slaughter seeped into the city.

Barton had fired thirty-nine shots at Momentum and All-Tech. He hit twenty-two people. Nine of them died. Seven hovered near death in Atlanta hospitals. Compounding the horror, police had also found the bludgeoned bodies of his wife and two children in the Stockbridge apartment, along with an ominous promise to "kill as many" of his enemies as he could.

Twelve people were dead and a deranged killer was still on the loose. Although nobody had yet done the math, it was already the second deadliest workplace shooting in American history and one of the country's twenty worst mass murders.

Police simply didn't know whether he was finished.

Just before sunset on that day, a strange man casually walked up to a woman getting into her car in the parking lot of a shopping mall in the Atlanta suburb of Kennesaw, more than 15 miles (24 kilometers) from the carnage in Buckhead.

"Don't scream or I'll shoot you," he warned.

But she ran back into the mall as another woman watched Barton get back into his green minivan. She recognized him from the news and called police.

Within minutes, unmarked cruisers were tailing Barton's van. They surmised he was looking to steal a car to make another ingenious getaway.

Then Barton's van turned into a gas station in suburban Acworth and circled slowly. But he'd made his last mistake. Police cars had blocked both exits. Barton stopped as more police cruisers and news crews descended on the spot where he was boxed in.

A cop on a bullhorn thundered orders at Barton, who sat trancelike in his driver seat. "Open the door very slowly and throw out your gun. Then climb out and lie facedown on the pavement!"

No response.

"Barton, throw out your weapon and get out of the van!"

Nothing.

Barton was cornered. He had no place to go. The phalanx of cops surrounding him could afford to wait him out.

A single gunshot.

Barton was obsessed with escape, and he had done it one more time. With the Glock at his right temple and the Colt at his left, he'd intended to fire both at the same time, but only one went off. It tore off the back of his skull and splattered

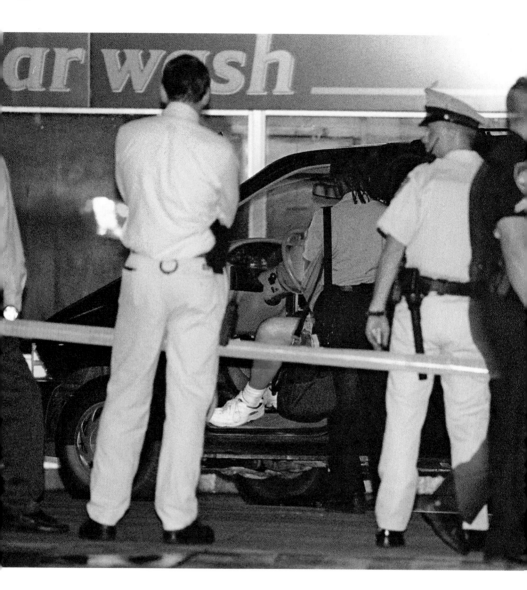

his brains all over the van's ceiling. On the seat beside him was his arsenal, some loose antidepressant pills, a cell phone, and a considerable amount of cash. In his glove box was a copy of his new will, in which he left everything to his mother and expressed a wish to be buried next to the two children he had just murdered.

On the day Mark Barton killed twelve people then blew his own brains out, the Dow dropped one

hundred eighty points and they called it a bloodbath.

GOING NASDAQ

At the same moment Mark Barton's brain was disintegrating, surgeons were piecing Brent Doonan back together.

His abdominal cavity had filled with 7 pints (3 liters) of lost blood. One-third of his liver had been blown away and was bleeding unchecked. His spleen had exploded. A rib was smashed. His diaphragm was a sieve. Part of his left lung was irreparably damaged. His pulse was so weak that the surgeon was literally squeezing his heart to keep it beating.

And beneath his right eye ran a raw furrow left by a .45-caliber slug that missed being his fifth serious wound by less than the depth of his skin.

For four and a half hours, surgeons worked to save Brent's life. Each time they plugged one bleeding hole, another showed itself. He'd lost twelve units of blood—his body's entire blood supply— and he was still alive.

Once out of surgery, he was hooked up to life support. Doctors left a 5-inch (12.7 cm)–wide hole in his side to let an infection drain. His raw, suppurating wounds were pinned together with more than three hundred stitches and staples.

A tenacious fever spiked at 103°F (39°C). The slugs had damaged several nerves, maybe permanently. For several days, he flinched at every shadow, every sudden movement, every waking dream. Night terrors gripped him, and he often awoke in a cold sweat.

Mark Barton still haunted him. The killer was dead, his family told him, but Brent asked again and again about him.

Five days after the shooting, Brent's father brought a copy of the *Atlanta Journal-Constitution*, in which a story on page eight detailed the cremation of Mark Barton in a country crematorium far from the city, far from Brent. His former in-laws had forbidden his last wish to be buried beside his children, who were buried in the same plot as their mother and Barton's first wife (and likely victim) Debra, so his ashes—if not his soul—were without a home.

"The bastard won't have to wait to get to hell," Brent's father said. "They already burned him."

It comforted Brent to know Barton wouldn't hurt anyone anymore, but he was freighted with guilt. Why didn't he see Barton's threat coming? Why didn't he jump on Barton when he had the chance? Why did he run? If he'd been a bigger man, a better man, would he have done something different? He replayed the whole sad movie over and over again in his troubled mind.

From that day forward, though, his physical condition slowly improved. Georgia governor Roy Barnes visited, reporters lurked around every corner, and thousands of well-wishers sent flowers, cards, and letters.

Even the boss of the Texas chemical company who had fired Barton so many years ago came to visit. He apologized to Brent for "letting Barton off the hook" after he had stolen company secrets. "But yesterday is gone," he told Brent. "All we have to do is work on today and tomorrow."

The man's words made him feel better, but Brent was still consumed with guilt. He asked the hospital staff to deliver all his flowers to the graves of Barton's victims. And he visited Scott and the permanently blinded Kathy—whose last vision was the face of Mark Barton—in their rooms, looking for answers, making apologies, fumbling around for the right words.

While Brent was on the mend, the North American Securities Administrators Association issued a critical report on day-trading that said nine out of every ten day traders lose everything. The *Wall Street Journal* published an article calling it "a lifestyle that is a petri dish for neuroses." Regular traders took to calling the occasional psychotic outburst in down markets "going NASDAQ."

On August 8, 1999, Brent celebrated his twenty-sixth birthday in a hospital room, surrounded by his family. Had he not been so young, so healthy, and so determined, he would have never seen this day.

Five days later—two weeks after Mark Barton shot him and killed twelve people in an insane spree—Brent Doonan wheeled out of the hospital into a different life.

THE LAST ESCAPE

On the first day of Brent's new life, as he was recuperating at his parents' home in Kansas, he was sued by the widow of an All-Tech victim. She claimed the company had failed to foresee a predictable meltdown by a distraught day trader. A dozen more suits would follow. Eventually, all of the lawsuits would be dismissed, but they hung over Brent for six years, and the legal entanglements prevented him from making the apologies he desperately wanted to speak to the families of his customers and friends.

Mark Barton continued to haunt him, too, mostly in nightmares, where he once saw Barton standing at the foot of his bed, aiming a gun at him.

After a couple months of rest, Brent went back to work at All-Tech, but even being in the refurbished offices—where the blood stains had been scrubbed, the bullet holes patched, and the carpets removed—made him ill. He developed panic attacks to accompany his lingering guilt. Worse, the markets were in a historic swoon, and All-Tech was hemorrhaging cash. Bills were piling up.

On August 8, 1999, Brent celebrated his twenty-sixth birthday in a hospital room, surrounded by his family. Had he not been so young, so healthy, and so determined, he would have never seen this day.

The only bright spot came at Christmas, when Brent was set up on a blind date with Sarah Poe, a beautiful, polished, athletic nurse from Augusta. They hit it off, and soon he was spending his weekends with her in Augusta, away from the city and away from the memories. For six months, she didn't know about Barton's attack, partly because the only time he felt truly relieved of all his demons was with her, partly because he didn't want to relive it.

In the fall of 2000, Brent was done with All-Tech. He sold his interest in All-Tech to his partner, Scott Manspeaker, who had also recovered from his wounds. Brent invested in a new online real-estate venture, but it tanked, taking nearly his every last dime. At the end of the day, he had almost nothing left, except Sarah and his family.

And that was enough.

By the time they married in the fall of 2001, day-trading was dead. His old life was dead. Mark Barton was dead. Brent and Sarah moved home to Kansas, the source of his strength, back to where he belonged. They got work, built a new life, and soon had a son, Jaxson, who quickly became the center of Brent's universe.

He also spent a year writing a book about his fateful encounter with Mark Barton. *Murder at the Office* was published in 2006—just one year before the Virginia Tech shootings—to scant notice, but it purged some of Brent's demons.

He wanted to forgive. Himself, as much as Barton. He wanted to give Barton, in death, more of a chance than Barton had given twelve people. He began to see every day since July 29, 1999, as a "freebie." When his friends complained about a bad day at work, Brent laughed.

"I wanted to show you could go through a day or week from hell and come back," he said.

For Barton's part, nobody yet knows what caused his deadly implosion. Many blithely blamed the stresses of day-trading for his collapse, although the evidence points to a complex and long-standing series of psychoses, behaviors, and events that probably had a much more profound influence on Mark Barton. Day-trading might have been more of a symptom than a cause of his catastrophic flameout. His rage might just as easily have resulted from his loss of control over his life, which his stock-market losses most certainly symbolized.

Barton's psychopathic tendencies showed themselves long before he discovered day-trading: his youthful criminal fantasies; his dysfunctional work life; his mask of intellect, humor, and charm; his remorseless, calculated response to accusations of grave criminal behavior, including the hyper-brutal bludgeoning of his wife and mother-in-law; even the killing of a family cat. All that—and more—pointed to a much more deeply disturbed, explosive psychopath, not a momentarily angry good guy who snapped over financial problems.

Was he, as one *Newsweek* writer suggested, a symbol of the angry American male, a victim of a telemarketed, outsourced economy that forced him to gamble on abstractions and put him at the mercy of distant events and corporations? Take a look in the cultural mirror, the article suggested, and see "a man in a room alone—isolated from his fellows, unneeded by his family, staring into a computer screen on which he seeks a disembodied fortune or, if that fortune fails, types a suicide note."

Or had he lapsed back into a paranoid and frighteningly nihilistic religious fanaticism in which the wicked "system of things" had to be eliminated? Although somewhat less likely as a root cause, some experts have pointed to Barton's earlier retreat into strange zealotry as evidence of the possibility.

But nobody knows, and nobody ever will. Maybe all those things. Maybe none. Mark Barton, it seems, has eluded understanding, his last ingenious escape.

Doonan doesn't speak Barton's name, and he wishes fervently that no killer's name will ever become more familiar than any victim's.

Today, Doonan supervises the finance and insurance branch of his father's truck dealership in Wichita, a business his grandfather started decades before. He still sometimes dreams about that day in Atlanta, but less and less as time passes. When he's in public, he watches people more intently. Every day, his fingers tingle from lingering nerve damage, but he plays with his son as if he were a child, too.

He never questioned the existence of God, but he wasn't so sure about miracles until he survived Mark Barton's rampage.

Like everyone else, he still doesn't know why it happened. He no longer weighs himself down with those questions because, he says, "someday I'll find out." Until then, he doesn't speak Barton's name, and he wishes fervently that no killer's name will ever become more familiar than any victim's.

"The choice, as with all things in life, is ours; to become a survivor or a victim," he wrote in *Murder at the Office*. "Just for today, I will be unafraid. . . . We are simply part of nature anyway. Nature is the sum of creation. From the Big Bang to the whole shebang. It's making snow forts, it's spring moving north at about thirteen miles a day, emotions both savage and blessed, the harvest moon, fat rainbows, the courtship tunes of birds, the sparkle in the eye of a person you love, a new leaf struggling to move the earth skyward in your garden, a shaft of bright warm summer light spilling over my shoulder as I read a good book, a call out of the blue from someone I love, my dogs licking my cheeks, my son giving dad a big hug."

CHAPTER 3

SEVENTY-SEVEN MINUTES IN HELL

KEITH THOMAS AND THE McDONALD'S MASSACRE

ENSENADA WAS ALREADY A DISTANT DREAM to Keith and Matao. The beach town lay only 70 miles (113 kilometers) behind them down old Mexico 1, but it might as well have been another universe. The week of vacation with Matao's relatives at their little trailer, with the fish, the fireworks, Matao's first kiss, the scorpion they captured in a jelly jar, the sea, the cliffs, the pirate beaches, that breathtaking blowhole, the sunsets . . . now it was all sucked up and exhaled in a squalid breath of exhaust, car horns, and dry July heat. The highway along the edge of Baja's glossy sea had given way to a desert dotted with the rusting hulks of Ford Fairlanes and VW Buses abandoned among the ocotillos, and then to the electric, dirty, smoky, scary chaos of Tijuana's panting streets, full of loud, smelly traffic and sweaty vendors hustling velvet Jesuses, or a cure for cancer, or unspeakable acts nobody should see.

But Keith and Matao were just little boys and hadn't seen anything yet.

Although he was twelve, Keith Thomas had never had a friend like Matao Herrera. They shared a little boy's passion for toy soldiers, drawing fantastic pictures, baseball, *Star Wars*, and pretending to be heroes on magnificent quests in the backyard.

Keith's mom and dad had been divorced for years, and his mom worked hard to keep her son fed and clothed, but she was gone a lot. She'd already been

MATAO AND BLYTHE HERRERA, SHOWN HERE IN A FAMILY SNAPSHOT, HUNKERED IN FEAR BENEATH THEIR TABLE WITH RON HERRERA AND KEITH THOMAS ON JULY 18, 1984, WHEN AN ANGRY JAMES HUBERTY OPENED FIRE ON DOZENS OF INNOCENT DINERS IN A SAN YSIDRO, CALIFORNIA, MCDONALD'S.

Courtesy of Keith Martens

married three times before Keith was in fifth grade. And there were boyfriends, too. Keith was on his own much of the time until his mom took a new job as a telephone operator in the little Los Angeles suburb of Orange. On his first day of second grade in a new school, the teacher assigned the blond and freckle-faced Keith to show this playful little half-Mexican kid wearing a Yoda T-shirt around. Keith knew he'd like any kid who'd wear a Yoda T-shirt. They bonded instantly and became inseparable, two halves of the same whole.

Before Matao, Keith's existence was a blur. He moved around a lot. He remembered a goldfish dying, and some of the men, good and bad, with whom his mom fell in love. There was an imaginary friend, a cricket. And he recalled getting his first picture Bible as a gift and asking a lot of questions about God, but not much more stuck.

Matao's parents, Ron and Blythe Herrera, were just thirtysomething hippies who had fallen in love in high school. He worked as a precision inspector for an oil company, and she was the consummate earth mother. They came to treat Keith like their own kid, feeding him and including him in everything they did. Their little bungalow was small, but they knew Keith's house was empty. Keith loved Blythe's alfalfa-sprout sandwiches so much that he'd trade his hot school lunch to Matao for them. If he loved Matao like a brother, then he loved Blythe like another mother.

For four years, they spent so much time together that Matao's parents, Ron and Blythe, had invited Keith to tag along with Matao on this Mexican vacation and family reunion. It was a brilliant trip: For a week, the boys made their own adventures in the old fishing village of Ensenada, and everybody was happy. Now heading north toward the border, they were crawling through Tijuana, lining up to go through the tiny gap between Mexico and California, the always-clogged U.S. port of entry at Tijuana's San Ysidro Transit Center, the busiest border crossing in the world. It was midafternoon on a Wednesday, so the traffic was already congealing at the gates as north-bound travelers scurried to get to California before rush hour on San Diego's swarming freeways.

In the stinking stop-and-go, Keith pulled his Ensenada visor lower and studied the shining bracelet Matao had given him. It was a chain with a small silver plate bearing Matao's name, his school ID. Keith's mother had moved again, so they would be attending sixth grade in different schools in the fall, and the bracelet was a reminder of their friendship.

Keith felt like part of a family, and it made him smile so much his face ached. But although the holiday had been magical, Keith wanted to see his mother and ride his bike and just be home.

After what seemed like a lifetime in the mid-July heat and dirty air, the American border guards eyed Ron Herrera's car, asked a few questions, and finally waved him through. The Mexican asphalt suddenly blossomed into a sleek, six-lane interstate freeway in the poor San Diego suburb known as San Ysidro, a stepchild district of one of the nation's most prosperous big cities. Still, San Ysidro was a few steps up from Tijuana, and the sunlight softened into the pastel shades of California, like waking up on the other side of the rainbow. The roadsides were suddenly familiar again, with American hotel marquees, franchise brake shops, and billboards in English.

It wasn't hunger as much as a craving for American food that made them want to stop somewhere for a late lunch.

About a mile up I-5 from the border, they spied the golden arches of a McDonald's and got off the freeway onto San Ysidro Boulevard, the main drag. It was just before 4 p.m., and the restaurant's parking lot, between a doughnut shop and a post office, was already crowded with the early dinner rush, everyone apparently deserving a break today at the same moment. The place was packed with about fifty people.

A YOUNG BOY LIES DEAD BESIDE HIS BICYCLE OUTSIDE THE SAN YSIDRO MCDONALD'S, ONE OF TWENTY-ONE PEOPLE KILLED BY GUNMAN JAMES HUBERTY.
Associated Press

Inside, Ron and Blythe took the boys' orders— Keith loved these new things called Chicken McNuggets with sweet-and-sour sauce and fries— before they scampered into the PlayPlace, where

other children were already cavorting. A few minutes later, carrying their loaded trays of fast food, Ron and Blythe took a corner booth inside the restaurant near the play area, where the hungry boys quickly joined them. Blythe sat beside Matao on one side, Ron beside Keith on the other, with their backs to the kitchen and counter area. As they tore into their burgers and fries, they laughed and talked about their dreamy days in Ensenada.

A blast shattered their reverie into a million pieces.

There had been many fireworks in Ensenada, and Keith thought someone had set off a big firecracker. He turned to look toward the front of the restaurant where the sound had erupted but only saw frightened people ducking down as a deep and angry male voice boomed, "Everybody down!"

Keith slid down beneath the table with Matao and his parents as the room exploded in an endless shudder of deafening bursts. Blythe screamed and began to cry. Keith had never heard anything as horrifying as the earsplitting rake of semiautomatic gunfire, much less in the confined, peaceful spaces of a neighborhood McDonald's. Everything was upside down.

Under the seat and against the wall, shielded by Ron, Keith couldn't see anything except parts of other terrified people hiding under the next table and the camouflaged pants of a man walking deliberately, just feet away. The thundering continued amid shouts and screams.

"What's happening?" he asked.

"Be still!" Ron commanded him. The fear in his voice scared Keith. "Don't move!"

Blythe screamed again. She hunkered at Keith's feet, and Matao was balled up beside her, next to the aisle. She could peer between the seats and the table.

"He's coming down the aisle shooting everybody!"

Keith turned his face to the wall and closed his eyes.

He no longer wanted to see what might be coming. He already knew.

He was about to die.

SLAUGHTER

Just before 4 p.m., a balding man dressed in camouflaged jungle pants, combat boots, a dark maroon T-shirt, and sunglasses pushed a mother and child out of his way as he entered the San Ysidro McDonald's, set his canvas bag on the floor, and unzipped an ungodly arsenal of weapons and ammunition. James Oliver Huberty calmly fired a shotgun into the ceiling to get people's attention, then set to the task of killing everyone he saw.

Fresh from shopping and hungry for a fish sandwich, Jackie Wright Reyes—pregnant and cradling her eight-month-old baby, Carlos, in her arms—stood at the counter with a friend and some children. They had just gotten their order when Huberty fired and commanded everyone to get on the floor. Huddled on the cold

tile with everyone else, Jackie shielded Carlos and her eleven-year-old niece, Aurora Pena, the best she could, but the man just looked down on them and started shooting.

First, he killed Jackie's teenage friend María Elena Colmenero-Silva with a single shotgun blast to the chest. Then he shot Aurora's friend, nine-year-old Claudia Pérez, several times with his semi-automatic Uzi.

Aurora was hit in the leg by one of the Uzi bullets and curled herself against her aunt's body, her eyes closed tight, except for the split second when she saw the man aim his little black machine gun at her aunt.

Then Huberty fired.

Jackie's body jolted and shuddered as it absorbed the long, slow fusillade of bullets in her shoulders, breast, back, buttocks, left arm, legs, neck, and head. The coroner would later count forty-eight separate wounds.

Baby Carlos, splattered in his mother's gore, shrieked. Unable to walk, he simply sat in the pooling blood and wailed.

Huberty shouted angrily at the child in a red jumpsuit to be quiet.

When the baby wouldn't stop screaming, Huberty aimed his pistol and put a slug in the baby's back.

"I've killed a thousand, and I'll kill a thousand more!" he shouted.

The madman shot at everything as he prowled back and forth through the restaurant. He had weapons in both hands. He screamed profanities and talked to the people he was about to kill. He told them he'd been in Vietnam and it didn't bother him to kill everyone. He fired his handgun, shotgun, and Uzi into windows, walls, and lamps; at pedestrians on the street outside; at passing cars—at anything that moved or cried. He kicked bodies to see whether they were alive or dead, then shot them anyway.

With the Uzi, he lit up the dark corners where diners took refuge, firing under tables and chairs.

Some corpses still held hamburgers. Others had tried to stem their bleeding with McDonald's napkins but couldn't save their own lives.

The kids behind the counter hid wherever they could in the steaming kitchen. Some fled into a stale basement closet after the manager and three young servers were shot point-blank. In time, a woman with a baby joined them, and then a wounded man.

Huberty stood at the drive-up window and fired at anything that moved outside. He blasted through the windows at anyone who came close. He listened to a portable radio, waiting to hear the news that would make him famous. The berserk shooter took out the flashing lights on a police cruiser in the parking lot, sending the lone cop scurrying for cover. Then he shot at an ambulance on the street until it sped away. There'd be more soon, he knew.

Huberty just kept shooting and reloading, spewing vulgarity and murder, stopping only to sip a cup of soda pop. The acrid stink of gun smoke and burning food filled the place.

A wounded woman on the floor looked up at him, and he saw her. He swore and threw food at her, then sprayed her with the Uzi again.

Three boys on bicycles rode up outside to get ice cream cones. They were still on the sidewalk when Huberty bellowed at them and then cut them all down with his shotgun. Two died instantly. The other was gravely wounded but played dead.

An elderly Mexican couple, Miguel and Alicia Victoria, had come to buy hamburgers to take home to Tijuana. Even at seventy-four, Miguel doted on his beloved sixty-nine-year-old wife, but as he reached to open the door for her, Huberty met them face to face.

The first blast from Huberty's shotgun hit Alicia in the face and knocked Miguel backward. Staring in shock at her bloody body on the ground, he screamed at Huberty.

"Goddamn it, you killed her!"

Miguel collapsed to the ground and wiped the blood from his wife's face as he cursed Huberty.

But Huberty didn't take shit from Mexicans. He cursed back at the old man, then put the shotgun barrel to his head and pulled the trigger.

From what he could see, he had killed them all, and it had only taken ten minutes. So he just paced the killing floor and waited for the world to learn what he'd done.

And he waited for the cops.

A CLEAR SHOT

It took a while.

The first 911 call came at 4 p.m., but cops and paramedics mistakenly went first to a different McDonald's 2 miles (3 kilometers) away from where a frenzied Huberty was killing people.

Ten minutes after the first call, police established a command post two blocks away, and within ten more minutes, the restaurant was surrounded. Life Flight helicopters were standing by, and urgent pages were sent to the San Diego Police's SWAT commander, but there was no answer.

Huberty kept them all at bay, shooting through doors and windows at any movement outside. He had 175 cops pinned down all around him. The nearby interstate was closed, and six city blocks were locked down.

From what little they knew, the police suspected several gunmen were inside; too many different guns were fired for it to be just one guy. But they also couldn't see much because the restaurant's safety-glass windows had been broken in a semiopaque web of tiny cracks.

A half hour into the slaughter, somebody finally found the SWAT commander at a reception in Mission Valley, 20 miles (32 kilometers) north. Within fifteen minutes, SWAT snipers encircled the restaurant.

In the meantime, Huberty's wife had seen the shooting on TV, and her daughter told her that his car was parked in the McDonald's parking lot, which they could see from their cheap apartment. She called police and told them everything she could about him, including that her husband owned armor-piercing ammo and could shoot accurately with either hand. They quickly brought her to the perimeter to coax her husband out, but it didn't work.

At 5:05 p.m.—more than an hour after Huberty's first shot was fired—the SWAT commander was speeding toward San Ysidro when he heard sharpshooters given the green light to shoot the gunman if they had a clear shot. He immediately countermanded the order until he arrived at the scene nearly ten minutes later. He couldn't be sure the proper precautions had been taken for the safety of his officers and people inside the restaurant. He worried that the gunman might have hostages or had traded clothes with one of the innocent people inside.

Moments after a second green light was given, Huberty shot out the restaurant's front window along San Ysidro Boulevard. Cops fired two shots back, but they missed him.

He had fired 247 bullets and shells. Twenty-one people were dead or dying, and nineteen lay wounded all around him. Thirteen of the dead were shot in the head, seven in the chest, and one—little Carlos Reyes—in the back. Only a handful survived physically intact, and nobody escaped without psychological wounds.

Seventy-seven minutes after it all began, SWAT sniper Charles Foster, perched on the roof of the post office next door, saw his chance. Huberty was standing alone at the front counter, a clear kill-shot in Foster's sights.

He squeezed the trigger on his Remington .308.

The bullet hit James Huberty dead-center in the chest and exploded his spine and smashed his heart into bits.

"WAKE UP!"

Throughout the ordeal, Keith Thomas huddled under the booth and listened to the cacophony of death all around him.

The alarms of the deep-fat fryers incessantly bleating.

Babies crying.

Glass shattering.

The wounded choking and gasping for air.

Guns booming.

The metallic jangle of empty bullet casings hitting the tile floor.

The shooter cursing at the living and the dead and at nobody at all.

More shots.

Then silence.

A small child lay next to a man's legs near Keith's head. He didn't know whether either one was alive or dead. He peeked up through a hole in the bench above him and saw the gunman lurking near the front counter, lifting his gun. Firing at someone.

That's when Keith noticed his own left arm was bleeding. It must have been cut by flying glass, he thought. He surely wasn't shot because he never felt any impact, just a slight burn.

A STUNNED KEITH THOMAS SITS DAZED WHILE A POLICEMAN CHECKS HIS WOUNDED ARM IN AN AMBULANCE OUTSIDE THE SAN YSIDRO MCDONALD'S MOMENTS AFTER GUNMAN JAMES HUBERTY WAS KILLED BY A POLICE SNIPER.
Associated Press

He didn't want to run. He wanted to see Matao. He wanted to know what was happening. He wanted to do something. He wanted to fight back. Oh God, how he wanted to fight back. But how? He was a twelve-year-old kid with nothing more than a plastic fork, no match for the shooter. He thought of his mother. *If I die, she's gonna lose it.*

Keith felt Huberty's dark presence the whole time. It terrified him to teeter at the edge of death, but he was powerless to do anything else.

He found out later that every time he twitched, every time he moved his leg or his head, Huberty fired and hit Ron Herrera, who still curled protectively around Keith.

Keith drifted in and out of consciousness. Time got all mixed up. Minutes dragged out forever as he floated between waking and blackness. Had it been an hour? Two?

Suddenly, from his hiding spot, Keith saw more camouflaged pants just a few feet away. Were there more bad guys? He grew even more confused when he heard Ron Herrera talk to the combat-booted men who were budging bodies on the floor.

They were cops.

Keith wriggled around. Matao and Blythe were slumped under the bench, both seemingly asleep. Blythe was disarrayed, stained with blood. Matao had blood all over him, too, seeping from some holes on his bare legs.

Keith slapped Matao's leg.

"Wake up!" he yelled.

Just then, a cop with a mustache grabbed Keith from behind and pulled him from under the table. Keith fought him as he was hustled to the curb outside, where the cop left him sitting alone. He watched the chaos unfold around him as other wounded people and survivors were hurried to waiting ambulances, wailing and bleeding. Everything became a blur of uniforms and bloodstains. And he had never felt more alone in the world.

He also saw a bloodied Ron Herrera out there, sobbing as he tried to go back inside, seemingly unaware he'd been shot eight times. It began to dawn on him that maybe Matao was not asleep at all.

Another cop tried to remove Matao's bracelet from Keith's arm, which was streaming blood onto his shorts and legs. He refused to give it up and started to cry. A paramedic walked him to an ambulance where medics were treating a woman who'd been shot in the breast and a teenage McDonald's worker who was shrieking over a leg wound; the paramedics quickly moved him to another ambulance. He sat there with a little girl about his age whose mother and sister were wounded, too. They talked to each other as if they had not just come within an inch of dying.

The ambulance took them all to the hospital. There, doctors found one 9 mm bullet had grazed Keith's right wrist, and another had entered his left forearm and burrowed into his shoulder, where it ricocheted back down his arm and exited near the crease of his elbow.

His mother was late getting to the hospital, posing a horrible scenario in the little boy's mind: Was she dead, too? To him, the possibility that anyone could die at any time without any reason or explanation had suddenly become all too real.

His grandfather later told him what had happened in McDonald's, at least as much as anyone felt he should know. Blythe and Matao were dead, he said. But he didn't tell the poor kid that they'd both been hit several times, apparently as they tried to crawl toward a nearby door. They were slaughtered when they retreated back under the table.

Matao was the good one, Keith always said. He was a gentle soul. And now that he was dead, Keith began to wonder what kind of God would take the good one and leave . . . him? In those first days, he began to think he should have died instead of Matao.

Keith spent a week recovering from his wounds. When he could sleep at all, he heard the sound of gunfire in his vivid nightmares.

After he was released, his mother took him to Matao and Blythe's funeral. It was an open-casket affair; Matao's sweet little face looked swollen, which bothered Keith, but none of his wounds showed. Keith cried, but he was in a stupor through most of the service and barely spoke. Afterward, some reporters came up to him and asked to see his wounds, and he obliged them by removing his sling and exposing his healing holes.

Soon after the funeral, Keith visited Ron Herrera in the hospital, where he was still recovering. He took off Matao's bracelet and gave it to Ron, and they both cried.

Despite the incredible horror he'd endured, the worst was yet to come.

And there was a good chance he wouldn't survive his survival.

THE COMING HOLOCAUST

In the days after the massacre, the portrait of James Oliver Huberty developed slowly, like some sinister Polaroid in all the violent colors of grief.

He was born on October 11, 1942, in Canton, Ohio. His father, Earl V. Huberty, worked in a steel mill in nearby Massillon, about 10 miles (16 kilometers) west of Canton, and was well liked by his neighbors in the rural farming community where he and his wife raised their kids in a devoutly Methodist home. After he was hurt on the job, Earl retired to his family farm, which he sold off over the years, piece by piece, to keep the family afloat.

At age three, James contracted polio and wore braces on his crippled legs for several painful years while children teased him about his awkward gait and crooked knees.

When he was seven, his mother abandoned the family to become a Pentecostal missionary to an Indian reservation. James was crushed.

Although he was a good student, James was distant and quiet growing up. Before he became the most prolific mass shooter in American history, most of his public school classmates would have barely remembered him, even though his graduating class of 1960 in Waynedale, Ohio, had only seventy-four students.

His family was so fervently religious that some believed James would go into the seminary. But while many of his classmates dreamed of being doctors or lawyers or taking over the family farm, James dreamed of being an embalmer. He took funeral-science classes at Malone College in Canton, and then his father sent him to the Pittsburgh Institute of Mortuary Science in Pennsylvania. He came home to Canton for his final internship at a local funeral parlor, where he quickly proved to be far better with the dead than the living. He enjoyed embalming and the other morbid but solitary pursuits of a mortician's back rooms, but he was clumsy and abrasive with customers.

"He was intelligent, but he just couldn't relate to others," Canton funeral director Don Williams, Huberty's mentor, said shortly after the shooting. "He simply wasn't cut out for this profession. He acted like he just wanted to be left alone." Despite the bumps, Huberty finished his internship, and the Ohio embalming board licensed him in 1966.

During that time, James met Etna Markland, a California girl who was a substitute teacher at a local grade school. They married in a private religious ceremony, moved into a small, tidy house in Massillon, Ohio, and started a family. They eventually had two daughters: Zelia in 1973 and Cassandra in 1977.

But even then, James didn't seem right. Coworkers, neighbors, and even the pastor who married James and Etna saw a man shadowed by inner demons that were clawing at his guts. Even in calm moments, he seemed barely able to control his anger at the world.

He kept snarling German shepherd guard dogs and hoarded food in his basement in fear of a coming holocaust. He forced his two little girls to take karate lessons because he feared the people around him.

In 1969, not long after earning his license, James quit the funeral business for good and became a welder at a Canton power plant, piling up overtime and taking night courses at Malone College until he earned a bachelor's degree in sociology in 1976.

JAMES O. HUBERTY GREW INCREASINGLY FRUSTRATED AFTER LOSING HIS JOB AS A WELDER IN OHIO. HE MOVED TO MEXICO, THEN TO SAN YSIDRO, CALIFORNIA, IN SEARCH OF RICHES, BUT ONLY GREW ANGRIER.

San Diego, CA, Police Department

Etna kept the Massillon house in pristine order and, at least in the early years of the marriage, was generally considered a good woman raising two fine girls. James was another story. Neighbors often grumbled about the thumping they heard coming from the Huberty house at night. They didn't know for a long time that James had built a shooting range in the basement.

James's fascination with guns started in childhood. Neighbors said guns were displayed in almost every room of the little house, and James often sat just inside his front door with a shotgun on his lap. Just sat.

Local cops came to the house more than once, sometimes because the Hubertys were complaining about the neighbors, sometimes because the neighbors were complaining about the Hubertys. Twice, the Hubertys were hauled in on minor charges.

In 1980, police charged James with disorderly conduct in a dispute at a service station. The reporting officer said a belligerent James simply wouldn't calm down, even after police intervened. He pleaded guilty and was fined only court costs.

A year later, Etna was charged with four counts of "aggravated menacing" for waving James's Browning 9 mm semiautomatic pistol—the same gun he later used in the McDonald's shooting—at neighbors during an argument. The charge was reduced to disorderly conduct.

NOTHING TO LIVE FOR

In 1982, James Huberty's fragile world began to crumble.

He was laid off from his welding job of thirteen years when his employer, Babcock & Wilcox, closed the plant.

"I got no job or anything," he told Etna. "I've got nothing to live for."

A coworker recalled even more chilling words. An embittered James talked about "shooting somebody."

"He said that if this was the end of his making a living for his family," the coworker said later, "he was going to take everyone with him."

Etna believed James had a nervous breakdown after the layoff. His politics became frighteningly radical as he blamed irrational enemies—capitalism, secret government initiatives, America's rich, former President Jimmy Carter, minorities, or the shadowy darling of 1980s conspiracy theorists, the Trilateral Commission—for his ruin. Voices in his head urged him to kill himself. He told people he was a German, even though he wasn't. He feared a nuclear war was only days away.

Then he had a brainstorm. They would sell their house for a big profit and move to Tijuana, where they had once vacationed. There, James said, they would "make a lot of money," although he never truly had a plan.

"We're going to show them who's boss!" he crowed.

Unfortunately, the neat little Massillon house sold at a $69,000 loss, but in October 1983, they moved to the grubby little Mexican border town anyway. James, the Rust Belt refugee, hated it. It was polluted, and the cops often stopped him on his motorcycle. Distrusting Mexican schools, they drove the girls across the border every day to a San Ysidro school. It was too much. Within three months, he uprooted the family again and moved across the border to a $610-a-month, two-bedroom apartment, where the Hubertys were the only Anglos in a mostly Latino complex. And they were running out of cash quickly.

Then James saw an ad for a program that trained low-income, unemployed men to be security guards. He ranked near the top of his twenty-seven-student class but made no real impression on his trainers. In April 1984, he got his license, and a few months later, since he had no serious crimes on his record and a check of his FBI fingerprints didn't raise any red flags, he received a gun permit that let him carry a loaded .38 or .44 Magnum pistol on duty.

But the voices in James Huberty's head grew louder and his delusions more twisted. Once, he approached a police cruiser on foot and surrendered himself as a war criminal. An FBI check showed nothing, so he was simply told to go home.

The voices in James Huberty's head grew louder and his delusions more twisted. Once, he approached a police cruiser on foot and surrendered himself as a war criminal.

In June, the Hubertys moved again, this time to Averil Villas, a dowdy, stuccoed apartment building a block off San Ysidro Boulevard, a stone's throw away from the McDonald's.

A month later, on July 10, he was fired from his job as a security guard because his bosses were troubled by his skittishness and odd behavior. James was again crippled by his disappointment at yet another failure in his life. On July 17, Etna finally convinced him to call a mental health clinic, but because of a clerical error, his message was never delivered.

The next day—the last day of his life—James Huberty took his wife and daughters to breakfast before appearing in traffic court on a routine citation. Afterward, they ate lunch at a McDonald's in San Diego and visited the zoo. They came home in the early afternoon and James took a nap.

Etna grumbled that the mental health clinic hadn't called back, but James shrugged her off.

"Well, society had their chance," he said.

Before 4 p.m., the forty-one-year-old unemployed security guard got up, dressed in camouflaged fatigues, black combat boots, and a maroon T-shirt, then kissed Etna good-bye.

She asked where he was going.

"Hunting," he said. "Hunting humans."

The ominous comment didn't faze Etna. James was always saying weird things. He could have walked to the McDonald's in less than a minute—it was that close. But Huberty got in his black Mercury Marquis and drove. In his duffel bag were his Browning P-35 Hi-Power 9 mm pistol, a Winchester 1200 pump-action 12-gauge shotgun, and a semiautomatic Uzi, all legal weapons, all legally purchased. He also had more than five hundred cartridges and shells.

Slowly, the missed signs began to emerge.

After the massacre, Etna told a reporter that she regretted thwarting her husband's futile suicide attempt a year before. Or wished that she had killed him herself, which she tried to do during one of their many arguments thirteen years prior, but her gun jammed.

Neighbors and coworkers remembered moments that, in light of the killings, took on new, ominous meaning.

"He always did comment on how he wanted to go through a lot of people," his ex-foreman at the plant told the Canton paper the day after the rampage. "He had a lot of guns in his house, and he always said he wanted to kill a lot of people. We watched him a lot. We believed him. It was just a question of when."

An autopsy found no drugs or alcohol in Huberty's corpse but did discover elevated levels of the metals nickel and cadmium, likely remnants of his days as a welder. Two years after the shootings, Etna filed a $5 million wrongful death lawsuit against McDonald's and James's former employer, Babcock & Wilcox, claiming her husband's killing urges were triggered by a combination of monosodium glutamate in the chain's food and the poisonous metals. Together, she said, they caused delusions, kidney failure, and uncontrollable fury. The case was thrown out.

It had been almost twenty years since the nation's attention had been so viciously grabbed. The last time was Charles Whitman's 1966 shooting spree from the Texas Tower in Austin, which left fourteen dead and thirty-one wounded. (See chapter 6.) Americans had grown complacent in the intervening years. Now they were shocked all over again by the latest record mass shooting.

Neither of those slaughters clings to the cultural memory like an unbeatable cancer simply because of the body count. In both cases, place matters significantly.

Whitman's rampage was made even more frightening by the looming tower in which he perched above everyone like some bloodthirsty angel of death. And Huberty chose a place where every American had been, a shared space where children played, where Little League teams went after the game, where people stopped to satisfy cravings. Every town had a McDonald's. Walking through the door, people knew exactly what to expect. It was always a safe choice. But suddenly, Americans everywhere could imagine themselves under fire in PlayPlace.

Just days after the rampage, Joan Kroc, widow of McDonald's founder Ray Kroc, seeded a fund for survivors and victims' families with $100,000 of her own money; the corporation added another $1 million. Keith's mom eventually got $10,000 for his wounds. The company even took all its upbeat advertising off the air for a time, costing untold millions.

One night, a month after the tragedy, even before James Huberty's ashes were secretly buried in Ohio, crews leveled the darkened restaurant completely. McDonald's donated the property to a local community college and built a permanent memorial to the victims on the spot where they died.

The horror was not in vain. Of course, anti-gun politicians seized the

> James Huberty "had a lot of guns in his house, and he always said he wanted to kill a lot of people. We watched him a lot. We believed him. It was just a question of when."
> — a former coworker

moment, and others demanded to know why Huberty's call to the clinic went unanswered. But many American police departments quickly rewrote their tactical manuals to make faster life-and-death decisions, and the now common practice of rapid-response mental health teams evolved.

A few months later, Etna Huberty announced she planned to sell the movie rights to her story so she could raise her two daughters. Several TV networks passed on the movie. Eventually, in 1987, producers released *Bloody Wednesday*, loosely based on the massacre, but it was poorly received and disappeared from theaters quickly.

Huberty still had fans, however. One was an angry ex-seaman named George Hennard, who was fascinated with the McDonald's massacre. He watched videotaped documentaries of it again and again. And seven years after James Huberty set the grim standard for psychotic mass murderers, Hennard plunged himself into another family restaurant more than a thousand miles away to raise the bar one more time. (See chapter 4.)

One hideous event had sent forth a thousand bleak ripples.

And Keith Thomas was one.

COLLATERAL DAMAGE

Although a normally outgoing boy, Keith stopped talking altogether in the days after the massacre.

While his wounds healed, he withdrew into himself. And he began to get angry. At first, it was with the people who kept telling him that Matao died because God needed him and stupid shit like that. He couldn't imagine God needing a little boy so badly that he would allow him to be murdered, punctured a dozen times by a madman's bullets.

After he was released from the hospital, he went to his mother's house, where she lived with a boyfriend whom Keith hated. The man abused Keith's mom and was an unpleasant authoritarian. Keith's anger welled up every time the guy talked, and he became verbally abusive toward both his mother and her boyfriend.

Nobody had ever really talked to Keith about faith, but he remembered God from the picture Bible he had been given years before. He still sensed there was a God or something bigger out there, but now it suited him to be angry with this God. He believed God was there, but Keith was pissed off at Him.

Not long after the McDonald's shootings, his mother took him on a Mexican cruise, just the two of them. She thought it would be good for her damaged son. The nightmares hadn't subsided, though, and he couldn't sleep. One night on the ship, during an argument with his mother about what to wear to dinner, she reached out and touched Keith's leg. He kicked her across the room.

In school, Keith felt like a freak, as if he didn't belong there, didn't fit in. One day in school, an annoying classmate pushed him too far. Keith beat him ferociously, and it felt good every time he hit the kid. Afterward, as he realized what he had done, Keith wept.

Anger became a drug. Living mad felt good.

But once, just one brief moment, he felt peace. He was recuperating at his grandparents' home when the television set came to life on its own. The tube hissed with snow. He hadn't touched it, and he didn't know why he asked out loud, "That you, Matao?"

The set went off.

Keith sat mesmerized.

"If it's you, come back."

The set whispered back to life, then just as quickly went off again.

It was the first time Keith believed Matao might be watching him.

But things just got worse after that. When his mother couldn't handle him any longer, she sent him to live with his biological father, a former

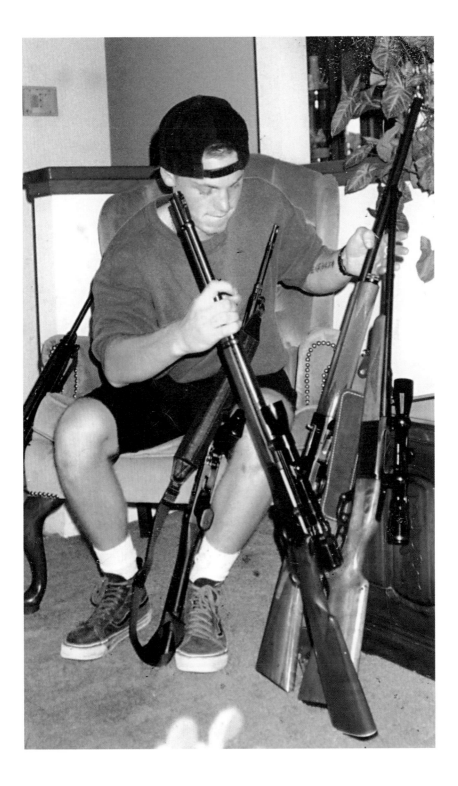

Army Ranger and Vietnam veteran living in Washington State and dealing with his own postwar nightmares. His father tried hard to restore the best parts of Keith, but they had burrowed too deep inside.

He spent much of his time in school staring out the window. He fell in with the kids who skateboarded and liked punk rock music. The first time he heard the Sex Pistols, the band's rage spoke to him. Like them, he was angry at everything—authority, heaven, the way life used to be, the light. The dead.

Keith lived with his dad for about eight months, and then he went home to California to continue his agonizing slide into madness. At thirteen, he was a full-fledged skate punk. He carved a circled A—the symbol for anarchy—in his own forearm. He still jerked at loud noises or an unexpected touch. Once, a teacher grabbed his arm, and he slugged her.

He started running away, spending long nights in abandoned trailers or empty pool houses, living on shoplifted food. He developed an interest in guns. He smoked flattened cigarettes he found on the sidewalk. He stole beer from open garages and hid in ditches or alleys to drink himself into the perfect illusion that he was worth a shit. Sometimes he went back home on his own. Other times they had to drag him back.

As he pushed more people away, he grew more lonely, more disturbed.

That's when Keith dropped the surname Thomas and adopted his biological father's name, Martens. He was reaching for something solid in his liquid world, where his name had already changed each time his mother remarried. He wanted so badly to have something to hold on to that he tattooed the name in big, ornate letters on his arm.

Less than two years after the McDonald's murders, he wrote a poem to Matao. Why him, it asked in part. He had no sins, he never did anything to that man.

He fell in love with pot. It pulled a thin veil over his memories. At fourteen, he couldn't get enough of it. His mother feared the worst—that Keith was insane and killing himself bit by bit. One day, when she found him after he had run away again, his mother took him straight to a mental hospital, where Keith was diagnosed with an ordinary personality disorder and locked down in a ward with other kids just like him—misfits, dopers, rebels, and freaks.

After a few months, no less depressed, he was transferred to a new hospital. There, he mostly slept and partied with the kids—they called themselves "inmates"—who cheeked their meds and pooled them for late-night parties on the ward. He even tattooed his right forearm—his scars—with a question mark.

KEITH MARTENS HAS LEFT BEHIND THE HORRORS OF THE 1984 MCDONALD'S MASSACRE AND THE DARKNESS OF THE YEARS THAT FOLLOWED—EVEN THE LAST NAME OF "THOMAS"—TO START HIS OWN FAMILY AND A CAREER IN SOUTHERN CALIFORNIA, BUT THE MEMORY OF HIS BEST FRIEND WHO WAS SHOT TO DEATH BY KILLER JAMES HUBERTY IS NEVER FAR FROM HIS MIND.

Ron Franscell

Then he went AWOL for a while until his mother found him and took him back to the hospital. He escaped again, and this time he overdosed on a handful of NoDoz pills and PCP before he was taken back to the ward.

DRAGGING OUT THE DEMONS

His mother was desperate. Nothing was working. She began to seek out specialists who might be able to reach Keith, and she found Dr. Robert Pynoos, a UCLA psychiatrist who was just beginning to investigate the unexplored mysteries of the effects of violence on children. Pynoos was intrigued by Keith, whom he believed had been misdiagnosed; Keith probably didn't have a personality disorder, he thought, but was likely suffering from posttraumatic stresses directly related to the McDonald's massacre.

Pynoos gave Keith a test. His Childhood Posttraumatic Stress Reaction Index was the first scale designed to measure the extent of a child's damage from violence. A score of 60 indicated a "very severe" reaction to whatever original trauma the child had suffered. Keith scored 75.

> **Keith was so damaged, Dr. Pynoos warned, that he was unlikely to live until he was eighteen.**

Pynoos immediately assigned one of his key aides, Dr. Kathleen Nader, to meet Keith. She was the director of UCLA's Trauma, Violence, and Sudden Bereavement Program, which researched and provided counseling to innocent young victims of violence, disasters, and war.

But Pynoos told Nader not to get her hopes up. Keith was so damaged, Pynoos warned, that he was unlikely to live until he was eighteen. The first time they met, Keith looked much younger than fifteen.

Keith hated Nader and he hated the bullshit therapy. He cropped his hair closely and bleached it blond. He had inked a skull and crossbones with the words "Dead Kennedys Society" on the sleeve of his oversized, olive-drab jacket. He told Nader that he didn't need whatever she was peddling and just wanted to be out of the hospital, on his own, with the motley crew of friends he was assembling among the "inmates."

Nader quickly saw how extraordinarily complicated Keith's psychological wounds were.

Even more than two years after the massacre, he was still having nightmares. Memories of the horrors still intruded at odd and all-too-often moments, yet sometimes he reenacted parts of the experience. He was unable to function in a classroom. Good kids avoided him. He was emotionally detached, seriously depressed, blamed himself for living, and couldn't control his impulses. If he wasn't lashing out at anyone who tried to talk about the massacre, he was literally beating his head against the wall until they shut up.

Nader saw Keith's unresolved grief for Matao, whose death was all tangled up in the memory of that horrible day. Keith couldn't properly grieve for his friend without reliving the whole grotesque moment and triggering a new series of horrifying symptoms.

The loving, intelligent, self-assured little boy Keith had been before the McDonald's incident had been swallowed up by his own damaged, traumatized, angry, antisocial shadow.

Just keeping him alive—much less fixing him—would be more complicated than peeling back the layers one by one. Keith was an unfathomable tangle of survivor guilt, rage, depression, self-destructive behavior, hostility, drug abuse, pessimism, emotional detachment, feeble self-esteem, obsessions, poor impulse control, self-mutilation, nightmares, and identity problems—all traceable to that day at McDonald's, all left untreated for more than two years, and all on the razor's edge of a little boy's adolescence. Worse, Keith's unstable childhood before the massacre left him especially vulnerable to the horrors the massacre heaped upon him.

Under Nader's care, Keith was released from the hospital and started seventh grade in an affluent school near the beach. He was the only skate punk, still doing drugs, still hanging out with old friends and skipping classes, still picking fights just to avoid being the victim again. He got high and listened to Black Flag, the Exploited, and other hardcore punk bands. In time, the school kicked him out. He went to a new school, where he still didn't fit in.

Things continued to get worse, not better. He had sessions with Nader once a week, but he skipped many of them and then stopped going altogether. She was still trying to drag out all his demons, and he was still resisting. The fights, the school, the drug use—mostly pot—were getting worse.

Still in junior high, he graduated from huffing aerosol Scotchgard to dropping acid, doing speed, and then snorting cocaine. He held himself together by selling marijuana to buy booze and more drugs. He was still running away, sometimes sleeping under the piers at the beach. Each time, his mother brought him home, but he never stayed long.

As if his life had become some kind of psycho-drama, Keith began acting out various roles he had witnessed in the McDonald's massacre. At different times, he wore the masks of the aggressor, the victim, the rescuer, even the information gatherer.

He became obsessed with books and movies about killers. Even as he tried on the parts of victim and rescuer, he always returned to the killer. He started dressing in fatigues and tight black T-shirts, like Huberty. He instigated fights and surrounded himself with kids who reinforced his aggressive behavior.

In one treatment session with Nader, Keith created a paper doll that looked just like him, down to his bleached hair and the green jacket with an inky symbol on the sleeve. He then proceeded to beat the doll, break its arms, slap it on the table, and hang it.

By the time he was sixteen, Keith was working dirty jobs for cash, partying constantly, and getting more violent. He loved to fight, especially bullies. He fell in with a punk gang, then with the skinhead underground, which embraced his violence with fiendish gusto. He quit working altogether and sold pot to make ends meet.

One dark night, while he waited in San Ysidro for a cab ride into Mexico, he started thinking about what had happened there. He started to cry, then started to drink just to numb himself. He blacked out.

During those days, the law was starting to catch up with him. In 1992, after a violent attack with some of his skinhead thugs, Keith did some jail time for misdemeanor assault and he spent more than a few nights in lockup on other charges, but it didn't dampen the rage in him.

At a club one night, Keith—now playing the rescuer role—rushed to defend a buddy who was being trounced in a brawl. He was stabbed in the belly and the knife broke off inside him. Keith's friends took him home, anaesthetized him with a bottle of whiskey, and dug around in his wound with a pair of needle-nose pliers until they found the broken blade, unwittingly carving up his intestines with their bumbling first aid. The resulting infection landed him in the hospital, where he quickly discovered the bliss of opiates.

Back on the street, he got into a garbage can of drugs, including a daily dose of heroin. He'd fallen in love with smack because it took away all feeling. He loved to stick his needles in the scars left by James Huberty's bullets. He even got a kick out of sucking his blood up into the syringe, then downing the whole mess again.

Incredibly, Keith's life would get even darker from there.

Although he had started seeing Nader again—mostly to mollify his mother and keep her on the hook for more drug money—he drifted in and out of jails, rehab clinics, and drug houses. He lived on the street or with other junkies. He tried detoxing a couple of times, unsuccessfully. He was busted for going into a bar with a gun. And he always went back to the junk.

He was twenty-two—ten years after the McDonald's massacre—when an odd pain developed in his legs. When he couldn't ignore it any longer, he went to a hospital, where they told him he had endocarditis, a heart infection likely caused by his intravenous drug use. The prognosis was poor because he had waited too long and the infection was too advanced. His heart was literally falling to pieces. He could stroke out at any minute.

After a month of antibiotics, doctors repaired Keith's damaged valves in open-heart surgery. Surprising everyone, he lived and was eventually released from the hospital—back to his angry, strung-out life. He picked up with the heroin where he had left off, pushing his limits even farther than before. His incisions were still fresh when he overdosed in a park and came close to dying again. He could feel the warm China White crackling in his brain cells.

He counterfeited money and stole tires right from under cars for cash to buy more heroin. He was a junkie who knew the stuff would kill him, and he was okay with that. Many of his relatives had written him off. He woke up every morning dope sick and went back out to hustle enough money to buy his next fix. He lived dirty and bloodied inside and out; even his underwear were perforated with little burns from nodding out with cigarettes between his fingers.

He wanted to die. At least, in the few times he prayed, that's what he asked for.

THE ROLE OF RESCUER

Keeping up a habit is hard work, especially when the goal of dying proves elusive.

Keith wasn't dying, and he was tired of merely being miserable.

Some tiny part of him, the child who survived the McDonald's shootings, wanted to live, goddamn it. And that part of him finally spoke up. If he wasn't going to die, he wasn't going to live like this any longer.

In 1996, twelve years after James Huberty turned his world upside down, Keith decided for himself to come clean. He felt guided by an unseen hand.

Metropolitan State Hospital was an old insane asylum. He spent his first week of nonmedical detox—old-fashioned cold turkey—in the Spartan "wet room," where they caged the worst cases who would puke, shit, and piss on everything in their delirium. When he was ready, he was sent to a halfway house where he met people just like him. Suddenly, he realized he was not a freak of nature. Everyone had his or her own demons.

Drifting through halfway houses for a year, his depression, insecurities, anger, obsessions—all his defects—were on full display. With the help of other addicts, he wrestled with each of them.

It wasn't easy. He cleaned himself up, inside and outside, not in one grand sweep, but slowly, one day at a time. He clawed his way through frozen, polluted layers toward the child buried alive beneath. He fought the foul urges that came in weak moments. He still couldn't let anyone come close to him, physically or emotionally. He retained some vestiges of the hostage-taker.

But he was clean and sober, had come to terms with God, and for the first time since that day at McDonald's, he stopped being a victim. Victims were not responsible for what happened to them. To take responsibility for himself, Keith had to stop playing that role.

Three years into his sobriety, Keith met the woman he would eventually marry. They had a son, who focused Keith in a way he'd never known. But his problems were not behind him: The day his son was born, Keith was undergoing a second emergency surgery on his damaged heart.

He eventually went back to school and got his GED, then started taking some college classes.

The 9/11 attacks dealt a blow to his recovery, so he entered a new phase of therapy. Among his therapist's first exercises was for Keith to list his resentments. James Huberty was there. One by one, Keith had to make amends with his resentments as a way to move forward, but Huberty always hung him up.

Keith began to imagine himself as an adult talking to the twelve-year-old boy who had been lost so long ago. Not Matao, but Keith. He felt an overpowering urge to save the child from James Huberty and everything that would follow. He reassured his younger self that everything would be all right.

The Rescuer.

He finally crossed Huberty off his list.

Keith was clean and sober, had come to terms with God, and for the first time since that day at McDonald's, he stopped being a victim.

For many years, Keith wouldn't set foot in a restaurant of any kind. When he finally did, he would sit with his back against the wall, facing the door. Today, he still won't go inside a McDonald's, but he often uses the drive-through window. Baby steps.

For a long time, he was haunted by two distinct moments at McDonald's: his poking at Matao's dead legs and his being snatched from his hiding place by cops who he thought might be killers. He no longer lashes out instinctively at people who touch his legs or arms, although some physical contact still reminds him of his near-death experience.

Keith now works as a project manager for a Southern California company that builds high-tech, high-end home theaters for wealthy clients. He also dabbles in oil painting, preferring themes of light and dark, inside and out.

These days, Keith still feels emotionally distant from most people except his son, but he's working on it. He also still blanches at the sound of beeping deep-fat fryers in fast-food joints. He continues to discover who he is and wrestles every day with stubborn old demons, but he's finally got the upper hand.

He has grown comfortable in the role of the rescuer and no longer endangers himself in violent situations. He counsels anyone who needs to hear his story and learn what he has learned.

And he still talks to Nader, his own rescuer, every couple of months, no longer as the patient but as a friend. A pioneer in childhood PTSD and a veteran of dealing with later school shootings, mass murders, the Gulf and Balkan wars, and even the World Trade Center attacks, Nader now lives in Texas and is one of the nation's leading authorities on the long-term effects of catastrophic trauma on children.

Some days, Keith thinks about Matao. He still has some of his friend's drawings, but he has never gone back to the cemetery where he was buried. He's not there. Keith feels Matao watching him every day. An angel, no longer a ghost.

He hasn't seen Ron Herrera since the day he handed back Matao's bracelet. Keith often thinks about the man who saved his life, but he doesn't know what he'd say if they met now, and he doesn't want to revive bad memories for a husband and father who lost nearly everything. He knows the awful power of memory.

His mother never gave up on him, even when he lashed out at her, took her money, and failed her in so many ways. She was the one constant in a life spent on the wind. She remains his most ardent protector.

The McDonald's massacre shaped Keith Martens. It's still a part of his life that he doesn't completely understand. But he knows this: James Huberty doesn't own him anymore.

"I used to fantasize about pissing on his grave," Keith says today. "But not anymore. I don't care about him now.

"It's just easier to get over it than it is to hang on to it."

CHAPTER 4

NIGHTMARE AT NOON

SUZANNA GRATIA HUPP AND THE LUBY'S MASSACRE

SUZANNA GRATIA REALLY DIDN'T HAVE TIME FOR LUNCH. She had a dozen errands to run and a full afternoon schedule at her chiropractic clinic in Copperas Cove, Texas. She was just thirty-one, a single woman struggling to build a small business in a small town. She refused to waste a sunny autumn weekday slacking off. She'd already declined a lunch offer from a friend who managed the Luby's Cafeteria in Killeen, about 10 miles (16 kilometers) up US-190. Time was money, and Suzanna needed both.

So when Suzanna's retired parents, Al and Suzy Gratia, dropped in after their Wednesday morning golf game and invited her to lunch, she begged off. After all, she saw them almost every day. They lived next door, and Suzy, a former executive secretary at Boeing in Houston, closely watched the clinic's administrative operations, while Al, who'd recently sold his heavy-equipment dealership, kept Suzanna's books.

Less than two weeks before, the Gratias had celebrated their forty-seventh anniversary with a big family party. Al and Suzy were anything but fragile geezers waiting to die. Al was seventy-one and Suzy was sixty-seven, but they traveled and golfed most mornings. Al spent his afternoons writing a book and local newspaper columns. Still, they had more time on their hands than Suzanna, and today she needed her lunch hour to do more pressing things.

So mom and dad bartered for her company: If Suzanna would eat lunch with them, they'd run some of her errands for her.

Suzanna couldn't refuse. She called her buddy, Luby's manager Mark Kopenhaffe, and accepted his offer. On the way, she and her mother dreamed up plans for Al and Suzy's fiftieth anniversary party. When they arrived at Luby's a little after noon, the parking lot was already packed. It was the day after payday at Fort Hood as well as National Boss's Day, and employees around Killeen didn't have too many other choices for a cheap, fast lunch with their supervisors.

Suzanna parked her Mercedes in a side lot. But before she got out, she slipped her Smith & Wesson .38 caliber handgun out of her purse. Soon after she graduated from chiropractic school and moved to Houston, one of her patients—a prosecutor—suggested she carry a gun for protection in the big city, even though concealed weapons were against the law in Texas. "Better to be tried by twelve than carried by six," he joked.

So a friend gave her a gun and taught her to shoot it. She was licensed to carry it, but Texas law forbade her from taking a hidden weapon into a public place. So now, rather than risk losing her hard-won chiropractic license by breaking the law, she tucked the snub-nosed revolver safely out of sight, behind her front passenger seat.

Besides, she only carried a gun for menacing moments, lonely roads, and dark places where young women needed protection from monsters—not crowded family restaurants on warm, sunny days in small central Texas towns.

What Suzanna didn't know was that at the same moment a young man not much older than her, his head filled with demons and his pockets filled with bullets, was barreling toward a bloody cataclysm the world never saw coming.

A BEAUTIFUL BOY

George Hennard was an unfinished soul.

Born October 15, 1956, in Pennsylvania, this son of an authoritarian Army surgeon father and a doting, narcissistic mother grew up a loner. The Hennards moved a dozen times before George was eighteen. Partly because he moved around so much and partly because he was frightfully strange, George never quite fit into any school cliques and was a mediocre student.

Some who knew him as a boy said he was outgoing and cool, but his personality and behavior literally changed overnight after an argument with his tyrannical father, who chopped George's long dark hair with a scalpel. He was so embarrassed by his haphazard haircut that he ran away, but when he was returned home, an enraged Dr. Hennard shaved him bald.

"He was never the same after that," a classmate said later. "He was completely introverted."

His relationship with his mother, Jeanna, who had two children from a prior marriage, was turbulent. A pretty woman who tended to dress far younger than her years, she cooed and called young George her "beautiful boy." But almost from the start, their bond was far more complicated. Their fights were often vile screaming affairs that sometimes became physical—and then at other times, they were warm and loving. Although he deeply craved his mother's approval, years later Hennard would call her a bitch and draw Jeanna's head on the slithering body of a rattlesnake.

By the time he transferred from Maine to a new high school at White Sands Missile Range in New Mexico, Hennard—who now preferred to be called Jo Jo, the way his baby sister Desiree pronounced "George"—yearned to be accepted, especially by the girls, who always kept him at arm's length. But he cloistered himself in his room with his rock music and marijuana. The pot mollified the beast inside, submerging him in an artificial serenity.

Jo Jo also bought a drum set, but his rock-star dreams evaporated with every jam session when he plunged into his own alternate musical reality, ignoring the rest of the band, even the music they were playing.

Hennard grew to be a handsome man, just over 6 feet (about 2 meters) tall with a trim, 185-pound (84-kilogram) physique and dark, wavy hair. Women found him attractive at a glance, but up close, his piercing black eyes were unsettling, spooky. Even when women saw past his eyes, he spoke awkwardly and had trouble communicating. Nothing ever went far.

After graduating from high school in 1974, Hennard joined the Navy. Although he hated taking orders, detested the minorities on his crew, and chafed at the tedium of shipboard work, part of him thrived at sea. He especially loved exotic ports of call, where he could marinate his unsound soul in easy drugs and easier women, who never rejected him.

During George's unruly Navy years, his father was given command of the hospital at Fort Hood, near the small town of Killeen, Texas. When Dr. Hennard retired from the Army in 1980, the family settled in the nearby village of Belton, where they bought a sprawling, four-bedroom colonial brick mansion built on four lots.

Life was not so easy for their son. After being disciplined for minor offenses in two captain's masts on the fleet oiler USS *Mississinewa*, Seaman Hennard was transferred to the destroyer tender USS *Dixie*, where he kept his nose clean but earned low performance scores. Three years after he joined the Navy, George's enlistment ended, but the Navy

AL AND SUZY GRATIA, SHOWN HERE, HAD SPENT THE MORNING AT A LOCAL GOLF COURSE AND WERE INTENT ON SHARING A LUNCH WITH THEIR BUSY DAUGHTER, CHIROPRACTOR SUZANNA. THEY CONVINCED HER TO JOIN THEM AT LUBY'S CAFETERIA IN KILLEEN, TEXAS, ON OCTOBER 16, 1991, UNAWARE OF THE DANGER THAT AWAITED THEM.

Courtesy of the Hupp Family

7706

didn't give him a chance to re-up. Although he was honorably discharged, across the bottom of his service record was printed "Not Recommended for Reenlistment."

A LIFE UNMOORED

At twenty, George Hennard was adrift. Dark squalls were brewing inside him again. The sea had been taken from him. For the first time in his life, nobody—not his father, his captain, or his absentee conscience—could tell him what to do, and Hennard had never made good decisions on his own.

Four months and a minor pot bust later, Hennard went back to sea. He took a job in the Military Sealift Command, a government-run agency that delivered supplies to the military. After a few more months, he joined the Merchant Marine as a seaman aboard a variety of civilian freighters steaming out of ports on the Gulf of Mexico.

In 1982, Hennard assaulted a black shipmate, and his seaman's license was suspended for six months. He went to ground in Texas, near his parents' home in Belton, where he pursued his volatile love-hate relationship with his mother, his loathing of women, and his unrestrained pot habit. A roommate at the time later recalled that Hennard "hated blacks, Hispanics, gays. He said women were snakes. He always had derogatory remarks about women—especially after fights with his mother."

When Hennard returned to sea, he sailed out of San Pedro, California, the main harbor for Los Angeles. He earned up to $5,000 a month, and with few expenses beyond his $90-a-week flophouse room, he banked most of it. After Jeanna divorced Dr. Hennard in 1983, George generously loaned her large amounts of money. He also paid cash for a brand-new 1987 Ford Ranger pickup with a scintillating metallic blue paint job, and financed a new Cadillac for his mother—a luxury car he obsessively tended for her.

Hennard loved being at sea so much that he spent his vacations in distant ports of the Far East and Central America, where he could satisfy his overwhelming cravings for drugs and obedient, nonwhite prostitutes.

As it had been all along, it was precisely George Hennard's cravings that sparked his final, fatal decline. In May 1989, marijuana was found in Hennard's shipboard cabin. He was suspended again and sent to a two-week drug treatment program in Houston. Not long after his release, his own father—a medical doctor—would tell a relative that he believed Hennard was schizophrenic. When this got back to George, it caused a final rift between father and son, who never spoke again.

On August 23, 1989, George Hennard's seaman's license was revoked for good. This was the darkest moment in his dark life. Though he would appeal, he would never go back to sea.

While he prepared his appeal, he worked odd jobs, from steam-cleaning to construction, never staying anywhere very long. He stayed off and on at the now-vacant Belton mansion, which his mother had won in the divorce but was trying to sell. He tried to join an Austin blues-rock band, but his heavy-handed, manic style and his habit of drifting into a different groove again doomed him. He carped profanely about the women he met and always ended up with compliant hookers. His white-hot rage at the world simmered, and his paranoia grew profoundly creepy.

When his rootless lifestyle had consumed most of his savings, Hennard moved into his divorced mother's two-bedroom apartment in Henderson, Nevada. Their tangled lives remained sometimes affectionate, sometimes violent.

Once, Jeanna fixed her son up with a single woman who worked with her at Miss Faye's Nail Salon in Henderson. During the short, strange courtship, Hennard took her on a macabre pilgrimage to the site of America's bloodiest mass murder to date: James Huberty's seventy-seven-minute lunchtime rampage at a McDonald's restaurant in San Ysidro, California, where twenty-one people died before Huberty was killed by a police sniper in 1984 (see chapter 3).

ALONG WITH HIS SUGGESTIVE LETTER TO NEIGHBOR JANE BUGG'S TEENAGE DAUGHTERS, GEORGE HENNARD ENCLOSED THIS ODD SNAPSHOT OF HIMSELF PLAYING HIS DRUMS IN THE BADLANDS. ON THE BACK, HE SCRAWLED, "MY NEW 'HANGOUT' IN THE DESERT NEAR LAS VEGAS. BEAUTIFUL PLACE AT NITE TIME!"

Courtesy of Jane Bugg

The relationship grew tenuous soon after Hennard went on a paranoid rant about being followed by police, and it finally ended after he had a stormy argument with mother on Christmas morning in 1990. That morning, a raging Hennard stomped out of his mother's house and sat revving his pickup's engine just outside the living room window. His shocked girlfriend feared he was planning to gun the truck through the glass, but instead he roared in reverse out of the driveway. She never saw him again.

DISTRAUGHT AND DELUSIONAL

Less than two months later, Hennard made a last-ditch appeal to get his seaman's license back. He wrote a two-page letter, claiming he'd suffered more punishment for smoking pot than the drunken captain of the ill-fated Exxon Valdez, who was suspended for only nine months. Playing every angle, Hennard also begged the U.S. Coast Guard (which regulated merchant seamen) to help him kick his drug habit by allowing him to go back to sea—because if he couldn't work as a seaman, "I honestly do not believe I could be rehabilitated from drugs.

"Any person can tell you who has known me that I am not readily adaptable to shore life," Hennard closed his letter. "It stinks! My home is the sea, and it is where I belong."

Despite his mushrooming desperation, Hennard's case wasn't hopeless. The commander of the Coast Guard's Marine Safety Office recommended clemency, but the final decision would take months. After eighteen agonizing months, George Hennard wasn't going to wait much longer.

Also in February and March 1991, an increasingly distraught and deluded Hennard bought two handguns, completely legally. He paid $420 cash for a Glock 17, a lightweight Austrian combat pistol capable of firing eighteen rounds as fast as the shooter can pull the trigger. Reloading with a new seventeen-round clip takes less than two seconds. A month later, he paid $354 cash for a stainless-steel Ruger P89, a workhorse semiautomatic pistol that could fire up to sixteen 9 mm bullets before reloading.

On June 5, 1991, Hennard visited the FBI field office in Las Vegas. He told the agent that his civil rights had been violated by a secret cabal of white women who conspired to thwart his love life by spying on him, tapping his phone, and spreading lies to prospective employers. Sometimes, he said, they stood in front of his car to prevent him from driving.

But apparently not all women were wicked. For obscure reasons, Hennard eventually developed an obsession with two teenage sisters, Jill Fritz and Jana Jernigan, both pretty and both blonde, who lived with their divorced mother Jane Bugg a few doors down from the Belton mansion.

The day after going to the FBI, on June 6, he handwrote a five-page, disjointed letter to Jill and Jana. In an increasingly delusional script, he cooed sweet hallucinations to the girls as he railed against the "mostly white, treacherous female vipers of [Belton and Killeen] who tried to destroy me and my family." Suggestively, he wondered if "the three of us can get together someday?"

"I will prevail in the Bitter End!" Hennard promised as he closed. Among the four photographs he enclosed in the letter was a self-portrait with his drums in the desert. It said: George—Grande, final solo.

Within a week of mailing the letter, Hennard was back in Texas as the caretaker of his mom's Belton mansion. There, he spent his days compulsively washing his truck; meticulously dusting the furniture; making copious notes to himself in journals, on calendars, and with tape recorders; and videotaping some of his favorite murder programs on TV, including a documentary about Huberty's massacre and the 1988 terrorist bombing of Pan Am Flight 103 over Lockerbie, Scotland.

> **Hennard also played, again and again . . .
> Steely Dan's "Don't Take Me Alive," a hard-
> rocking anthem about a killer holed up against
> enemies who laugh at him and spread lies—
> the killer determined to cling to his own
> dark delusions rather than surrender.**

When potential buyers toured the mansion, Hennard would stalk close behind. He kept some doors locked, including his bedroom. When he spoke to them, as he often did, he would list the home's flaws or chide children who wandered away from their parents. The house was his. Not theirs.

But it wasn't just about the house. When children ran after balls that strayed onto the expansive lawn at Hennard's mansion, he chased them away, shouting curses. Young girls walking past were peppered with suggestive remarks. One friend recalled him passing a girl on the street and yelling out his truck window, "Bitch!"

Darkness descended on George Hennard. He fell even deeper into his obsessions and paranoia. In the wee hours of the night, neighbors could hear his squeaking mountain bike passing up and down the dark streets, aimless and haunting.

Hennard also played, again and again, a song that to him coruscated like St. Elmo's fire. It was Steely Dan's "Don't Take Me Alive," a hard-rocking anthem about a killer holed up against enemies who laugh at him and spread lies—the killer determined to cling to his own dark delusions rather than surrender.

Some days, he followed Jill and Jana to their jobs, or to the market, where he might tease them by popping up unexpectedly from behind a car or playing catch-me-if-you-can in the aisles, before disappearing into thin air.

And in the darkest nights, Hennard sometimes crept beneath their bedroom window for hours, smoking cigarettes, tossing butts in a growing pile on the ground, and watching. A few days after the usually docile family shih tzu inexplicably began yelping wildly at shadows in the night, the dog dragged himself into the garage and died. He'd been poisoned.

The girls' mother, Jane, began to have nightmares about George Hennard. In one, she saw him as a night wraith phantom, circling their house until he came crashing through the living room's plate-glass bay window with blazing guns in each hand.

Jane awoke with a start in the electric darkness of her room. It was only a dream, she thought.

Only a dream.

"SOMETHING TERRIBLE'S GONNA HAPPEN"

Before dawn on Wednesday, October 16, 1991, George Hennard rode his creaky bike to the Leon Heights Drive-In for his customary fast-food breakfast. Most mornings, clerk Mary Mead hated to see him walk through the door. He was rude and scary, sometimes pushing other customers out of the way as he demanded service.

Sometimes, he'd spit on other customers' cars as he left.

One recent morning, he had glared at her and sounded a warning to no one in particular. "This town had better stop messing with me and my family," he growled, "or something terrible's gonna happen."

But not today. Hennard smiled and said good morning as he picked up his usual items: an orange juice, a sausage-and-biscuit sandwich, some doughnuts, and a newspaper. George's geniality was out of character. It vexed her.

"Three thirty-seven," she told him as she rang up his breakfast.

Hennard grubbed in his pocket, then smiled.

"I don't think I have it," he said. "Can I come back this afternoon and pay you?"

"Sure," she said as he gathered his food and pedaled off.

The day before, George Hennard had celebrated his thirty-fifth birthday alone. In his desk calendar, he had marked the date with these words: "I am not an animal nor am I a number. I am a human being with feelings and emotions."

He had spent part of his big day in downtown Belton, bitterly complaining about his water bill, blaming yet another conspiracy against him. At nightfall, he had driven to the Nomad, a roadhouse, snack bar, arcade, and gas station rolled into a single rusty corrugated metal building just outside the town limits, for his birthday feast of a burger and fries.

While he ate alone at a small table, he watched the TV over the beer cooler. The evening news was replaying clips of the Senate hearings on Anita Hill's sexual harassment charges against Supreme Court nominee Clarence Thomas. Suddenly, Hennard hurled his half-eaten burger across the room at the screen.

"You dumb bitch!" he had screamed. "Now you bastards have opened it for all the women!"

But that was yesterday, when things had been all wrong. This was another day—a day to set things right.

Hennard showered and dressed for the occasion. He buckled his freshly ironed, stonewashed jeans with a Southwestern-tooled leather belt. Over a white T-shirt that said "Ford, the heartbreak of today's Chevy," he buttoned up a short-sleeved, turquoise shirt whose yokes were embroidered with multicolored Aztec mazes and desert roses. He chose bright red socks from his drawer, put them on, and laced up his brown Rockport Oxfords. He wore no jewelry except his Casio quartz wristwatch with a gold face, and he pocketed his turquoise- and coral-studded jackknife.

Before Hennard put his personal destiny in motion, he ordered his belongings neatly in the big house. He threw out the birthday card his mother had sent, and put the garbage cans at the curb. Everything was laid out: the shipping boxes for his two guns, his videotapes, his Merchant Marine footlockers, his overseas photos, his journals and notes. And there was a fat folder of legal documents about his Merchant Marine troubles, which had culminated in his dismissal—exactly two years, minus one day, before.

Around 11 a.m., he wrote a note to his sister Desiree, who lived off and on at the mansion, too, and left it on the dining room table:

> Desiree,
> Enclosed is $100.00 to cover the Water and Electric Bill. Do not pay the phone bill! I am responsible for it. Southwestern Bell violated my Privacy Rights. Therefore they don't get paid. Don't let the people in this rotten town get to you like they done to me. Take care of yourself and be strong.
> Love you
> Brother Jo Jo

And on his desk calendar, in the square for October 16, 1991, he scribbled: "Life has become a stalemate. There is simply no hope and not a prayer."

SETTING THINGS RIGHT

So it wasn't hope Hennard carried. Instead, he stuffed a pack of Bristol cigarettes and four pre-loaded clips of 9 mm ammunition in his pockets, along with a fistful of loose cartridges. With two semiautomatic pistols and more than a hundred rounds, he was ready.

At 11:50 a.m., Hennard backed his Ford Ranger out of his driveway in Belton and soon turned onto Sparta Road toward US-190. In less than a half hour, he'd be in Killeen to set things right.

More than 150 diners jammed the Luby's dining room on this Wednesday lunch hour. A few were Suzanna's friends and patients, whom she greeted warmly as she came in. One of the benefits of living in a safe, small town.

The serving line was long and the Gratias' usual table by the restaurant's front windows was occupied, so they claimed a table on the far side of the dining room, beside a wall of floor-to-ceiling windows. Manager Mark Kopenhaffe

DURING THE LUNCH HOUR ON OCTOBER 16, 1991, AN ANGRY AND PARANOID GEORGE HENNARD CRASHED HIS FORD PICKUP THROUGH THE GLASS WINDOWS OF LUBY'S CAFETERIA IN KILLEEN, TEXAS, AND BEGAN HIS METHODICAL SLAUGHTER OF THE SHOCKED DINERS INSIDE.

Texas Department of Public Safety

joined them for lunch, sitting across from Suzanna, who he bantered about politics with while keeping one eye on the unrelenting stream of hungry people who continued to spill through the front door. It was going to be a big day. One for the books.

A little after 12:30 p.m., the swollen serving line slowed almost to a stop and several tables hadn't been bused, yet customers were still coming. Mark excused himself and went to the cashier's counter to speed things along.

The Gratias had eaten their fill and chatted idly while waiting to thank Mark for lunch. At 12:39, mellow Muzak played above the collective hum of friendly diners and the soft clinking of silverware in the dining hall. Hanging pothos plants, potted palms, the gentleness of pastel mauve and emerald green colors, and the sheer draperies softened the feel of a corporate cafeteria, made it innocuous and homey.

So at first, the startling crash was presumed to be a busboy who had dropped a big stack of dishes, usually the worst calamity to befall most commercial eateries such as this one. But when everyone in the place wheeled around to see not a pile of broken plates but a monstrous blue pickup truck exploding through the plate-glass windows and into the carpeted dining room, smashing tables, chairs, and people in a slicing shower of glass before coming to a stop twenty feet into the crowded restaurant . . . well, reason twisted in upon itself.

An accident! Suzanna thought as she rose from her chair to help. Somebody lost control of his truck and crashed into the restaurant. Maybe a heart attack! Maybe he needed help!

A few Samaritans rushed toward the truck to aid the driver. One was reaching for the door handle when the driver thrust his left arm out his open driver-side window and fired a gun four times into the serving line, and fired another with his right hand out the rolled-down passenger window. And before the driver's would-be rescuer knew what was happening, he had been shot three times. He died instantly.

"This is for the women of Belton!" the shooter yelled as he leaped from the truck, a Bristol cigarette still between his lips.

It's a robbery! Suzanna suddenly thought. *They're going to come for our purses!* She could hear the *pop-pop-pop* of gunfire, but her view was blocked by the truck, which sat just twenty feet away between her and the shooter. Suddenly, Al turned their table on its side and they crouched behind their meager breastwork, but Suzanna had to watch. She had to know.

After the first burst of pandemonium, an eerie silence fell on the entire tan-colored room as George Hennard began shooting the people closest to his truck, then hunting down others. The killing was easy. People hid under their tables, cowering and trying desperately to make themselves small, invisible, but they couldn't make themselves small enough. Isolated cries erupted with each shot, then died.

"This is for what Bell County did to me and my family!" he shouted cryptically as he fired at anyone who stood or fled. "This is payback! Was it worth it? Was it worth it?"

Suzanna saw his face for the first time less than a minute after he crashed through the window; it was intent and calm. Hennard came around the front of his truck toward her, stopping to aim point-blank at a wounded man's head and pulling the trigger. He shot another one, then another one. Always in the head.

What's wrong with this guy? Suzanna's rational brain was spinning, trying to make sense of the bedlam. Like so many women who'd crossed paths with George Hennard, she was sucked into the paradox of his handsome looks and his behavior, which people often don't associate with beauty. *He's not bad looking. What could be so wrong? I'd go out with him . . .*

Suzanna reached for her purse lying a couple feet away, but she realized to her horror that her Smith & Wesson wasn't in there. It was safely under her passenger seat a hundred feet away, and a lunatic killer stood between them.

Then the ghastliness of his purpose dawned on her. This wasn't a robbery. It was a mass murder, like the one she remembered had happened at that McDonald's in California seven years before. She had thought at the time she would have been able to shoot Huberty with her gun if she was there that day. Now here was this freak, methodically slaughtering frightened people as calmly as an altar boy lights candles, and he would kill everyone unless he was stopped.

She had a gun! She had a clear shot, a place to steady her aim, and he was less than six paces from her. She'd dropped smaller targets much farther away. She couldn't miss.

"WE HAVE TO GET OUT OF HERE!"

I've got him! she thought.

Suzanna reached for her purse lying a couple feet away in the warm goo of her uneaten chicken tetrazzini—but then realized to her horror, even before she lifted it from the congealing mess, that her Smith & Wesson wasn't in there. It was safely under her passenger seat a hundred feet away, and a lunatic killer stood between them.

"Wait till those fucking women in Belton see this!" Hennard hollered as he shot into a group of school teachers. "I wonder if they'll think it was worth it!"

There was no time for regret. Suzanna began to consider her other alternatives, all bad. She thought of breaking the window and running but knew it would only call attention in her direction. She thought of stabbing the gunman with a steak knife, throwing a saltshaker at his head, whacking him with her goopy purse while he inserted a fresh clip at the next table.

"The women of Belton and Killeen are vipers," Hennard shouted as he pumped three bullets into the chest of Kitty Davis, a new grandmother who'd come to celebrate a former coworker's engagement.

Hennard prowled the floor, cool and deliberate, executing crouching patrons point-blank in the head or chest, pausing only to rack new clips into his guns. Witnesses later said he often passed over men to shoot women.

The entire restaurant was eerily silent, except for the *pop-pop-pop* of Hennard's guns and his profane ranting. Frightened diners hid the best they could, sometimes protected by nothing more than their hands covering their heads, hoping not to attract the killer's attention. Paralyzed by fear. Waiting quietly to die.

"I have to do something," Al Gratia told his daughter as they hid behind their overturned table. "If I don't, he'll kill everyone in the restaurant!"

"Yeah, and he'll kill you, too, you son of a bitch!" she screamed as she clung for dear life to her father's golf shirt. She kept waiting for a cop to take the killer down. A seventy-one-year-old man shouldn't be the one. Where were the cops? There were always cops in here!

Al had been a crew chief for a U.S. Army Air Corps bomber squadron in World War II, but he was no John Wayne. He didn't own guns and didn't fish because he couldn't inflict pain on the fish. He taught his children how to shoot with a BB gun, but after Suzanna's brother killed a mourning dove, nobody picked up the gun ever again.

Al just couldn't sit and watch people die, one by one, at the hands of a lone madman. And he knew his wife and daughter would die, too, if he didn't act.

In a split second, Hennard turned away and Al leaped out of his daughter's grasp. He'd taken only a few steps when Hennard turned back and shot him once in the chest. Al dropped onto his side in the narrow aisle and groaned. He was alive but mortally wounded—and Suzanna knew it.

Instead of coming for Suzanna and her mother, Hennard turned to his right and picked up the systematic slaughter in the front area of the cafeteria. Later, she would realize that her father's body probably blocked Hennard's path to them, and with so many other targets, it wasn't worth the trouble of Hennard making his way to them.

Hennard moved back to the serving area, where many people tried to hide. "You trying to hide from me, bitch?" he yelled at a woman huddled in a corner just before he killed her.

He emptied his Ruger into several more people with a cool affect. When he used up all his preloaded Ruger clips, he just set the useless gun on a plate of fried chicken and hush puppies and continued to kill with his Glock.

Returning to the center of the dining room to investigate a mysterious heavy thud, Hennard cornered Olgica Taylor and her daughter Anica McNeil, who clutched her four-year-old daughter Lakeichha.

"Tell people I ain't killing no babies today!" Hennard shouted. "Tell everyone Bell County was bad."

He stepped aside to let Anica and her child flee, and when the young mother wavered, he yelled again, "Get out of here before I kill you both!"

Then he shot Olgica in the face before making another pass through the dining room, killing others as he circled.

In the chaos, people tried desperately to hide. One woman hid in a walk-in freezer and was later treated for hypothermia. A teenage food preparer curled inside an industrial dishwasher and didn't come out until the next day. Some got away, but most were frozen by their fear, trapped like rats in a box.

Suddenly, another explosion of glass rattled the restaurant, this time from the back. Suzanna feared it might be a second attack by an accomplice, but it wasn't. A 6-foot-6, 300-pound (about-2-meter, 136-kilogram) mechanic named Tommy Vaughan, a Luby's regular, had thrown his linebacker body through one of the immense windows at the rear of the dining room, and panicked diners now frantically scrambled behind him through the jagged glass.

"Mom, we have to get out of here!" Suzanna yelled, but Suzy had just watched her husband of nearly fifty years gunned down. She was frozen by fear, slumped against the window. Suzanna stood and turned her back to the gunman, fully expecting to feel the thump of a bullet as she lifted her mother to her knees. She knew she'd only feel the impact at first. The burning pain would come later.

"You've got to follow me, Mom!" she commanded as she sprinted toward the open window, stumbling over someone and losing a shoe as she fell headlong into a bramble of glass shards outside. Blood streamed from cuts on her hands and arms as she ran, with one bloody, bare foot, across the asphalt toward Mark Kopenhaffe, who'd just emerged from an emergency exit.

"My father's shot in the chest . . . he's down . . . ," she told her friend as she looked around expecting to see her mother right behind her. "My God, where's my mom? I thought she was right behind me!"

Suzy hadn't followed.

Suzanna tried to go back, but police had finally arrived on the scene and a cop kept her outside. Her mother wasn't with the others who'd escaped, and the restaurant's reflective glass hid the carnage inside. The shooting continued as she limped to the relative safety of a nearby apartment complex with other survivors.

There, a tenant loaned Suzanna a phone so she could call her sister in Killeen.

"Get over to Luby's now. There's been shooting. Mom and Dad are in trouble" is all she said.

She tried to call her brother in Lampasas, too, but only got his answering machine. In the background of her message were gunshots. Hennard was shooting the straggling diners who had been wounded or hesitated to escape when they had the chance.

GOING DOWN WITH A FIGHT

When the first cops arrived, they couldn't be sure who the shooter was. One rattled survivor told them it was a black man carrying an assault rifle. And if they saw a man with a gun inside, they couldn't be certain if it was the killer, a vigilante civilian defending himself, or another undercover cop.

But any doubt was erased when State Police Sergeant Bill Cooper, standing outside the shattered window where it all began eleven minutes before, watched a dark-haired white man in a blue, short-sleeved shirt firing at wounded people on the floor and then executing an old woman next to the windows on the far side of the dining room. It was Suzy Gratia.

"Police!" one of the cops yelled, but Hennard ignored them.

WHEN HIS RUGER P89 RAN OUT OF BULLETS DURING HIS DEADLY 1991 ASSAULT, INSANE KILLER GEORGE HENNARD LAID IT ON A PLATE OF FOOD AT THE LUBY'S CAFETERIA IN KILLEEN, TEXAS.
Texas Department of Public Safety

A Killeen undercover detective, Ken Olson, was one of the first lawmen on the scene. When Hennard showed himself, Olson fired his Browning 9 mm from his hip. His bullet passed through the killer's right forearm and lodged below the skin in his chest. Stunned, Hennard retreated to a confined alcove outside the restrooms. He was cornered.

But he wasn't going down without a fight. He fired more shots and taunted the cops, who shot back.

"Drop your weapon and come out with your hands up!" Olson's partner Chuck Longwell hollered.

"Fuck you!" Hennard yelled.

"Fuck us? Fuck you!"

"Fuck you! I'm going to kill more people," Hennard taunted again.

A handful of cops slowly closed in on Hennard's hiding place, crawling over dead and wounded bodies as they tightened the noose. This guy wasn't getting out alive unless he surrendered, and that didn't look likely.

After trading a few more shots, Hennard was hit in his left thigh, throwing him against the alcove's back wall. Although he now suffered from at least four flesh wounds, the undaunted Hennard unleashed another fusillade.

"I have hostages!" the killer yelled.

The cops could clearly see he didn't. The skirmish continued.

"You don't have any fucking hostages," Olson said.

"I do, too!"

"Show 'em!"

Then Hennard spied a cop crawling belly-down through a breach in the ruined dining room. An easy kill. He raised the Glock for a clear shot and—nothing. His gun jammed. A live shell stuck awkwardly out of the breech. In all the chaos, Hennard had mistakenly shoved a Ruger clip into the gun. He dropped to his stomach, hastily cleared the breech and substituted a full Glock magazine he found on the floor, then racked the slide.

It was too late to kill the cop, who now had the drop on him. But it wasn't too late to make things right.

Hennard rolled onto his back, pressed the Glock against his right temple and pulled the trigger. The bullet exited his left temple and hit the alcove wall, releasing a spew of blood, fragments of brains, and whatever demons haunted him.

The numbers were horrifying. Twenty-two innocent people—eight men and fifteen women—lay dead around Hennard, and another woman died of her wounds later. Seventeen were wounded by gunfire, and sixteen more suffered cuts, broken bones, and shock. More than one hundred rounds had been fired in little more than twelve minutes.

One small town wondered why.

And George "Jo Jo" Hennard, who died with his frightening eyes open and lay in a congealing puddle of his own gore, had fired the last shot in the deadliest mass shooting in American history.

The world had missed every sign, every omen.

THE HORROR OF THE LUBY'S MASSACRE PROPELLED SUZANNA GRATIA HUPP (SHOWN HERE WITH HER FAMILY AFTER SHE TOOK OFFICE) INTO THE TEXAS LEGISLATURE, WHERE SHE CHAMPIONED LAW-ABIDING CITIZENS' RIGHTS TO CARRY CONCEALED WEAPONS. HER CRUSADE REVERBERATED THROUGH MANY STATES AND ALL THE WAY TO CONGRESS.

Courtesy of the Hupp Family

MONSTROUS MOVIE

Al Gratia outlived his killer.

When the shooting ended, paramedic Robert Kelley found Al alive but in shock, rolling from side to side, unable to speak or breathe. His pulse was weak, and he was turning a deathly blue as he slipped toward unconsciousness. At a glance, Kelley knew Al was mortally wounded, likely drowning in his own blood. Because other lives might be saved in these precious minutes, Kelley made a harsh triage decision. He mentally labeled Al as a likely death.

"Let's get this guy out front, on oxygen," Kelley told an EMT with a stretcher as he continued the grim task of sorting the dead from the living. Muzak still played and a phone rang incessantly somewhere as the Vietnam combat vet circled the wrecked room. Gun smoke and the smell of death hung in the air as he covered each corpse's face with a green linen napkin, a sign to his fellow medics that this one was beyond help.

When he was almost finished, Kelley checked another lifeless man's pulse.

"Is he dead?" asked the police officer standing over him with an assault rifle.

"Yeah."

"It's a good thing," the cop said, and that's when Kelley knew the dead man was the killer himself.

> **Suzy Gratia refused to save herself**
> **because it would require leaving**
> **her beloved husband Al behind.**

As Kelley hurried to help with the wounded outside, Suzanna tried in vain to get back into the restaurant to find her mother and father. Refused reentry at the broken window where she'd escaped, she looked for her lost shoe and limped around to the front of the building, where ambulances were shuttling the wounded to local hospitals, along with a steady stream of med-evac dustoffs from Fort Hood. She pushed her way through a growing throng of reporters, frenzied survivors, overwhelmed first responders, and curious onlookers.

There under the Luby's atrium, out of the direct sun, she found her father's body strapped to a backboard. He had just died. His open eyes were empty and flat, and blood pooled on the asphalt beneath his stretcher. She cursed herself for being slow getting there, for the cuts that slowed her, for worrying about a goddamned shoe. She might have been able to spend her father's dying seconds with him.

"Is there anything I can do?" she asked Kelley, who covered Al's body with a sheet.

"He's gone," the veteran paramedic answered.

Suzanna's sister and brother-in-law, Erika and John Boylan, suddenly burst through the crowded chaos.

"Dad's gone," Suzanna told her as Erika dissolved into tears.

"What about Mom?" Erika asked when she regained her composure.

"I've got a bad feeling," Suzanna said, close to breaking. "The way the guy was shooting . . ."

The news about Suzy Gratia came later, when survivors were gathered in the neighboring Sheraton Hotel, when Suzanna's friend Mark Kopenhaffe appeared at the door of her first-floor room.

"Thank God you're okay!" she said, hugging him.

"Suz, your mom's dead," he told her. "There's nothing I could do."

"How do you know?"

He told her how the cops had watched Hennard kill Suzy, how her death strangely might have saved lives. "Him shooting her . . . that's how they knew he was the bad guy," Mark said.

SUZANNA GRATIA HUPP TURNED HER GRIEF AND ANGER INTO ACTION BY BECOMING ONE OF THE NATION'S MOST VISIBLE ADVOCATES FOR INDIVIDUAL GUN RIGHTS.

Ron Franscell

Suzy and Al Gratia died as they had lived most of their adult lives: together.

Suzanna didn't sleep that night. The monstrous movie just kept replaying in her mind, and always with the same bloody ending. In her waking nightmare, her mother Suzy refused to save herself because it would require leaving her beloved Al behind. And every time the horror show looped back on itself, she died with him. No matter how hard she wished, Suzanna couldn't change the ending in her imagination or in reality.

And that night, sleep didn't come easy for Robert Kelley, either. In a nightmare, he watched a giant hand materialize from an angry, black cloud, pointing down at him reproachfully. He bolted upright in a cold sweat, frightening his wife. He thought of the old man who reached out to him without words or breath, the man he decided would soon die. How could he have been sure? Was there more he could have done? Numbed by all the death around him, did he give up too quickly on Al Gratia?

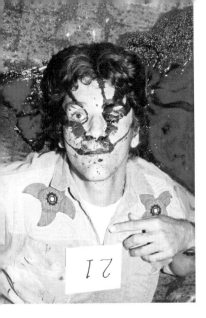

Two weeks after the shooting, Al and Suzy Gratia were buried together in the national cemetery in San Antonio to a bone-rattling 21-gun salute that curdled Suzanna's blood. The acrid stink of gun smoke in the crisp fall air made her sick.

Thankfully, a cadre of psychological counselors had recently been moved to nearby Fort Hood in anticipation of heavy Desert Storm casualties, so survivors and the families of victims received quick attention to their emotional trauma. (The first irony is that Killeen lost twice as many citizens to the Luby's killings than to the brief Gulf War; the second is that almost exactly nineteen years later, an Army psychological counselor named Nidal Malik Hasan would open fire with two handguns on soldiers just after lunch at Fort Hood, killing thirteen and wounding at least thirty in Killeen's second major mass murder in two decades.)

After Hennard's ashes began their journey to the sea, Suzanna joined a small group of survivors on a clandestine tour of the killing floor.

Locals had been gossiping that the cafeteria, like the McDonald's in San Ysidro, might be torn down, erased from the community's memory altogether. Instead, Luby's had gutted the restaurant, ripped up the bloody carpeting and scrubbed the bloodstains off the concrete beneath, patched the bullet holes, expelled the stink of burned gunpowder and death, dumped all the furnishings . . . exorcised everything but the ghosts that haunted the place.

But on the asphalt outside, in the exact spot under the atrium where her father breathed his last, a dark stain lingered.

It was Al's blood.

A ONE-WOMAN CRUSADE

The massacre was not yet finished for Suzanna. In her mind, amid the guilt and cold rationale that had failed her when it mattered most, the slaughter of her mother, father, and twenty-one others became part of a bigger battle for survival. If she could replay the day, she would risk everything by carrying her gun into Luby's for a shot at George Hennard, but there were no replays.

She began to think she could change the past by changing the future.

The people of Killeen wore yellow ribbons while troops from nearby Fort Hood were fighting in Iraq and switched to white ribbons after Hennard's rampage. They left flowers and heartfelt messages outside the empty Luby's shattered windows.

And Texas governor Ann Richards spoke passionately about the need to control the sale and possession of automatic weapons, even though Hennard had purchased his guns—both semiautomatic weapons—completely legally. "Dead people lying on the floor of Luby's should be enough evidence we are not taking a rational posture," she said.

For them, that was enough, but not for Suzanna.

Suzanna launched a one-woman crusade to allow Texans to carry hidden loaded handguns if they pass a safety course and get a license. And in 1996, five years after George Hennard's rampage, it became law, although concealed weapons remained illegal in places such as churches, stadiums, government offices, courts, airports, and restaurants serving alcohol.

Now married to Greg Hupp, the man she was dating at the time of the Luby's shooting, Suzanna ran for the Texas legislature and won handily. She continued her crusade for gun rights, testifying passionately in Congress and states where fear of random crime had forced a legislative response.

"I've lived what gun laws do," she told them all. "My parents died because of what gun laws do. I'm the quintessential soccer mom, and I want the right to protect my family. What happened to my parents will never happen again with my kids there."

The media beat a well-worn track to her door. She got airtime with all the major networks and ink in most of the country's magazines and newspapers. She became the first woman ever honored with a life membership to the National Rifle Association.

After serving five terms in the Texas legislature, Suzanna retired with Greg to raise her two sons on her central Texas horse farm. She has written an unpublished manuscript about her life, the Luby's massacre, and gun rights, but mostly she jealously guards her time with her children—worrying about lack of time is one of the posttraumatic effects she must endure.

Suzanna now carries a gun with her almost everywhere, hidden in a purse or holster. She even has a special gun purse for her evening wear. She still eats out at restaurants, preferring places where she's known—and where she knows almost everyone. She always sits where she can watch the door, usually near the back. If a strange, lone man saunters in, she pays closer attention. If a dropped glass shatters on the floor, she freezes for a startled moment.

But she's ready.

And she never mentions George Hennard's name, denying him the notoriety that even a single whispered breath grants. He is just "the gunman" or "the killer," her way of reducing him to the pathetic, unfinished, nameless soul that he will always be to her.

CHAPTER 5

DEATH FROM ABOVE

TIM URSIN AND THE HOWARD JOHNSON SNIPER

A COLD SKY, WATERCOLORED IN SHADES OF GRAY, hung low over the parish voting hall on Election Day 2008. Tim Ursin hunkered into his coat and inched along in the long line outside, trying to keep warm. The brisk wind carried a hint of Gulf salt. He'd spent his whole life in these bayous, going on sixty-six years now, and he loved the water, but today wasn't a good day for fishing. Today was for voting. A black man talking about hope looked like he might win this historic presidential election, not just for Louisiana, but for the country and maybe the world.

"Cold one today," said the young African American man in his mid-thirties in line ahead of him. He turned his back to the wind, facing Tim.

"It is."

"Line's movin', but I wish it was movin' faster."

"Got nothin' else to do today," Tim said. "Can't fish."

"I hear ya," the man said. "I love to fish, but today just ain't the day."

The young man introduced himself to Tim. He was a truck driver with a family.

"What do you do?" he asked.

"I'm a fishing guide," Tim said. He reached in his pocket for a business card and the young man saw the silvery steel hook where his left hand once was.

"I hope you won't be offended," the curious man said, "but what happened to your hand?"

Tim smiled. People always wanted to know about the hook, even if they didn't ask. He was used to it. And, hell, he'd told the story so many times in the past thirty-five years, he didn't mind telling it again.

"It's okay. I was a firefighter. I've been retired from the New Orleans Fire Department since '75. I was shot a long time ago, in '73, by a sniper at the Howard Johnson. Lost my arm up to here," he said, wrapping his good right hand around the stump of his left forearm.

The young man's eyes flickered with recognition as Tim told about that other cold morning in New Orleans when he crossed paths with a killer.

"I heard about that guy! I was just a little kid, but my parents talked about it," he said. He stumbled slightly over his next words. "He was . . . he was a black guy, wasn't he?"

"Yeah, but he . . . ," Tim started to say.

"I'm sorry, man. I mean, that you were shot by a . . . a black man."

"Hey, you didn't do it," Tim assured him. "I appreciate that, but you don't have to be sorry or feel bad for what somebody else did. Didn't matter what color he was then, and doesn't now."

"Thanks, man," he said. "But if it happened to me, I just don't know how I couldn't be bitter . . ."

They talked about the shooting as long as they could. Inside the voting area, they parted ways in front of the poll workers' table.

"I admire you," the young truck driver said. "I mean, the way you look at it."

"Life goes on," Tim said. "Doesn't do any good to dwell on something that happened a long time ago, you know? Everything has a purpose. Every day's a gift. You just never know. I just gotta keep moving forward . . . and not just for me, but for the people around me, too."

The man smiled, shook Tim's hand, and was gone.

It's funny, Tim thought, how the murky water of memory gets churned up on cold mornings.

STRAIGHT UP TO HELL

A chilly drizzle fell on New Orleans all night. For a few hours between the last late-night jazz riffs in the Quarter and the first peal of St. Louis Cathedral's bells, the only sound was rain. The greasy blue Sunday morning streets, absolved of Saturday night, lay empty under leaden January skies.

Before dawn on January 7, 1973, Lieutenant Tim Ursin kissed his wife and three sleeping children good-bye, left his house, and arrived at New Orleans Fire Department, Station Fourteen, a little before 7 a.m. He was only twenty-nine but already a nine-year firehouse veteran and one of the NOFD's most promising young officers, maybe even a future district chief. He had spent part of his rookie year at Engine Fourteen, as it was known in the department,

and now was coming back to help out his short-handed buddies.

Engine Fourteen was a busy station near the center of New Orleans, surrounded by Charity Hospital, City Hall, downtown hotels, some dreary ghetto housing and projects, and one of New Orleans's forty-two cemeteries, where big rainstorms had been known to pop airtight caskets right out of the waterlogged earth like macabre bubbles. In New Orleans, death and water have always had an uneasy kinship.

But Tim loved New Orleans, the city where he was born. His father had played drums with the great Pete Fountain and some of the Dixieland bands that set the rhythm for the beating heart of the Crescent City. He'd met his wife here and was raising three kids here, too. It had everything he ever wanted, and he never needed to leave. Sure, there was crime, pervasive corruption, decadence, and dreadful poverty, but the city hid it all behind a mask of Old World architecture and sumptuous menus of bayou cuisine, iron-lace balconies, and endless revelry.

Rainy winter Sundays were usually slow for firefighters, so Tim spent the morning helping with mundane chores around the station, sweeping floors, making beds, and washing the trucks. Because nobody cooked on leisurely Sundays, the firefighters usually ordered takeout.

Tim was the extra man today, so he volunteered to make a lunch run to a local burger joint a couple blocks away. He took everybody's order and was heading to his car when somebody hollered for him to wait while they called another local place to see if they had hot lunches. When nobody answered, he turned to leave, but the firehouse radio beeped twice—the signal for a working fire with visible smoke someplace in the city.

"Engines Sixteen, Fourteen, Twenty-seven, Truck Eight, Three-oh-two," a dispatcher blared at 10:45 a.m. "Go to Howard Johnson Motor Court, three-three-zero Loyola. Working fire."

The Howard Johnson was just two minutes from Engine Fourteen, damn near a straight shot. Firefighters scrambled as Tim quickly yanked on his bunker gear and grabbed a jump seat behind the pumper's cab.

As they pulled up in front of the seventeen-story high-rise hotel, Tim saw black smoke belching from windows on the eighth or ninth floor. This was no mattress fire.

Worse, just six weeks before, a mysterious arson fire had swept through the top three floors of the seventeen-story Rault Center—a luxury office and apartment complex right next door to the Howard Johnson—killing six. Five had leaped to their deaths from fifteenth-floor windows because the firefighters couldn't pump water high enough and had no ladders tall enough to rescue them. The New Orleans's Fire Department had reason to be edgy about another skyscraper fire.

Truck Eight, an aerial-ladder truck, pulled up in front of the hotel just ahead of Engine Fourteen, a water pumper. The operator was already setting his stabilizer jacks so he could extend his ladder to snatch frantic hotel guests who were already screaming from upper-floor balconies. But even if he were perfectly positioned, his ladder would only reach the ninth floor. Visions of the Rault Center were already starting to sweep through the heads of the firefighters on the ground.

A district fire chief grabbed Tim amid the chaos of running firefighters, civilians, and cops.

"Come with me," he barked. "Let's see what we've got here."

They entered the hotel's lobby as frightened guests streamed down stairwells from their rooms above. Anxious to know exactly what they faced, Tim instantly made a plan: He would take an elevator up to the sixth or seventh floor, then scramble up the stairs to the fire above. He grabbed two firefighters and started for the elevator but was quickly stopped by armed cops.

"Can't go up there," they said. "We got a guy with a shotgun trapped in the elevator, and we're trying to get him out."

Blocked from the stairs, too, Tim went back outside. Truck Eight sat empty, its crew working elsewhere. Its stabilizers were set, but there was nobody to operate its ladder.

Except Tim Ursin. He had trained on Truck Eight and knew how to deploy its life-saving, hundred-foot (30 meter) ladder.

He leaped up to the console on the back of the truck and began to maneuver the ladder into position, swinging it around toward the burning hotel, then extending it slowly to just below a ninth-floor balcony where he saw people yelling and waving hysterically. Some already had their legs over the railings, ready to jump. The whole operation might have taken four minutes, but it seemed like a lifetime to Tim.

Once the ladder was in place, he looked around. Firefighters were dashing everywhere but none was ready to go up.

"I can't wait around," he shouted to a cop nearby. "I'm going up. Gimme that washout line."

Tim stuck his right arm through the coiled inch-and-a-half (4 centimeter) line—a sixty-pound (27 kilogram) hose that he could plug into a standpipe in the hotel's internal fire suppression system—and stepped onto the ladder.

"Here's your belt," a passing firefighter said, tossing up the safety strap commonly used in ladder rescues. Tim would be more than eighty feet (24 meters) up, standing on the wet, narrow steps of a flexing ladder, wrestling with panic-stricken people.

"Ain't gonna use it," Tim said as he started up. "I'm going straight up and not stopping." As he climbed, the washout hose's five-pound (2 kilogram) brass nozzle slapped against the back of his knee, slowing him down. He paused at the seventh floor and told the people on the balcony twenty feet (6 meters) above to calm down. Steadying himself with his left hand on the rung at eye level, he reached behind his leg with his right hand and grabbed the dangling nozzle, which he tucked between his chin and left shoulder.

IF YOU FALL, YOU DIE

A loud bang erupted somewhere off to Tim's left. The shock jolted his left arm as he reached up the hand rail, and he felt a soft rush of heat ripple across his face.

Somebody up there is tossing cherry bombs, he thought. *These people could die, and they're playing with fireworks?*

Then his left arm began to burn, just a little at first. He looked down at the heavy sleeve of his fire coat to see lumpy gore spilling out, as if someone had opened a bloody faucet.

Tim pivoted, turning his back to the ladder. He tried to gather his wits, but he could literally feel his blood pressure dropping. He didn't know what had happened, but he could tell from the thick flow of blood and the searing pain that he'd been hurt badly, and he wasn't sure he'd make it to the ground alive.

Stay awake! he commanded himself. *If you fall, you die.*

He started down the ladder on his heels, steadying himself with his good hand.

He began to shout, to firefighters below, to the people above, to God . . . to anybody who could hear his act of contrition.

My God, I am sorry for my sins with all my heart . . .

His left arm seemed to be on fire, as if someone had jammed a white-hot poker up his sleeve into the soft flesh of his forearm.

. . . in choosing to do wrong and failing to do good . . .

He saw cops with rifles and handguns below, shooting up toward him. He realized he was caught in some kind of crossfire.

. . . I have sinned against you whom I should love above all things . . .

Could anyone hear? He wanted people to know he'd confessed his sins before he died up there.

. . . I firmly intend, with your help, to do penance, to sin no more, and to avoid whatever leads me to sin . . .

Growing woozy, Tim saw his friend Huey Brown, a beefy tillerman on the ladder truck, hurrying up the ladder.

"I'm coming up to get you!" Brown yelled.

"No, get down!" Tim yelled back. "He's gonna shoot you, too."

Brown kept coming. "Fuck it!" he shouted.

Brown reached Tim and wedged his brawny shoulders under the wounded fireman's legs. Slowly, rung by rung, he eased Tim the last twenty feet (6 meters) down the precarious ladder, knowing somebody was above them with a gun. Tim's gushing blood streamed over Brown's helmet, his shoulders, his face, and hands as he lowered his comrade to safety.

A New Orleans cop met Brown at the bottom of the ladder, while another officer covered them with a shotgun. They lowered Tim's body off the fire truck's rear turntable to a safe spot on the pavement behind Engine Fourteen, out of the line of fire.

A fireman cut off Tim's heavy coat, exposing a gaping wound that looked like it was inflicted by a dull pickax on the meaty part of his left forearm. The bullet had passed completely through, shattering bone and nearly sawing his arm off completely. The fireman wrapped Tim's black leather, NOFD-issue belt with a shiny silver buckle around Tim's upper arm to stanch the bleeding before they loaded him in an ambulance.

LAST RITES

At Charity Hospital's emergency room, nurses pushed Tim's gurney against the wall as more shooting victims rolled in behind him. The place was pandemonium. The wounded were crying and moaning as overwhelmed doctors and nurses rushed around. Cops and firefighters scurried among them all, confused and in shock. Blood stained everything.

Tim fought the worsening pain. He begged for painkillers, but nobody was listening. They couldn't give him anything until they knew the precise extent of his wounds.

Orderlies finally rolled Tim into an examination room, where he was transferred onto the cold, bare stainless-steel table beneath a bright light. He was fading fast. Except for the blinding light over him, the rest of the room appeared to be dark. Ghostly figures worked all around him, removed his clothes, searched for more wounds, probed his butchered arm, emptied blood from his boots, and murmured in uneasy tones words he couldn't understand.

The bullet had blown away a biscuit-sized chunk of Tim's arm flesh and smashed his radius, one of the two bones in his forearm. It severed his radial nerve and ruptured both arteries in his left arm. He had already lost more than three pints of blood, about one-third of his life fluid.

As he floated at the brink of consciousness, a prayer rose above the pain. Then a hand from the darkness daubed his forehead, eyes, and lips with oil, and made the sign of the cross over him.

"... may the Lord pardon thee whatever sins or faults thou hast committed ..."

He knew the voice. It was Father Pete Rogers, the fire department's chaplain. He was giving last rites.

"... I grant you a plenary indulgence for the remission of all your sins, and I bless you. In the name of the Father and the Son and the Holy Spirit ..."

It was the last thing that Tim wanted to hear. He wasn't even thirty. He had three kids and a wife. He didn't want to die. He wasn't ready.

He didn't know that God or destiny or maybe just dumb luck had already intervened to save his life. The 240-grain, .44 Magnum bullet that mangled his left arm had passed completely through the thick sleeve of his fire coat and lodged in the annoying brass hose nozzle he had just tucked under his chin. It had stopped the slug from tearing into his neck.

And he didn't know that the sniper took aim at him a second time, but maybe by the same trick of providence or fluke, his gun didn't fire.

Tim drifted into unconsciousness on the table. The next thing he remembered was waking up in a dark hospital room. He heard moaning and solemn voices he didn't recognize. In a few hours, he learned there were three gravely wounded cops with him there in the dark: Officer Skeets Palmisano had been shot in the back and the arm as he ran across a grassy mall in front of the hotel. Patrolman Chuck Arnold had been shot in the face as he stood in the window of an office building across from the hotel, and although his jaw was nearly gone, he had walked a few blocks to the nearest hospital. Officer Ken Solis was trying to keep onlookers back when a single bullet blew a massive hole in his right shoulder and his belly.

Tim could hear something else. Not in the room but somewhere outside in the night. Distant but chilling.

He could hear gunfire.

AN INVADING ENEMY

The first shots were fired a week earlier, on New Year's Eve, 1972, although some would argue later that this war began centuries before.

A phantom gunman lay in wait in a vacant lot across from New Orleans's Central Lockup on Perdido Street—where prisoners are booked, fingerprinted, and photographed—just before the jail's 11 p.m. shift change. When two police recruits came into view, he cut loose with seven shots from a high-powered rifle, killing nineteen-year-old unarmed police cadet Alfred Harrell and wounding a lieutenant.

Police searching the empty lot found a dropped .38 caliber blue-steel Colt revolver, spent .44 Magnum shell casings, footprints, several strings of firecrackers, and other evidence left behind, but the shooter had melted into the night.

But eighteen minutes later, another cop, thirty-year-old K-9 officer Ed Hosli, was mortally wounded while investigating a burglar alarm less than a quarter mile (half a kilometer) from the jail at a warehouse in Gert Town, a poor, black neighborhood where crime and hatred of cops flourished. Spent casings and other evidence at the scene—including a leather bag containing two cans of lighter fluid and some firecrackers—pointed to the same assailant who shot up the city lockup.

The next day, when police flooded Gert Town looking for the assailant, they were treated as an invading enemy. Armed black men shadowed the cops. NOPD switchboards were swamped with callers reporting dozens of fake sniper sightings. After nightfall, some locals shot out streetlights, making the investigation harder and adding an element of menace.

Even before the New Year's Eve shootings, tensions between New Orleans cops and the city's poor blacks had been high. In the past year, Police Superintendent Clarence Giarrusso had created the Felony Action Squad, an elite unit assigned to target violence in the city's most crime-ridden neighborhoods. Announcing the squad's formation in 1972, Giarrusso proudly told reporters that if any of the unit's twelve undercover agents encountered armed robbers, rapists, or murderers, they could "shoot to kill."

A series of armed conflicts with Black Panthers and several other black revolutionary organizations in New Orleans's Desire public housing projects only made matters worse.

Louisiana was smoldering with racial friction. The previous January, two Black Muslim militants had been shot to death by police at a Baton Rouge race riot in which two white deputies also died; among the thirty-one wounded, fourteen were cops. And on November 16, 1972, two black student protesters had been shot and killed at Southern University in Baton Rouge, but their killer (allegedly a police officer) was never identified.

So when the Gert Town sweep wrapped up, the NOPD had precious few clues as to their sniper's identity or whereabouts. It was clear that the same shooter (or shooters) shot three cops on New Year's Eve, probably with the same .44 Magnum rifle. They also knew he had wounded himself while trying to break into the warehouse because he left a trail of bloody handprints and spatters.

The investigation wasn't dead by a long shot. One bit of evidence looked like a promising piece of the puzzle.

A young, slightly built black man had broken into a black Baptist church in Gert Town the night of the shootings. When he was surprised by the pastor the next day, he fled, leaving a satchel of bullets, bloodstains all around the sanctuary, and an apology: "I am sorry for breaking the lock on your church door, but pastor at two o'clock I felt I had to get right with the Lord. You see I was a sinner then, walking past your church . . . I was drinking . . . I then broke the door and fell on my knees in prayer. Now I have managed to get it together. I will send you the money for a new lock. God bless you."

And some potential clues were never fully investigated or simply missed.

Two days after the shootings, a local grocer named Joe Perniciaro told police a young black man with a bloody bandage on his left hand had come into his store just a couple blocks from the warehouse where Hosli was shot. The kid wore a dark jacket and Army fatigues, and Perniciaro feared he might rob the place, but he left without incident after buying a razor.

On Perdido Street, just two blocks from Central Lockup, patrolmen found an abandoned two-door, blue 1963 Chevrolet with Kansas plates and the keys still in the ignition. When they ran the license number, LYE 1367, it came back to a Mark James Robert Essex, age twenty-three, of 902 Cottonwood Street in Emporia, Kansas. With no priors and no warrants, the kid checked out, so police wrote it off as a stalled vehicle and cleared young Essex.

But before the New Year's Eve sniper investigation could unfold fully, before New Orleans could rest easier, even before the coming week was finished . . . a bloody, one-man race war would erupt in the worst carnage the city had seen since the War of 1812.

And police would hear the name Mark Essex again.

FROM CHOIRBOY TO REVOLUTIONARY

Mark James Essex's private war began in the peaceful prairie town of Emporia, Kansas, an American Gothic village once described as "grassland, stoplights, grassland again."

Emporia was a meatpacking town of fewer than thirty thousand citizens, but fewer than five hundred of them were black in the 1960s. Jimmy—as his friends and family called him—was the second of five children born to Nellie and Mark Henry Essex, a foreman at one of the local meat plants. The seven of them lived in a modest white frame house on the eastern edge of town, near the Santa Fe Railway tracks, an area where most of the town's minorities also lived.

Jimmy grew up happy but soft-spoken, congenial but unremarkable. He was the kid nobody noticed and few remembered. He loved to fish and hunt, and he was a crack shot. He attended church faithfully enough that he talked about becoming a minister someday. He mowed neighbors' lawns for pocket money. Jimmy Essex was, both literally and metaphorically, a Boy Scout and a choirboy, not a loner or rebel.

In school, Jimmy was a C student who probably had Bs in him, but he never pushed himself that hard. Short and skinny, he didn't play sports, although he played saxophone in the Emporia High School band for three years. When it appeared he was better with his hands than with his mind, Jimmy spent his last two years at a vocational-technical school, where he focused on auto mechanics.

In January 1969, after one listless semester at college and worries about being drafted to fight in Vietnam, Jimmy Essex enlisted for four years in the U.S. Navy. After graduating from boot camp with outstanding ratings, he went to dental technician school, where he graduated with the highest honors before being assigned to the clinic at the naval air station in Imperial Beach, California.

Jimmy wasn't in Kansas anymore. Back home, he'd never seen racism as virulent as he saw in the Navy, where he came to believe black men were still treated as second-class citizens. He suffered racial slurs, ridiculous and meticulous searches of his car when he came and went from the base, harassment in the barracks, extra guard duty, trifling orders from white superiors intended only to exasperate—all irritations that most black sailors encountered but shrugged off.

But not Jimmy Essex.

Although only 5-foot-4 (1.6 meters) and less than 140 pounds (64 kilograms), Jimmy fought back physically. Sometimes he complained bitterly to officers about the racist behavior he experienced. In letters home, he wrote that "blacks have trouble

MARK ESSEX'S FAMILY AND FRIENDS BELIEVE THE MILD-MANNERED, SMALL-TOWN KANSAS KID ENCOUNTERED UNEXPECTED RACISM IN THE U.S. NAVY. ANGERED BY IT, HE FELL UNDER THE SWAY OF RADICAL BLACK MILITANTS.

Getty Images

getting along here." His constant skirmishing often landed him in hot water and marked him as a troublemaker.

Eventually, Jimmy befriended a black sailor named Rodney Frank, a convicted rapist and armed robber from New Orleans who hid behind his own militant bombast. Frank introduced Jimmy to radical Black Panther literature, to the revolutionary writings of Eldridge Cleaver and Huey Newton, and to Black Muslim fanatics off-base.

In a matter of months, everything changed. Jimmy Essex, the quiet choirboy from Kansas, was dead. Mark Essex, the angry revolutionary, stood defiantly in his place.

On October 19, 1970, Essex went AWOL. He packed a duffel bag and boarded a bus back home to Emporia. When his parents picked him up at the bus depot, he told them he had come home "to think about what a black man has to do to survive."

He was angry, bitter, and isolated, obsessed with the wrongs he had suffered and adamant about not returning to the Navy. His worried mother asked the Reverend W. A. Chambers, the Baptist minister who'd baptized Jimmy at age twelve, to speak to her son. Essex wanted to hear none of it. He was not only disillusioned with the world, but with God, too.

"Christianity is a white man's religion," he told his former minister, "and the white man's been running things too long."

Twenty-eight days later, Essex returned to his base to face a court-martial.

Although he had already pleaded guilty to being absent without leave, Essex's defense was that the Navy's entrenched racism was to blame. Hate made him do it. "I had to talk to some black people because I had begun to hate all white people. I was tired of going to white people and telling them my problems and not getting anything done about it."

The court actually gave credence to Essex's claims of discrimination and handed out a relatively insignificant sentence, but within weeks, Essex was given a special discharge for unspecified "character and behavior disorders" after a Navy psychiatrist had concluded that Essex had an "immature personality." In his report, the psychiatrist noted that Essex exhibited no suicidal tendencies, but "he alludes to the fact he 'might do something' if he doesn't get what he wants."

In the end, the Navy washed its hands of Seaman Mark James Robert Essex, who served for little more than half his enlistment.

Starting in February 1971, Essex spent a few months in New York City, where he voraciously consumed Black Panther Party propaganda and fueled the flames that were beginning to flicker deep inside. He studied the Panthers' urban guerrilla warfare tactics and started calling cops "pigs." He also learned that one of the Panthers' weapons of choice was the .44 Magnum

semiautomatic carbine, a light and powerful hunting rifle that was devastating at close range.

Back in Emporia, Essex couldn't adjust. His
few childhood friends had all moved away, and he
yearned to live in a black man's city. He worked a
series of odd jobs for a year or so, but never with
any enthusiasm. His hatred, however, continued
to simmer.

Then one day, he walked into the local Montgomery
Ward store and bought himself a .44 Magnum Ruger
Deerslayer rifle, which he practiced firing in the coun-
tryside until the gun had become an extension of him.

Whether Emporia had become too claustrophobic or Essex had decided
to launch a new front in his private race war, nobody knows. But in the summer of 1972, he picked up the phone, called his old friend Rodney Frank—also
recently drummed out of the Navy as an incorrigible—and decided to move to
New Orleans.

To the outside world, Mark Essex appeared to be just another young black
man who didn't know exactly where he was going or why. He entered a training
program for vending-machine repairmen and rented a cheap apartment in the
back of a shabby house.

But inwardly, he was reaching an ugly kind of critical mass. His defiant, revolutionary outlook grew darker. He began calling himself *Mata*, the Swahili word for a hunter's bow. He was devouring militant newspapers and books. And he was filling every inch of the pale brown walls in his little two-room apartment with a hateful scrawl of angry anti-white slogans like "My destiny lies in the bloody death of racist pigs," "Political power comes from the barrel of a gun," "Hate white people beast of the earth," "Kill pig Nixon and all his running dogs."

All references to whites, and that was most of them, were daubed in red paint. The rest were black. He even wrote on the ceiling, taunting the police he knew would eventually visit his frowsy sanctuary: "Only a pig would read shit on the ceiling."

In November 1972, when Essex heard the news that two black students had been gunned down at Southern University while protesting the white man's oppression, he declared his own personal war on whites and cops.

After Christmas, he handwrote a note to a local TV station announcing his bloody intentions:

> *Africa greets you.*
> *On Dec. 31, 1972, aprx. 11 pm, the downtown New Orleans Police Department will be attacked. Reason—many, but the death of two innocent brothers will be avenged. And many others.*
> *P.S. Tell pig Giarrusso the felony action squad ain't shit.*
> *MATA*

The attack happened as Essex had promised, although the letter was not opened at the TV station until days later. It was revealed too late to prevent the murders of Alfred Harrell and Ed Hosli. Nevertheless, it would not only link Mark Essex undeniably to those New Year's Eve shootings—in which his first victim, ironically, was a black man—but also foretold a bigger, bloodier butchery to come.

"THE REVOLUTION IS HERE"

On the rain-shrouded morning of Sunday, January 7, 1973, Mark Essex girded for battle.

Almost a thousand miles away, Nellie Essex prepared for church, where she would cry and pray for her son's wayward soul.

Tim Ursin kissed his children good-bye before going to work.

And a whole city awoke to a misty, gray day that would be unlike any before it.

Shortly after 10 a.m., Mark Essex walked back into Joe Perniciaro's market and stood in the doorway holding his .44 Magnum hunting rifle in his right hand. With his wounded left hand, he pointed at Perniciaro.

"You. You're the one I want," Essex shouted. "Come here."

Perniciaro recognized him as the bandaged young man who bought the razor five days before. He started to run toward the back of the store. Essex, believing Perniciaro had fingered him to the cops, had come for revenge.

Essex fired one booming shot, blasting a gaping hole in the grocer's right shoulder and knocking him to the floor, before he turned and ran down the street.

Four blocks away, a fleeing Essex ran up to a black man sitting in front of his house in a beige and black 1968 Chevrolet Chevelle.

"Hi, brother, get out," Essex told him.

"You crazy, man?"

Essex leveled his rifle at the stunned man's head.

"I don't want to kill you, brother. Just honkies," he said calmly. "But I will kill you, too."

As the man leaped out, Essex jumped into the car and peeled out in the stolen Chevelle, sideswiping another vehicle before disappearing into traffic.

Police radios crackled with nearly simultaneous reports of a shooting and an armed carjacking in the Gert Town district. Cruisers scrambled to respond, but the stolen Chevelle eluded them. All they had was a description of a slim, young black male, up to 5-foot-4 (1.6 meters), weighing about 140 pounds (64 kilograms), wearing a green camouflage jacket and olive-drab fatigue pants. He was carrying a hunting rifle onto which he'd tied a red, green, and black handkerchief—later identified as the Black Liberation Flag.

While police searched for the stolen Chevelle, Mark Essex careened into the parking garage of the Howard Johnson Hotel on Loyola Street and left the car on the fourth level. He ran up the stairwell to a locked fire door on the eighth floor, where he pounded until two black maids came to the door. He told one he wanted to visit a friend who was staying on the eighteenth floor.

She hesitated. She could lose her job if she let a stranger through the fire door.

"Are you a soul sister?" he asked one of them.

She said she was.

"Sister, the revolution is here," he said. "It's one for all and two for one."

But the maid still wouldn't let him enter, so Essex climbed another flight of stairs to the ninth floor, where he again pounded on the fire door and was again turned away by a maid.

On the eighteenth floor, he found a fire door propped open and went into the hallway, where he encountered two frightened maids and a houseman, all three of whom were black.

"Don't worry, I'm not going to hurt you black people," he reassured them as he hurried past. "I want the whites."

But before Essex could get to an elevator, a white guest, twenty-seven-year-old Dr. Robert Steagall, saw him with the gun and tried to tackle him. They wrestled desperately for a few seconds before Essex shot the doctor in the chest. When Betty Steagall ran to her husband's aid, Essex coolly put the muzzle of his carbine against the base of her skull and pulled the trigger. She died embracing her dead husband.

Essex untied the Black Liberation Flag from his gun and threw it near their corpses.

Inside the Steagalls' room, Essex set the drapes on fire and ran to the nearest stairwell.

Moving quickly through the hotel, he started several fires on various floors by soaking phone books with lighter fluid, then igniting them beneath the draperies. The whole time, he would shoot at any white folks he saw and would set off firecrackers in smoky halls and stairwells to create the illusion that many snipers and arsonists were prowling the hotel's eighteen floors and killing at random.

On the eleventh floor, he shot the hotel's assistant manager point-blank in the head, blowing most of it away. On the tenth floor, he mortally wounded the general manager. On the eighth-floor patio, a gut-shot hotel guest floated in the hotel pool for two hours, playing dead.

On the eighth floor, Essex heard sirens outside. From the balcony of one room, he saw a firefighter scrambling up an aerial ladder toward hysterical guests on the floor above. He took careful aim and squeezed the trigger, hitting the fireman. He racked another cartridge into the chamber and took aim again, but the gun didn't fire. He didn't have time for another shot. Cops on the ground were firing back, so he ducked for cover.

By 11 a.m., less than a half hour after Mark Essex laid siege to the Howard Johnson, police had set up a command center in the lobby, and hundreds of cops surrounded the hotel. Sharpshooters had taken positions atop nearby buildings while other cops tried to keep curious onlookers out of the line of fire.

But it was fruitless. Local TV stations were going live, and their feeds were being picked up by networks for wall-to-wall coverage. Mark Essex's war was being televised. Worse, word was leaking out that the snipers were militant black revolutionaries, and many angry African Americans were gathering on the street outside the Howard Johnson to yell things like "Right on!" and "Kill the pigs!" every time shots were fired from the balconies above.

From his perch on the eighth floor, Essex began to pick off cops who were scurrying around the streets below. One after another, they were falling wounded and dead.

In the meantime, some cops—led by the NOPD's second-in-command, Louis Sirgo—began to work their way through the choking black smoke into the bowels of the hotel, searching for what they believed were at least three snipers. In a darkened stairwell just above the sixteenth floor, Essex shot Sirgo in the spine almost point-blank, killing him.

For several hours, police exchanged fire with the phantom shooters, who continued to set fires. A circling police helicopter even took fire from the hotel. Descriptions of the shooters varied so widely that police were convinced they faced a small army of cold-blooded militants who held key strategic positions throughout the hotel. They were everywhere . . . and nowhere.

At 3:30 p.m., police began securing the hotel, floor-by-floor, hoping ultimately to corner the snipers on the top floor, where fires were burning unabated.

Sometime around 4 p.m., more than five hours after the first shots were fired, police believed they had pushed the snipers onto the hotel's roof, where they had taken refuge in a concrete cubicle at the top of the stairwell and elevator shaft. It was a nearly impregnable bunker, especially since police were neither close enough nor armed with sufficiently powerful weapons to penetrate its thick walls.

Cops hiding in the stairwells below the cubicle could hear somebody moving around, cursing at sharpshooters on nearby buildings. "Africa! Africa!" he would chant. At odd intervals, a sniper would run out on the graveled roof, fire several shots at police, then scamper back into the safe pillbox.

"Come on up, you honky pigs!" Essex yelled once as he fired down into the stairwell. "You afraid to fight like a black man?"

"Fuck you! Fuck you! Fuck you!" they screamed back. But all they could do was scream.

Even then, nobody knew exactly how many shooters were up on the roof, how they were armed, or how much ammo they had.

A HAIL OF GUNFIRE

One of the many Americans intently watching the violent drama unfold on television was Marine Lieutenant Colonel Chuck Pitman, a tough helicopter pilot who'd flown 1,200 combat missions in Vietnam, been shot down seven times, and won four Distinguished Flying Crosses. After the Rault fire, local Marines and Coast Guard chopper crews drew up contingency plans to help local police and fire departments in case of another high-rise fire. *So where is the Coast Guard?* Pitman wondered.

Fog, wind, and low skies made flying too dangerous, a Coast Guard commander told Pitman.

But Pitman knew the cops needed his help. At least seven people were dead and more than a dozen wounded. The snipers had the high ground and the firepower to do even more damage.

"Shit," Pitman said. "It's not too bad for me. I can fly up the river."

Within an hour, Pitman and his crew were inching up the Mississippi River toward the city, sometimes only inches above the water. By 5:30, Pitman and three police marksmen were aloft in a twin-rotor military helicopter, with shoot-to-kill orders. Incredibly, they were about to strafe the roof of a downtown hotel in an American city—but this was a war.

Over the next several hours, Pitman played a cat-and-mouse game with the shooters. Time after time, the chopper took fire until it rose over the roof, then . . . nobody. The airborne police sharpshooters were pouring thousands of rounds into the concrete cubicle, but they couldn't see anyone. Yet when the helicopter would move away, police observers on nearby buildings saw somebody run out and resume shooting.

Essex was hiding by climbing a water pipe and wedging himself under the bunker's ceiling. So when the chopper hovered above, police marksmen couldn't see him and their bullets ricocheted harmlessly all around him.

But once Pitman's crew figured this out, a simple tactic was employed: While a fire truck on the ground pumped water into the hotel's system, one of

Pitman's sharpshooters poured a stream of tracer bullets into the pressurized pipe. It exploded.

Cops on the chopper unleashed a ferocious storm of fire on the cubicle. Forced from his hiding place by a spewing pipe and flying concrete chips, Essex ran from the cubicle holding his rifle and looked straight up at Pitman.

He yelled something nobody heard and raised his fist in one last defiant act before he was slaughtered in a hail of gunfire.

A little before 9 p.m., Mark Essex lay dead on the roof of the Howard Johnson, but the war wasn't finished. Police kept firing into his body without mercy, and they shot his rifle into bits so none of his accomplices could use it. Throughout the night, police radioed that other snipers were shooting at them, or that they saw gun flashes in the dark or heard taunts from hidden corners of the hotel.

And they watched the corpse of Mark Essex all night. An occasional night breeze would sometimes flutter through the shreds of his fatigues or his black turtleneck sweater and they would swear he was still alive. Somebody would shoot him again, just to be sure.

The next morning, after the sun had risen, cops stormed the roof and found only Mark Essex's ruined body. It had been hit by more than two hundred bullets and was virtually unrecognizable. One leg was nearly severed. Pieces of him were scattered for yards around, including his jaw and tongue, which had been blasted across the roof. One witnesses said the body was so ravaged that "we nearly had to use a shovel to scoop him up."

Essex's racist rampage was among the worst mass shooting in American history, even if it fell out of the public consciousness unusually quickly. Firing more than a hundred shots, Essex had killed nine people and wounded thirteen more. Five of the dead and five of the wounded were police officers. Of Essex's twenty-two victims, only one was black.

To this day, some cops believe with all their hearts that there were other snipers, but the official police ruling was that Mark Essex had acted alone. Police found no metal casings that matched any other gun but Essex's .44 Magnum carbine.

Nevertheless, the Rault Center arson fire six weeks before is now generally believed to have been a dry run for Essex's attack at the Howard Johnson. If true, his death toll would rise to a grim fifteen innocent people.

Black outrage erupted within hours of Essex's death.

A QUICKLY FORGOTTEN STRUGGLE

Even before Essex's body had been shipped back to Emporia in a simple wooden crate, black militant leader Stokely Carmichael praised Essex for "carrying our struggle to the next quantitative level, the level of science."

And within days, columnist Phil Smith of the *Chicago Metro News*, an activist black weekly, eulogized Essex as a "new hero in an old struggle."

"Essex may not have been in love with white people, but that made him as normal as 3o million other Black people," Smith wrote.

He suggested Essex was framed by a "sick white racist society" bent on the "systematic extermination of young Black men." No young black man, he said, would ever "go berserk and kill white people for no reason.

"White people hate the idea that Black people, by virtue of their very existence, force whites to deal with their own dishonesty, deceit and criminal intent . . . White people truly believe 'the only good nigger is a dead nigger,'" Smith seethed. "If there was one lesson that [Essex] had learned in his short life, it was that Black men are the most dispensable item in this country."

Even Essex's mother, resolute in her conviction that racism had transformed her cheerful little boy into a monster, was almost defiant when she spoke to reporters a week after the rampage.

"I do think Jimmy was driven to this," she said. "Jimmy was trying to make white America sit up and be aware of what is happening to us.

"I don't want my son to have died in vain," Nellie continued. "If this terrible thing will awaken white America to the injustices that blacks suffer, then some good will have come from it."

Although the Howard Johnson attack swiftly resurrected the ghosts of Charles Whitman's 1966 Texas Tower massacre (see chapter 6), it quickly fell out of the national media spotlight. Many observers believed stories about black rage ran counter to the media's efforts to portray a nation where African Americans should be seen as innocent, noble, civilized victims of white oppression—more Rosa Parks than Nat Turner, a messianic slave who, inspired by an eclipse of the sun, led the mass-murder of at least fifty white people in 1831.

So black rage neither began nor ended with Mark Essex, but he became one of its most powerful symbols.

In 2002, snipers John Allen Muhammad and Lee Boyd Malvo shot sixteen people, killing ten, in a reign of terror as the "D.C. sniper," even plotting to kill white police officers in one grand finale. Muhammad was a twelve-year-old boy in Baton Rouge, Louisiana, on the day Mark Essex laid siege to the Howard Johnson, and it seems unlikely that he was not affected somehow by a case that drew stark divisions between whites and blacks.

Nellie Essex buried her son's bullet-shredded body in Emporia six days after the shooting. There were no military honors. At his funeral, one memorial wreath bore a sash that said "Power to the People."

The Black Panthers of New York sent a telegram to the family applauding Mark Essex as "a black man, warrior, and revolutionary."

For many years, Mark Essex's grave sat unmarked in Emporia's Maplewood Cemetery, not far from the grave of legendary newspaperman William Allen

White. But his family eventually placed a modest granite stone, and local veterans now mark Essex's grave with a small bronze military medallion.

Among the many ironies and enigmas still surrounding the Howard Johnson massacre, there's this one: An American flag is planted on Mark Essex's grave every Memorial Day.

"IT JUST WASN'T MY TIME"

Tim Ursin had never heard of Mark Essex, never looked him in the eyes. Their paths had never crossed until that miserable January morning at the Howard Johnson hotel.

He heard fragments of the story as he drifted in and out of sedation at the hospital, but he didn't hear the full story of what happened that day until about three weeks later. By that time, he was involved in a different kind of fight.

During his six weeks in the hospital, Tim endured excruciating pain to save his arm.

As many as ten times, his wound was debrided, an agonizing procedure to strip away dead, rotting flesh from his wound. Doctors laid moist pig skin over the mutilated tissue to protect it from infection.

Later, surgeons planed paper-thin ribbons of skin from Tim's thigh to seal the wound permanently and to finally offer some relief from the electric ache of air hitting the exposed meat and raw nerves.

But within his first two weeks, a repaired artery in his forearm burst. Rather than repair it, surgeons simply sealed it off—a risky move. A few weeks later, as a doctor examined his gangrenous thumb, he accidentally thrust his finger through the squishy rotten tissue of Tim's hand. So they removed the thumb in hopes of saving the rest of his left hand.

Things didn't get better. To stabilize the remaining palm and fingers, doctors inserted a stainless-steel pin in the wrist end of his shattered radius, but the pin eventually worked its way out through the skin of his hand.

His hand was now useless.

Tim had made many difficult decisions in his life, but the next one was easy. He asked his doctors to remove his mangled left hand entirely and replace it with a prosthetic stainless-steel hook.

While he was still in the hospital, the fire chief asked him to take on the department's public information job, but Tim wasn't a desk rider. If he couldn't fight fires, he didn't want to be around the firehouse, where he'd be reminded more of his weaknesses than his strengths. If he couldn't ride a truck, he knew he would always be on the periphery of the brotherhood.

He leaned hard on his wife, Mary, in those dark days. A daughter and sister of firefighters, she never gave him a chance to feel sorry for himself. While he tried to keep himself together, she kept the family together. When people would stare at his hook, he felt more embarrassed for Mary and the kids than for himself.

When Tim's sick leave ended in 1975, he drifted. He worked as a concrete tester, a boat salesman, and a sporting-goods clerk. He bought a boat and taught himself how to handle a fishing rod with his hook.

At first, friends were asking him to take them out on the bayous. Then he started doing a few weekend charters for rich fishermen from the interior.

By 1982, he was chartering fishing expeditions full time from Delacroix Island and then from Shell Beach, fishing the inland marshes and the outer bays for speckled trout and redfish. And he began to use a marketing moniker that, for better or worse, had literally come from above: Captain Hook.

When his fishermen ask, he often spins a wild tale about a hungry shark because it makes people laugh, but he makes no effort to hide the real story. Everybody on the water knows him as Captain Hook.

He still feels his phantom hand. He can tell you the exact position of it because when they clipped the tendons and tied them off, its sensory pose was fixed forever. The thumb is extended, the index and middle fingers spread apart, the ring finger curled in . . .

And he keeps the brass nozzle that saved his life. It still bears the bullet hole that might have been in his neck if not for the simple intervention of a different unseen hand.

But he seldom imagines what he might say to Mark Essex if they were to meet, finally, face to face. It no longer matters. He wants only to live without the hate that consumed the man who tried to kill him for no better reason than the color of his skin.

Every morning, Tim Ursin, more than ever a devout Catholic, says a prayer and thanks God for another day. And at the end of every Saturday, he attends Mass without fail.

But he's philosophical about it. He bears no malice for Mark Essex, although he rarely speaks the name. He's lucky to be alive—and most important, he knows it.

"I've been living on borrowed time for more than thirty-five years," he says today. "It just wasn't my time."

The evening after he voted, Tim was watching television when the phone rang. It was the young black man he'd met at the election hall that morning.

"Look, I've been thinking about our conversation all day," the man said. "I came home and told my wife that I met you and that you told me your story, and, well, I just kept thinking all day that you have a good way of looking at a bad thing."

"Thanks, man," Tim said. "I appreciate it."

"I'm sorry about the man . . . a black man . . . I don't feel that way . . ."

"Hey, this was one man," Tim said. "It wasn't personal and it doesn't make me feel any different about black people who don't think that way. You can't spend your life blaming others for what only a few bad people do. Hate will eat you up, man."

"Yeah, well, I guess you taught me some things, and I just wanted to say . . ."

The man paused for a long moment.

"I just wanted to say I won't ever forget you."

And for the first time in a long time, Tim cried.

CHAPTER 6

THE DARKEST TOWER

ROLAND EHLKE AND THE TEXAS TOWER SNIPER

A MIDSUMMER THUNDERSTORM WAS BREWING to the west. A warm mist had settled over Milwaukee.

Reverend Roland Ehlke rolled up his car window against the sultry air and listened to the radio as he drove on his afternoon hospital rounds.

Then a newscaster broke in with a bulletin about a sniper who was killing people from a perch in a tower high above the University of Texas campus in Austin.

Reverend Ehlke turned up the volume and listened closely. After all, his twenty-one-year-old middle son, Cap, was on the UT campus, being trained for a Peace Corps job overseas.

"But it's a big campus," the pastor silently reassured himself. "He won't be involved in this."

Later, the newscaster came back on the air with more details about the unfolding tragedy in Texas. And again, Reverend Ehlke thought about his Cap. He was a little disappointed that Cap, who'd recently graduated from a Lutheran college, had skipped going directly to seminary and decided instead to go adventuring. When Cap joined the Peace

IN 1967, LESS THAN A YEAR AFTER THE TEXAS TOWER ATTACK, CAP EHLKE VISITED WITH SOME OF HIS PEACE CORPS CLASSMATES IN THE MIDDLE EAST AFTER RECOVERING FROM HIS WOUNDS.

Courtesy of Roland Ehlke

Corps and got assigned to teach English to Iranian kids, he couldn't exactly find Iran on the globe, but he didn't care. He was going to see the world.

The Peace Corps had sent him to Austin for the summer with other volunteers to learn basic Farsi and about Iranian customs and Muslim culture.

Now the world was watching as a madman with a high-powered rifle sprayed the college with bullets from a lofty tower.

"... many people have reportedly been wounded," the man on the radio said, "and some are dead ..."

Misty rain streamed down the Ford's windshield. Cap was a fresh-faced Midwestern boy from Wisconsin. The son of a preacher knew how to detour around trouble, his father reasoned. And Austin was a big enough city. What were the chances? Good kids didn't just find themselves in the crosshairs of lunatics.

Cap wouldn't be involved, the Reverend Ehlke told himself.

One thousand two hundred miles (1,931 kilometers) away, Cap was indeed involved.

UNREST AND UPHEAVAL

By the long, hot summer of 1966, the simmering fever of Americans' unrest with the war in Vietnam, with the status of women and blacks, with the old sexual ethos, with the establishment—with almost everything that represented the previous generation's sensibilities—had exploded into a furious furnace of violence and disorder. Time had inexplicably sped up. The world was in upheaval. Wars raged between nations, races, sexes, faiths, young and old, fathers and sons.

It seemed like everything was falling apart that summer. A president had been assassinated fewer than three years before. Race riots were erupting in major cities. More American soldiers were dying than South Vietnamese in "their" war. Armed troops and demonstrators were squaring off in the street. Draft cards and bras were being burned in spectacular fires of discontent. The sexual revolution was redefining relationships between men and women while sowing seeds that would rock the rest of the century. Some professors were encouraging their students to use psychedelic drugs. A new kind of book about mass murder, Truman Capote's *In Cold Blood*, became an instant best seller. And a homeless ex-con named Richard Speck had raped, stabbed, and strangled eight student nurses in Chicago in one of the most horrifying American crimes ever committed.

There were a lot of ways to get hurt in those days of rage. Some people simply went mad.

And college campuses were among the most dangerous of danger zones. The ivory towers and tree-lined quads had become incubators for protest, radicalism, and experimentation.

Yet the national unrest had pretty much skipped the University of Texas at Austin. Maybe because Austin was a tiny island floating in a sea of more conservative values, unlike Berkeley, Rutgers, or even University of Wisconsin-Madison in their liberal enclaves. Or maybe because Austin already had the reputation of going against the grain. But outside of minor incidents of civil disobedience, mostly over race issues during the civil rights movement, the UT campus had so far been spared the roiling turbulence of the 1960s. So far.

Roland Cap Ehlke was a preacher's kid, as white and impressionable as a fresh sheet of paper. Born of good German stock in the tiny lakeside village of Two Rivers, Wisconsin, he had grown up in a middle-class neighborhood on Milwaukee's south side, where his father pastored a Lutheran church. A soft-spoken kid, Cap loved school, played intramural tennis, dated a few girls casually, and stayed out of trouble. His parents always hoped he would go into the ministry someday.

After graduating from a prep school, Cap entered Northwestern College, a small school established at the end of the Civil War in Watertown, Wisconsin, to train Lutheran pastors. Most of Cap's classmates intended to graduate and continue their theological studies to be ordained as ministers, but by the time he graduated in 1966, Cap had different ideas.

It wasn't that he didn't wish to be a pastor. He just wanted something else more. Or first. Or for now. He didn't even know what it was. He couldn't give it a name or point to it on a map. He just knew it wasn't the cloistered life of a Wisconsin seminarian on a long slide into the life of a Wisconsin clergyman in a cold Wisconsin village.

He let it be known that after graduation he would be joining the Peace Corps, a fledgling army of young American volunteers dispatched to the most desperate corners of the earth to put a human face on the United States as they lent a helping hand. By 1966, a record fifteen thousand volunteers—almost all idealistic young students—were digging wells, teaching school, harvesting crops, and administering medicine throughout the Third World.

The president of Northwestern himself tried to talk Cap out of it. He said the ministry was more important, that he could affect far more lives as a pastor than by spending a couple years on the other side of a troubled world. Besides, he reminded Cap that he might have to repay Wisconsin's Lutherans for his "free" education if he didn't take the next logical step into seminary in the fall.

But Cap stood his ground, shaky as it was. The next chapter in his young life would be an adventure, not more books and Wisconsin winters. When the Peace Corps assigned him to teach English to Iranian children, he consulted an atlas to see where exactly in the world Iran was located. After a summer training course at the University of Texas, he would ship out in the fall to begin his two-year tour of duty in a place he didn't know, far away from the only place he had known.

First stop: Austin.

"OOZING WITH HOSTILITY"

Charlie Whitman was an enigma wrapped in a man-child. An Eagle Scout and altar boy with a high IQ, he grew up in a family that could afford the better things in life. Charlie learned to play the piano very young, took up a paper route, and learned to shoot so well that his proud father once crowed, "Charlie could plug a squirrel in the eye by the time he was sixteen." Outgoing and ambitious, he grew to be a popular athlete and model student at his parochial high school in Florida, where he graduated seventh in his class in 1959.

But Charlie had a tense relationship with his domineering, abusive father, who demanded perfection from his wife and children—and who beat them when they disappointed him. Just before Charlie's eighteenth birthday, when Charlie came home from a party drunk, his father beat him fiercely and threw him into the swimming pool, where he nearly drowned. It was the last straw for Charlie, who enlisted in the U.S. Marine Corps a few days later. He wanted nothing more than to be better and smarter than his cruel, semiliterate father. That would show him.

Early on, he thrived in the Corps, as he had under his father's authoritarian watch. With his blond crew cut and skinny frame, he might not have looked the part of a leatherneck, but he developed into a good one on active duty in Guantánamo Bay, Cuba, one of the world's Cold War hot spots. Qualified as a sharpshooter, he excelled at rapid-fire marksmanship, especially with moving targets.

In fact, Whitman was such a good Marine that he won a special military scholarship to study engineering and set himself on track to become a commissioned officer. In the fall of 1961, Whitman enrolled at the University of Texas in Austin and declared his major in mechanical engineering, still a Marine but beyond the daily control of his superiors.

Without the rigid discipline he had known for his whole life, school was a disaster. Whitman's grades tanked. He gave up studying for gambling and began wearing a .357 handgun under his shirt, ostensibly as protection against enemies he made in his late-night, high-stakes poker games.

One night, Whitman sat on the balcony of his dorm room and peered across the campus at the 307-foot (94-meter) Tower, a Spanish colonial building that stood at the dead center of the sprawling campus. Austin's tallest building—even taller than the nearby state capital dome—the Tower was the city's first skyscraper when it was built in 1937. Rallies and debates took place on its steps, and it loomed over all graduation ceremonies. Deep inside were twenty tons of bells, and its limestone walls were regularly swathed in orange floodlights after major sports victories.

The Tower was not just the most visible symbol of the University of Texas; it was its beating heart, as well.

"A person could stand off an Army before they got to him up there," the Marine sharpshooter mused. He would love to shoot people from up there, he said to nobody in particular. But nobody took him seriously. After all, Charlie was a good soldier, a mature guy, and a joker at heart. He couldn't be serious.

In February 1962, Whitman was introduced to a freshman coed named Kathy Leissner, who was studying to be a teacher. After a starry-eyed courtship, they married six months later.

If marriage improved Whitman's attitude, it didn't improve his grades. A semester after the wedding, the Marine Corps withdrew his scholarship and ordered him back to active duty at Camp Lejeune, North Carolina, while Kathy stayed in Austin to finish her education.

The return to regimented military life was claustrophobic. No longer a good soldier, Whitman rebelled. He was court-martialed for gambling and busted back to the rank of private. Desperate to get out, he turned to an unlikely ally, his father, who used his political connections to cut Charlie's enlistment. Charles Whitman was honorably discharged in December 1964 and returned to Austin, where he reenrolled at UT in the spring of 1965. His new major: architectural engineering.

He took a part-time bank teller job for $1.25 an hour and worked as a Scoutmaster in his spare time. But he wrote secretly in his journals with a darkening hand about his lack of self-esteem, expressing frustration with the dysfunctions in his family, blaming himself for his problems, and meticulously listing ways he could be a better husband. He hated that Kathy, who worked at the local phone company, was a better breadwinner than he was, and he was ashamed of accepting money from his father. He feared that something was wrong inside his brain and that he was sterile. He openly declared he didn't believe in God anymore. He began to see himself as an all-American loser.

The psychiatrist concluded Whitman was unlikely to hurt himself or anyone else and asked him to come back in a week for another session. Charles Whitman never returned.

Whitman didn't know what a happy marriage looked like; his own father and mother had made for a poor example. As a result, if his spirit was willing to try to be a better husband, his flesh had no idea how a good husband behaved.

And he behaved badly. He was a perfectionist like his father, and he began almost from the beginning to expect more of Kathy than she could give. He would check for dust *behind* picture frames and talk about his sex life with friends while Kathy was in the room. He hit her on at least three separate

occasions during their marriage, and his journals reflected his regrets over being too harsh with her.

It grew worse when his parents divorced in the spring of 1966 and his mother, Margaret, moved from Florida to Austin to be near her son. She rented an apartment near downtown, not far from Charlie and Kathy's modest, five-room bungalow at 906 Jewell Street.

Worse yet, Whitman's abuse of amphetamines, especially Dexedrine, had gotten out of control. He needed the pills to stay awake, but friends recalled him tossing them back "like popcorn." During finals week, he reportedly stayed awake for five days and nights, slept over the weekend, and did it again—nearly two weeks hopped up on chemicals and without restorative sleep. He was also taking other drugs—some legal and some not—to combat the effects of the amphetamines and to deal with his depression and stress. His medicine cabinet at home contained thirteen different pill bottles prescribed by seven different doctors.

Kathy saw her husband's turmoil. She begged him to get counseling, but he resisted. At the time of his parents' divorce, he was suffering from severe headaches, and so he finally visited a university psychiatrist.

He told the doctor how much he hated his father. He lamented what a failure he had become. He even mentioned how he had fantasized about "going up on the Tower with a deer rifle and shooting people."

Although the shrink noted that Whitman "seemed to be oozing with hostility," he wasn't particularly alarmed. First, he saw Whitman as a man who had basically good values. Second, he'd been listening to troubled, suicidal students fantasize about the Tower for years, and it no longer startled him. The doctor concluded Whitman was unlikely to hurt himself or anyone else and asked him to come back in a week for another session.

Charles Whitman never returned.

"THESE THOUGHTS ARE TOO MUCH FOR ME"

July 31, 1966, was a Sunday, and it dawned Texas-hot. It would reach 101°F (38°C) that day, the hottest day of the year so far. That morning, Charlie drove Kathy to her summer job at Southwestern Bell, where she was working a split shift.

After he dropped Kathy at her downtown office, he paid cash for some Spam and small food items at a convenience store, then bought a Bowie knife and a pair of binoculars for $18.98 at an Army surplus store.

At 1 p.m., he picked up Kathy and they went to a movie followed by a late lunch with his mother, Margaret. They killed more time before Kathy

FORMER MARINE CHARLES WHITMAN'S REPUTATION AS A CLEAN-CUT ALL-AMERICAN KID MASKED DEEPER, TROUBLING ISSUES, MANY OF THEM ARISING FROM A BRUTAL CHILDHOOD WITH AN ABUSIVE FATHER.
Associated Press

had to go back for the late half of her shift by visiting friends, who later remembered Charlie as being unusually quiet.

At 6 p.m. he dropped Kathy back at work and went home to Jewell Street. Alone in the little house where he and his wife had so recently talked about having children, Charles Whitman went to the back bedroom, calmly rolled a sheet of paper into his typewriter, and began to explain as best he could why he was about to become a mass murderer.

Sunday
July 31, 1966
6:45 P.M.
 I don't quite understand what it is that compels me to type this letter.
Perhaps it is to leave some vague reason for the actions I have recently performed.
[Author's note: Whitman had not actually yet performed these "actions" but
was writing this note to be found after he had.] I don't really understand myself
these days. I am supposed to be an average reasonable and intelligent young
man. However, lately (I can't recall when it started) I have been a victim of
many unusual and irrational thoughts. These thoughts constantly recur and
it requires a tremendous mental effort to concentrate on useful and progressive
tasks. In March when my parents made a physical break I noticed a great deal
of stress. I consulted a Dr. Cochrum at the University Health Center and asked
him to recommend someone that I could consult with about some psychiatric
disorders I felt I had. I talked with a Doctor once for about two hours and tried
to convey to him my fears that I felt some overwhelming violent impulses. After
one session I never saw the Doctor again, and since then I have been fighting
my mental turmoil alone, and seemingly to no avail.
 After my death I wish that an autopsy would be performed on me to see if there
is any visible physical disorder. I have had some tremendous headaches in the
past and have consumed two large bottles of Excedrin in the past three months.
 It was after much thought that I decided to kill my wife, Kathy, tonight after
I pick her up from work at the telephone company. I love her dearly, and she has
been as fine a wife to me as any man could ever hope to have. I cannot rationally
pinpoint any specific reason for doing this. I don't know whether it is selfish-
ness, or if I don't want her to have to face the embarrassment my actions would
surely cause her. At this time, though, the prominent reason in my mind is that
I truly do not consider this world worth living in, and am prepared to die, and
I do not want to leave her to suffer alone in it. I intend to kill her as painlessly
as possible.
 Similar reasons provoked me to take my mother's life also. I don't think
the poor woman has ever enjoyed life as she is entitled to. She was a simple
young woman who married a very possessive and dominating man. All my
life as a boy until I ran away from home to join the Marine Corps

A knock at the door interrupted him. It was another couple, best friends of
the Whitmans, dropping in for a Sunday visit. Rather than shooing them away,
Charlie invited them in.

They talked for an hour or so about everything and nothing—the Vietnam
War, upcoming exams, Charlie's dream of buying some land near the
Guadalupe River. Charlie seemed upbeat to them and talked about Kathy with

more affection than he normally did. The pleasant visit came to a happy end around 8:30 p.m. when an ice cream truck passed and they all ran outside to flag it down. The ice cream tasted good because it had been a hot day and the night was not cooling off.

A little after 9:30 p.m., Charlie picked up Kathy in their new black Chevy Impala and took her home. The night was uncommonly hot and the Jewell Street house had no air-conditioning, so Charlie asked his mother if he and Kathy could come to her air-conditioned apartment to cool off before bed. Kathy begged off, but a little before midnight, Charlie drove over to Margaret's flat, while Kathy slipped naked into bed, hoping for the slightest Texas breeze through their little bedroom window.

Margaret met Charlie in the high-rise's lobby around midnight and escorted him up to her fifth-floor apartment. Alone inside, he strangled her with a piece of rubber hose before stabbing her in the chest with a hunting knife and either shooting her or bashing the back of her head violently. He also smashed her left hand with such force that the diamond flew out of her wedding ring, which became embedded in the ruined flesh of her finger. She was only forty-three.

He then sat down with a yellow legal pad and wrote another letter, explaining that he had killed his mother to relieve her suffering at the hands of her husband. He lifted her corpse onto her bed, covered her wounds with the bedspread, and laid the letter neatly upon her. A little after 2 a.m., he returned to the Jewell Street house, where Kathy slept peacefully.

Standing over her in the darkness, he plunged his Bowie knife into her naked chest five times, hitting her heart and killing her instantly. He pulled the blankets over her and washed his hands before he returned to the unfinished letter he had begun hours before. In his own handwriting—not typing, as he had started the letter—he scrawled in the margin:

friends
interrupted
8-1-66
Mon
3:00 A.M.
Both Dead

> *I was a witness to her being beaten at least once a month. Then when she took enough my father wanted to fight to keep her below her usual standard of living.*
>
> *I imagine it appears that I bruttaly [sic] kill both of my loved ones. I was only trying to do a quick thorough job.*
>
> *If my life insurance policy is valid, please see that all the worthless checks I wrote this weekend are made good. Please pay off my debts. I am 25 years old and have been financially independent.*
>
> *Donate the rest anonymously to a mental health foundation. Maybe research can prevent further tragedies of this type.*
>
> *Charles J. Whitman*
>
> *If you can find it in yourself to grant my last wish Cremate me after the autopsy.*

Not once did he mention the horror he was about to visit upon a city and a nation. He spent the rest of the night rereading his journals, writing good-bye notes to others, and gathering the supplies he needed for the daylight, just a few hours away. Many items that he packed in his old Marine footlocker spoke more of survival than death: a radio, a blank notebook, jugs of water and gasoline,

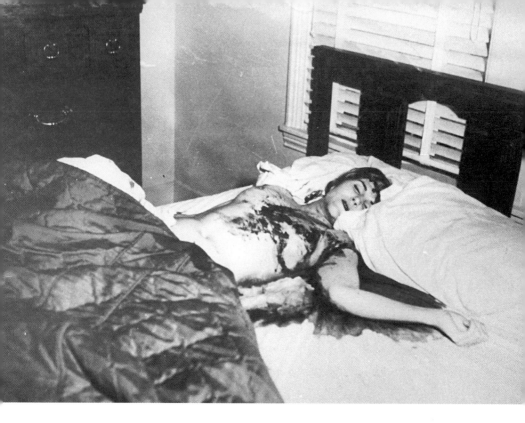

Spam and other food, deodorant, toilet paper, several knives and a hatchet, ropes, a compass, an alarm clock, a flashlight and batteries, a machete, several gun scabbards, matches, and various pieces of hunting equipment. He expected a long siege.

But some of it spoke of death, too. After the sun rose on another hot Texas day, he visited at least three Austin stores, where he bought more guns and ammunition and a dolly with which to wheel his deadly arsenal, which now included a high-powered 6 mm Remington rifle with a scope, two other hunting rifles, a sawed-off shotgun, three pistols, the large hunting knife he'd already used to kill his wife and mother, and an astounding seven hundred rounds of ammo.

He dressed in sneakers, jeans, and a plaid shirt under blue nylon overalls, trying to disguise himself as an inconspicuous workman hauling a dolly of equipment.

He scrawled a last note and left it in the house:

8-1-66. I never could quite make it. These thoughts are too much for me.

A little past 11 a.m., Charles Whitman closed the front door of the little bungalow on Jewell Street for the last time, loaded his footlocker into his car, and drove away toward the UT campus.

IN THE LINE OF FIRE

Cap Ehlke sat in a Peace Corps training class, watching the clock tick toward lunch. For more than a month, the preparatory classes had been droning on. It was intense, but not much different from regular college work. He was eager to get into the field and see the world, and another month of classes seemed more like an obstacle than a necessity.

Most days, he and some of his Peace Corps classmates would grab a quick lunch on "the Drag," as UT students called Guadalupe Street, a noisy thoroughfare that cut across the western edge of campus where many cafés and shops catered to the kids. Cap loved the college hangouts and the different people he met.

When class finally let out at noon, Cap and two friends, Dave Mattson and Tom Herman, started a long, hot walk to a school cafeteria, where they planned to meet a new friend, Thomas Ashton, for lunch. All four were headed to Iran in the fall.

The heat was oppressive and the humid air still as death as they walked three abreast down Guadalupe. Road workers were fixing the street, and the lunchtime traffic was heavier than usual. Kids passed them on the sidewalk, where newsstands displayed front pages depicting Vietnam, and many passing girls wore their hair long and straight. Cap noticed both.

As they passed traffic barricades in front of Sheftall's Jewelers, a little shop beside the university bookstore, Cap heard several pops. *Firecrackers*, he thought. *Or road workers with an air hammer, or maybe a stupid fraternity prank.*

Beside him, Dave shrieked. Cap looked down to see Dave cupping his right hand in his left. It was nearly severed from his wrist and bleeding profusely. *What the hell?* he thought. *Don't they know that firecrackers can hurt people?*

Then he noticed the left sleeve of his madras shirt was riddled with small holes and flecked with blood, and it made him angrier.

Suddenly, his upper right arm was jolted, as if he'd been punched by someone unseen. A deep gash in his triceps began to pour blood into his shredded sleeve.

"Take cover!" somebody yelled down the street.

Cap and Tom, who wasn't wounded, hunkered near the wall of the bookstore, but Dave simply crumpled in shock on the sidewalk, holding his dismembered hand and muttering to himself. People were running all around them, taking cover. Cap thought he saw a girl's lifeless body lying on the pavement up the street. His arm wounds were starting to burn.

A HEAVILY ARMED CHARLES WHITMAN PROWLED THE UNIVERSITY OF TEXAS TOWER'S OBSERVATION DECK, FIRING HIS HUNTING RIFLE AT PEOPLE 231 FEET (70 METERS) BELOW WITH DEADLY ACCURACY. ONE OF HIS VICTIMS WAS KILLED MORE THAN 500 YARDS (455 METERS) AWAY.

Associated Press

Nobody knew what was happening. He heard more distant pops, but there was so much confusion, and Dave needed help.

"We've got to get off the sidewalk," he hollered.

Cap and Tom left their hiding place and crawled to Dave. Together they dragged him across the hot concrete to the jewelry store's front door, just a few feet away. Little pings and puffs of dust erupted all around them as the mysterious, distant pops continued.

Jewelry store manager Homer Kelley saw kids crawling around on the sidewalk and was suspicious of a college prank—until he saw the blood. As the sixty-four-year-old Kelley ran outside to help drag the boys to safety, something hit him in the lower left leg.

Inside, Cap collapsed on the ripped carpet with Dave, still stunned. All around him, more than a dozen other people hid behind display cases and furniture as broken glass flew from the front windows. Some were also wounded. One man lay bleeding from his belly while others made bandages from handkerchiefs.

Cap could hear gunshots behind the store. It slowly dawned on him that they'd been hit by bullets fired in front of the store, and they continued to fly from the opposite direction. It made him think they were caught in the crossfire of a spectacular gunfight, or maybe a jewelry store robbery.

The frightened people around him were coming to the same fearful conclusion.

"It's a whole gang out there," somebody said. "They're coming in here!"

Then Cap noticed that the left thigh of his tan jeans was perforated with tiny holes, and blood welled up in a widening stain. He had been wounded three times. He didn't know his friend Thomas Ashton, who the three boys were on their way to meet, was already dead. And he didn't know why anyone would shoot at him.

ENDING THE SIEGE

There was no reason. There was no gang. There was no robbery.

Just one berserk killer in a tower.

Pretending to be a janitor, Charles Whitman had wheeled his arsenal into the University of Texas Tower, killing three innocent people there before barricading himself on the Tower's observation deck.

At 1 p.m., with his weapons arrayed all around him in his impenetrable fortress, Charlie Whitman took aim at a heavily pregnant young woman walking with her

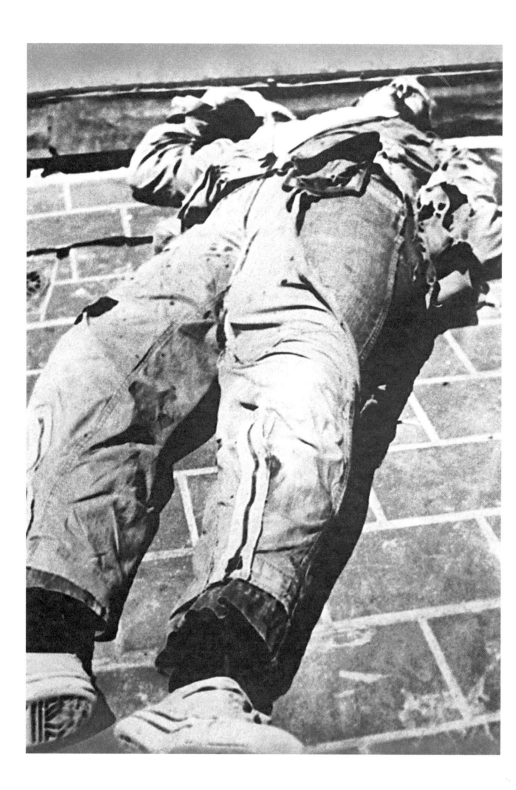

boyfriend on campus. He hit her in the belly, and as she fell, her boyfriend crouched over her. Charlie shot him, too.

He commenced shooting anyone he could see. He had a 360-degree field of fire, and he proved lethal.

For the next ninety-six minutes, Whitman killed with uncanny precision. He hit some victims up to 500 yards (457 meters) away, and zeroed in on frantic, running bodies with deadly accuracy. He dropped them all: first, the pregnant freshman and her boyfriend, who tried to shield her . . . then the young math professor . . . Peace Corps volunteer Thomas Ashton, who was simply walking toward the sound of gunshots . . . the student running away . . . the cop who peeked out from his hiding place . . . the Ph.D. candidate with six kids . . . the new high-school graduate and his girlfriend who dreamed of being a dancer . . . the city electrical repairman who just wanted to help somebody . . . the seventeen-year-old girl who attended the same school where Kathy taught . . . the electrical engineering student who'd take another thirty-five years to die from his wounds . . .

With one hundred fifty bullets, Whitman hit almost fifty people.

All the while, a CBS television crew was filming inside the free-fire zone, and news photographers were risking their lives to snap images for the next day's paper. Citizens all over the city—including Whitman himself—had dialed their transistor radios to listen to the live coverage.

Minutes after the first shot, Austin police scrambled to the scene, where one of them had already been killed. A police sniper was sent aloft in an airplane, but Whitman drove them away with his gunfire. As word spread on the radio, dozens of angry citizens arrived with deer rifles and returned fire at the Tower.

As police slowly moved across the killing ground toward the Tower, they helped the wounded as best they could, even as Whitman continued to fire at the ambulances trying to save them.

A handful of policemen finally got to the Tower. Once inside, Officers Ramiro Martinez and Houston McCoy—with the help of a civilian deputized on the scene—crept to the observation deck but found the door wedged shut. When McCoy finally breached the door, they both snuck toward the sound of Whitman's shots, even as bullets from the ground ricocheted off the walls around them.

McCoy caught Whitman's eye for a split second, then blasted him in the face with a shotgun. Charlie's head flipped back and his body spasmed as McCoy hit him with another blast in the left side of his head. At the same moment, Martinez emptied six shots from his service revolver into Whitman.

He was dead, but McCoy and Martinez ran to his twitching body and each fired a last shot at point-blank range into him. As Whitman's blood drained into a rain gutter near his shattered head, McCoy grabbed a green towel from Whitman's footlocker and waved it to the people on the ground.

The siege was over. At 1:24 p.m., Charles Whitman was dead.

PUTTING THE PIECES TOGETHER

Whitman was likely already dead when Cap and the others hiding in the jewelry store—and most people on the ground—escaped into an alley and scrambled over a wooden fence into the arms of paramedics on the other side. In the alley, Cap saw ordinary people aiming their rifles toward the Tower, and a few more pieces of this bloody puzzle fell into place.

Several injured people were already in the ambulance, including the driver himself, who was critically wounded. Driver Morris Hohmann was responding to the victims on West Twenty-Third Street when one of Whitman's bullets pierced his leg artery. His partner used his belt as a tourniquet and took him to Brackenridge Hospital with the other victims.

At Brackenridge, the dead and wounded were piling up in the city's only full-service emergency room. Chaos reigned in the hospital's hallways, where cops, reporters, and relatives rushed around among the dead and dying. Meanwhile, hundreds of local citizens lined up at Brackenridge and the local blood center to donate.

In the ER, somebody told Cap what had happened: A madman in the Tower had been shooting innocent people, and many were dead.

When a doctor finally saw Cap, he found serious shrapnel wounds in his upper left arm, the front of his left leg, his back, and his left hand—all caused by Whitman's soft-tipped bullets splattering against his friend Dave's wrist bones and the walls and sidewalks of Guadalupe. He had also been hit directly in the soft flesh of his upper right arm; the bullet furrowed 6 inches (15.2 centimeters) across the meat of his triceps. None of the injuries were life-threatening, but all had come close to something much more serious.

Brackenridge soon transferred Cap to the University Health Center, where he spent a week recuperating from his wounds, some of which suppurated for months. There, he was told that Thomas Ashton, his Peace Corps buddy, had been killed. And he began to contemplate how close he had come to death.

Outside of his hospital window the Tower loomed. This edifice, seemingly within an arm's reach, had come to symbolize so many things to so many people, including Charles Whitman. Now it became a symbol of something else to Cap Ehlke: the nearness of death.

"As I lay in the clean, white bed at the clinic, I could look out the window and see that lofty tower," he wrote later. "At night it was lit up. Piercing into the dark sky, it gave me an eerie feeling, as stark as death itself. It made me think about the ultimate meaning of things."

After he was released, Cap joined up with another Peace Corps group that had been sent to Mexico to practice teaching before shipping out to the Middle East. He was assigned to a high school in

NOW A PROFESSOR OF RELIGION, WRITING, AND LITERATURE AT WISCONSIN'S CONCORDIA UNIVERSITY, CAP EHLKE FINALLY FULFILLED HIS DREAM OF SEEING THE WORLD BEFORE COMING HOME TO MILWAUKEE, WHERE HE GREW UP, TO BECOME A LUTHERAN MINISTER.

Ron Franscell

Mexico City for a few weeks, but he felt out of sync with the group. His wounds weren't healing properly, and he was still obsessed with his brush with death. Or with God.

The shooting had jolted him back into a spiritual focus. He still wanted adventure, but maybe it wasn't as far as Iran or all the other places he never knew. Maybe it was closer than all that.

He picked up the phone and called the seminary. The new semester had already begun, he was told, but they took him anyway.

The next summer, he went to Iran to visit some of his old Peace Corps friends, including Dave Mattson, whose hand had been reattached by surgeons. He explored Europe that summer, too, before traveling to Jerusalem six weeks after the Six-Day War between Israel and Egypt. The air was electric in those days, and it thrilled him.

Later, he attended the Hebrew University of Israel before finishing at seminary. He was sent to a small church in Little Chute, Wisconsin, and made a family. He was, at last, the minister his father expected him to be.

In time, he returned to Milwaukee as an editor for a Lutheran publishing house, where he worked for fifteen years. Cap eventually collected four master's degrees and a doctorate, and he took a teaching position at Concordia University, a Lutheran college on the shores of Lake Michigan in Mequon, a northern suburb of Milwaukee.

For many years, he kept the bloodied pants he wore that day in Austin, but they have disappeared. So have some of the memories he thought he'd never forget. Somewhere there's a box full of clippings and mementos from those dark days, but he has lost track of them. Reading other people's memories might somehow taint his own.

"I just have never looked at my survival as some kind of great accomplishment," he says now. "It was just something I was involved in. In some ways, it seemed kind of morbid to want to revisit it."

He feels no animosity toward Charles Whitman, partly because he never saw it as a personal attack.

"What he did was terrible, and he went over the edge," Cap says. "It was like being hit by lighting, being touched by some force outside of me. I happen to have been shot by him, but my relationship to Charles Whitman is no different than someone's who wasn't even there.

"If anything, it made me aware of how we are always close to death. An inch or two either way can make all the difference."

WORKMEN USE WIRE BRUSHES TO REMOVE BLOOD STAINS FROM THE CONCRETE SIDEWALK IN FRONT OF THE UNIVERSITY OF TEXAS TOWER IN AUSTIN, THE DAY AFTER CHARLES WHITMAN'S ASSAULT.
Associated Press

THE ENIGMA IN THE TOWER

In ninety-six horrifying minutes, Charles Whitman had killed fourteen people and wounded thirty-one. The discovery of his wife's and mother's corpses brought the day's grim toll to sixteen.

A long line of American mass murderers preceded Charlie Whitman, and a longer line came after, but the Texas Tower massacre became an archetype for wholesale slaughter possibly because of the iconic Tower itself. Or possibly because it would be twenty-two years before another crazed shooter—James Huberty, at the San Ysidro McDonald's in 1984—would exceed Whitman's grisly body count (see chapter 3).

In the days after the orgiastic slaughter in Austin, an autopsy showed that Whitman had a malignant, walnut-sized tumor deep in his brain, just as he had feared. But doctors concluded that it was unlikely to have caused his rampage, even though they believed it might have killed him within a year.

Some scoff at the suggestion that a tumor, drug abuse, insomnia, or anything but raw evil caused Whitman's rampage.

"Charlie Whitman knew precisely and completely what he was doing when he ascended the University of Texas Tower and shot nearly fifty people," wrote Gary Lavergne, whose meticulously detailed book, *A Sniper in the Tower*, stands as the definitive account of the crime. "He could not have done what he did without controlled, thoughtful, serial decision-making in a correct order to accomplish a goal. Nothing he did remotely appears undisciplined or random . . . [He] was a cold and calculating murderer. Those who say they can't believe he would commit such a monstrous crime are only admitting that they didn't really know him."

Charlie Whitman died as he had lived, an enigma.

Ironically, he was buried beside his beloved mother—his first victim—in a Catholic cemetery in Florida. A priest blessed Charlie's gray, flag-draped casket as it was lowered into hallowed ground, saying he had obviously been mentally ill and was therefore not responsible for the sin of murder.

Kathy Leissner Whitman, only twenty-three when her husband stabbed her to death, was buried in Rosenberg, Texas, not far from the little town where she grew up.

As so often has happened after gun crimes, a groundswell of anti-gun hysteria erupted after the Tower massacre. But it was stillborn: Charlie Whitman was a military-trained marksman who possessed legal weapons that he legally purchased. He had no previous criminal record and knew more about firearms than most gun owners do. As many pointed out at the time, he could have taught the gun-ownership courses that any state might have mandated.

For many, it wasn't what Whitman knew or what he couldn't control that caused his crimes. He was in complete control of his actions and understood their profound consequences.

"Charles Whitman knew that what he was doing was evil," Lavergne concluded in *A Sniper in the Tower*. "[He] became a killer because he did not respect or admire himself. He knew that in many ways he was what he despised in others.

"He wanted to die in a big way . . . he died while engaging in the only activity in which he truly excelled: shooting."

For two years after the mass murder, the Tower's observation deck was closed. After it reopened in 1968, a series of suicide leaps forced it to close again in 1974. Finally, after several safety improvements, it reopened in 1999.

Nine years after the killings, when Hollywood proposed a TV movie about the massacre, starring a post-Disney Kurt Russell as Whitman, the University of Texas refused to allow filming at the Tower, saying it would be an affront to the still-raw emotions in Austin. *The Deadly Tower* was eventually filmed at the state capital building in Baton Rouge, Louisiana, and aired in late 1975 to luke-warm reviews. The movie itself is five minutes shorter than Whitman's real-time shooting spree.

The Tower's symbolism is so potent that for years UT offered a college course, "The UT Tower and Public Memory."

"After more than thirty years of institutional repression and silence," its teacher, professor Rosa Eberly, wrote in 1999, "UT has been presented with an opportunity to come to terms publicly with one of the most troubling incidents in its history. The university . . . has, at least institutionally, begun to heal and move beyond the violent effects of Charles Whitman's actions in 1966 and the enduring pain of those who witnessed or were otherwise affected by the several suicides there."

Forty years later, in 2006, the university mounted an inconspicuous bronze plaque beside a turtle pond just north of the Tower as a memorial "to those who died, to those who were wounded, and to the countless other victims who were immeasurably affected by the tragedy." This is the only memorial to the massacre on the UT campus.

For a long time, the Tower bore the pockmarks where bullets had hit, but they were all eventually patched, and the divots are barely noticeable. Today, Tower tour guides are instructed not to talk about the Whitman massacre, as the university tries to minimize the memory of August 1, 1966. All visitors must first pass through a metal detector at ground level, and an armed guard accompanies all tour groups to the observation deck.

But many people will never forget. Officer Houston McCoy, who suffered from posttraumatic stress for years after he killed Whitman in the Tower, is one.

"If I get to heaven and see Charles Whitman," he once said, "I'm going to have to kill him all over again."

CHAPTER 7

EVIL ON THE FRONT PORCH

DIANNE ALEXANDER AND THE SERIAL KILLER DERRICK TODD LEE

THE LANGUID BROWN WATER OF BAYOU TECHE runs slow as a cemetery. It twists and turns among giant moss-bearded oaks, haunted swamps, and decaying mansions built with sugar money.

The meandering bayou's name comes from a local Indian word for "snake" because, in the Indian culture's mythic history, a giant snake attacked their scattered villages, and it took many years for an army of warriors to kill it. The serpent's enormous corpse sunk into the Louisiana mud and rotted where it lay until the rain filled its death hole with water.

Muddy Bayou Teche is the sclerotic artery through the heart of Cajun country, where crawfish boils and Mass are both religious sacraments. On its shifting banks, Longfellow's Evangeline waited for her long-lost lover. And its syrupy water nourishes the very roots of Cajun history in the former French colony known as Louisiana.

Cecilia is one of the farming villages that settled on the rich soil of Bayou Teche more than two hundred years ago. Today, it's one of those backwater places few people go unless they live there, but residents are friendly enough to answer the door when somebody needs directions.

After all, people have been known to disappear into the *petite pluie fine*—the mists—of Bayou Teche.

SAFE AT HOME

Gospel music poured from the radio like light. Dianne Alexander was humming along as she fixed lunch for her son, Herman, who'd soon be home from his morning classes at the University of Louisiana at Lafayette, a half hour away.

She'd spent her morning running errands in Breaux Bridge and Lafayette, picking up groceries, gassing up, and stopping at the post office. A nursing student, Dianne had just started working the evening shift for her clinical studies at Lafayette General Medical Center, and she was grateful for a morning off. She only wished her husband, Oliver, a delivery driver for a local seafood company, could be there to share that sultry morning of July 9, 2002, with her, but he was off on a run to Houston and wouldn't be back until after she was at work later that night.

The errands took all morning, but Dianne's timing was perfect. She had time to make lunch and start dinner. She'd gotten home to the comfortable mobile home where she had lived for twelve years, plopped her purse on the kitchen counter, and took off her wedding ring, which she always did before cooking. While some turkey necks sizzled on the stove, she set up an ironing board in Herman's room so she could press her student nurse uniform after lunch.

The daughter of a construction worker, Dianne was the second of seven children. Her strict father worked hard, but the family barely scraped by. She grew up with eight other people in a tiny, three-bedroom wood-frame bungalow in the black section of Breaux Bridge. They had a TV, but Dianne liked to listen to rhythm-and-blues shows on the radio while she helped her mama do the laundry on an old wringer machine on the back porch. She went to class in homemade clothes and played the xylophone in the school band.

Education wasn't a priority for her devoutly Catholic parents, but church was. Because Dianne was the family's only driver at age thirteen, this little girl who peered in the mirror and spoke to God quit school in the eleventh grade.

Dianne grew up tall and pretty. A light-skinned African American woman with striking hazel eyes, she caught plenty of boys' attention, and she liked it. Although she'd met Oliver in high school, she was pregnant at eighteen by another boy. When that marriage fell apart, she and Oliver found each other again and eventually married.

She also found Jesus. Although faith ran through her like the beat in one of her beloved R&B songs, she had never been a staunch churchgoer until she picked up an evangelistic tract from a nearby church one day. "God knows the number of hairs on your head," it said. The notion intrigued her. So she and a friend drove to the church one night and were caught up in a frenzy that excited her, made her feel good. She was saved that night.

By age forty-six, she lived with a hardworking man she loved in a house that sat on two acres of land in Cecilia, just up the road from where she grew up. Life hadn't always been easy, but she was a wife and a mother of four children, one going to college. She'd earned her GED years before and had been taking college classes since 1992 to become a nurse. She not only felt loved as she cooked and sang along to the gospel station, but she also felt safe.

Then came a knock on her door.

A MYSTERIOUS VISITOR

Dianne opened the door to find a burly young black man standing on her covered porch. He was tall and good-looking with a neatly trimmed mustache and light brown eyes. His hair was closely cut. Although he was slightly heavy, he was well dressed in a striped golf shirt, denim shorts, and sneakers with white ankle socks. He smiled as she opened the door.

"May I help you?"

"Hi, my name is Anthony," he said, shaking her hand. "I'm from Monroe. I'm supposed to be doing construction work for the Montgomerys. Do you know them?"

No, Dianne said, she didn't know of any Montgomery family in the area. But this man was well spoken and pleasant, she thought, and she wanted to help if she could.

"Well do you think your husband would know them?"

"No, he wouldn't."

"Do you think I could use your phone? Maybe a phone book?" the young man said. "Maybe it'll have their address."

Dianne retrieved her cordless phone and directory from the kitchen and handed it to the man on her porch. While he flipped through the pages, she pushed her front door closed—leaving it open just a crack—and went back to the turkey necks cooking on the stove for Oliver's dinner while she hummed along with the radio. When the man started peeking through the thin gap at the door, she went back.

The man smiled at her.

"Oh, I ain't gonna do you anything," he said, smiling big. "But are you sure your husband doesn't know these Montgomerys?"

Dianne was adamant. "No, he doesn't know them."

He could hear the gospel music playing inside.

"I used to sing in a gospel choir," he said, stepping closer. "Maybe you've heard of us . . ."

DIANNE AND OLIVER ALEXANDER MET IN HIGH SCHOOL AND FOUND EACH OTHER YEARS LATER AFTER PRIOR MARRIAGES. IN THE PAINFUL DAYS AFTER DERRICK TODD LEE'S ATTACK, OLIVER BECAME DIANNE'S STURDIEST SUPPORTER.

Courtesy of the Alexander Family

He gave Dianne a name she didn't recognize. She told him she hadn't heard of him, and she began to get a little annoyed at this chatty guy at her door. She had work to do.

"Are you sure you and your husband don't know the Montgomerys?" he asked again.

Dianne had heard enough from this annoying guy.

"Look, my husband isn't home," she said and started to close the front door.

The man suddenly plowed into the door to force his way inside. She tried to barricade the metal door but in the blink of an eye, his big hands were around Dianne's throat, and he shoved her against the door.

"Take me to your bedroom!" he demanded, as he pulled a blade out of his back pocket. "I have a knife! I'll stab you in the eye!"

Everything in Dianne wanted to scream out, to fight back, but she couldn't. Nothing seemed real. A stranger was in her home and she didn't know why, but she knew she couldn't lose her nerve. Instead, she tried to clear her head and speak as calmly as she could to her attacker, who gripped her windpipe. She didn't want to go to her small bedroom because there was only one way out.

"We don't have to go into the bedroom," she managed to whisper. "We can just stay right here."

With his hand still around her throat, the man walked her a few steps to the living room and eased her down onto the carpet.

"Take off your panties!" he told her.

"I can't. Your hand's on my throat," Dianne rasped, realizing exactly what was happening to her.

He removed his hand, and Dianne lifted her long denim skirt to slip off her panties. He spread her bare legs, propping one on the couch as he unzipped his shorts and played with himself. He touched her, trying to arouse himself. Bending down, he laid his freshly shaved cheek against hers.

"I'm just going to do this and then I'll leave," he said, almost tenderly.

"I'm not going to tell anybody."

Then he kissed her lips lightly and whispered in her ear. "I've been watching you."

Sweaty and breathing harder now, he was trying to get an erection, but it wasn't happening. He even turned off the mobile home's humming air conditioner so he could focus better.

Then he put the knife on the floor and tried to concentrate on his flaccid penis. Dianne grabbed the knife, but the man took it away from her before she could use it.

"Where did you see me?" Dianne asked calmly. She was determined to be compliant, fearing he would kill her if she fought back, resisted, or just made him mad. She studied everything about him—in case she survived. She wanted to be able to describe every detail.

"Shut up! Shut up!" he shouted. Still no erection.

"Can I turn off the fire on the stove?" Dianne asked matter-of-factly. She worried she might be killed and the house might burn down, destroying all the evidence.

"Fuck the pot!" he yelled.

He told her not to move while he took off his shirt and laid on top of her, sweating all over her, trying to get it up but unable to.

"Bitch!" he growled.

Frustrated, the man stood up and looked around the room. His eyes fell on a phone cord connecting the computer to a wall outlet. He cut a length of the cord with his knife.

"You're not a bad-looking guy," she said, trying to stall.

"No, I'm not," he seethed.

He straddled Dianne's shoulders and lashed the cord around her neck, pulling it tight. Choking, she slipped a finger under the wire, but she couldn't fight against the man's weight pinning her to the floor. Unable to penetrate her or strangle her, he flew into a rage, beating her with his fists and finally smashing a heavy ceramic pot on her head.

The next day, St. Martin's Parish cops released a composite sketch of Dianne's would-be rapist. . . . What they didn't know at the time was that they were releasing the first public portrait of a serial killer.

She passed out, bleeding profusely from a ragged gash in her forehead. Drifting in and out of consciousness, she would sometimes wake to see him and feel him on top of her, still trying in vain to rape her but still unable to get an erection. She didn't know how long she lay there, half wake and half dead, while her attacker moved freely around her.

He was making one last effort to penetrate her when he suddenly looked up and listened intently. He had heard something he didn't expect: a car in the driveway.

Dianne watched him as he leaped up, dressed, and grabbed her purse and cordless phone. Frustrated at being interrupted—at losing control of the situation—he stomped Dianne hard in the stomach and fled out the back just as her son Herman came in the front door.

Dianne was numb and barely conscious. She felt no pain, just relief.

She was alive.

Herman had come home for lunch to find a strange car parked in his spot in the driveway. He noticed a gold-colored Mitsubishi Mirage with front-end damage and a front license plate advertising a local dealer, Hampton Motors. It belonged to nobody he knew.

He went inside, and everything was quiet until he heard his mother's distressed voice in the living room.

"Help!" she cried. "Get a knife!"

Dianne was splayed on the bloody rug, delirious, with her skirt pulled up around her waist. Her face was badly bruised and her eyes were swollen shut. Then Herman saw the back door swinging open and ran outside to see the gold Mirage speeding away down Highway 31, with a silvery cord hanging from a rear window. He ran back inside, got his keys, and peeled out of the driveway to chase the man who attacked his mother, but he quickly lost sight of him.

When he returned to the mobile home, he followed a trail of blood to find his mother, who had stumbled into the bedroom, called 911, and passed out.

When detectives arrived, they found Herman waiting for them in the driveway, furious. His fury was so intense he couldn't describe what he'd seen.

Dianne was Life Flighted to Lafayette General, where doctors found she had a skull fracture; many cuts and bruises around her neck, face, and scalp; and other injuries to the back of her head. They were unable to collect any of the attacker's DNA. Over the next five days in the hospital, while police scoured her home for clues, an investigator gently worked through the details with her and asked her to describe her assailant for a police sketch artist.

The next day, St. Martin's Parish cops released a composite sketch of Dianne's would-be rapist and a description of his gold Mitsubishi sedan.

What they didn't know at the time was that they were releasing the first public portrait of a serial killer. It never crossed their minds that this crime in little Cecilia could be related to a recent series of killings in Baton Rouge.

And they didn't know that Dianne Alexander was his first and only living victim. All the rest were dead. And there would be more.

THE WRONG PROFILE

Three days later, on July 12, Pam Kinamore, a forty-four-year-old mother and antique-store owner, disappeared from her Baton Rouge home one evening. Her nude, rotting corpse was found four days later under a swampland bridge 30 miles (48 kilometers) west of Baton Rouge, nearly decapitated by three vicious slashes across her throat. She had been raped.

The body, exposed to humid Louisiana summer heat and various bayou predators, was unidentifiable except for a gold wedding band on its left ring finger. It was Pam Kinamore's. But her husband noticed that the body was not wearing Pam's favorite thin silver toe ring.

$75,000⁰⁰
REWARD

For Information Leading to the Arrest and Conviction of the Person Responsible for the Murder of Pam Kinamore.

Justice for Pam. Justice for All

CALL 389-5000

Police also found a strand of phone cord near the body and collected it as evidence.

The medical examiner determined Pam had been alive when her throat was cut because there was blood in her lungs.

Two witnesses reported seeing a white pickup truck driven by a white man with a naked, frightened, white female passenger matching Kinamore's description on the night she disappeared. Other than the DNA collected from her body, that was all the local cops had to go on.

White man. White pickup truck.

Within two weeks, police announced that trace DNA evidence conclusively linked the murder of Kinamore, a one-time beauty queen, to the same man who had killed at least two other local women in the past year: Gina Wilson Green, a forty-one-year-old nursing supervisor found strangled in September 2001; and Charlotte Murray Pace, a twenty-two-year-old grad student whose throat was slashed in a townhouse near the Louisiana State University campus the previous May.

News of a serial killer among them stunned the citizens of Baton Rouge, and a flood of questions were only starting to be asked—but not answered very well.

Like Kinamore, the two earlier victims were attractive white women with chestnut hair, and there had been no forced entry into any of their homes. But that's where the common characteristics ended.

Pace and Green both drove BMWs, but not Kinamore. Pace and Green both jogged on the same lakeside path near LSU, but not Kinamore. Pace and Green had lived a few doors from each other on the capital's Stanford Avenue, but Kinamore didn't live nearby. Green and Kinamore both loved antiques, but not Pace. Green and Kinamore were both older, petite women; Pace was tall and young.

WITHOUT REMORSE

Less than a month after Kinamore's slaying, the Baton Rouge Multi-Agency Homicide Task Force was formed to find the serial killer, but it released precious little valuable information to the public, even though police agencies in the greater Baton Rouge area had more than sixty unsolved cases of missing or murdered women since 1985.

The task force lacked credibility almost from the start. The streets of the state capital were already alive with rumors, complicating the investigation. Scuttlebutt pegged the killer as a professor at LSU, a BMW salesman, or a cop. It said he played tapes of crying babies outside so women would open their doors. The police themselves fueled the hysteria by telling the frightened citizens of Baton Rouge the killer was a white man driving a white pickup.

Pride played a role, too. When criminologist Robert Keppel, an investigator credited with catching Ted Bundy and Gary Ridgway, the Green River killer, offered to help the Baton Rouge task force, it declined.

Women swarmed to self-defense classes and started carrying guns. Every white guy in a white pickup got suspicious looks from passing motorists and pedestrians.

Task force members wanted to bet on statistics. They put their faith in the tendencies of serial killers to use the same methods, stalk identical kinds of victims, and avoid crossing racial borders.

So the task force also dismissed other possibly related cases brought to them by other cops. The January stabbing of white, brunette Geralyn DeSoto was ignored because she had not been raped, her wounds were not as vicious, and the murder happened in West Baton Rouge, a decidedly different jurisdiction. Besides, her husband was the prime suspect in that crime.

Nobody had yet studied the DNA of human tissue found beneath Geralyn's fingernails, or they would have known that she, too, was killed by the same man.

FBI profiler Mary Ellen O'Toole built a portrait of the killer. She said he was likely between the ages of twenty-five and thirty-five. He was big and strong, weighing up to 175 pounds (97 kilograms). His shoe size was between 10 and 11. He earned an average wage or less—money was tight—and he probably didn't deal with the public in his job.

He blended into the community and was seen as harmless. When he lost control of a situation, he regressed to primitive anger. And he blamed other people when he lost control.

He hadn't expected Pam Kinamore's body to be found, O'Toole surmised, so he might have gone back to the crime scene to see where he screwed up.

> **When Dianne Alexander's composite sketch was shared with Baton Rouge cops, they dismissed it because her would-be rapist was black and drove a Mitsubishi. Their killer was a white man driving a white pickup.**

Going deeper into his psychology, O'Toole said the killer stalked his victims, who were likely to be attractive women of a higher social class. He might even have chatted with them before his attacks. He wanted to be appealing, but he was too unsophisticated to truly relate to them.

He likely gave odd, unexpected gifts to the women in his life, possibly even "trophies" he'd taken from victims. He didn't handle rejection well but was cool under pressure. Because he chose high-risk targets at high-risk times of day, he liked the excitement of the attack. Despite his planning, he was impulsive. In relationships, he was hot-tempered and irritable. He was, like most serial killers, without remorse or empathy. Worse, the killer was learning from his mistakes and evolving. And as time wore on, he was likely to become increasingly paranoid.

She didn't say whether he was white or black. But whether the police had watched too many TV crime shows or their suspicions had been influenced by witnesses who swore they saw a white man in a white truck, they were focused only on white men. For them, it was a safe bet because fewer than one in six American serial killers is black.

MOUNTING HYSTERIA

But profiles don't catch killers. Cops do. And in this case, Baton Rouge authorities were making a series of crucial errors, dismissing leads, and looking the wrong way. More than 1,500 white men were swabbed for DNA samples. The task force bought a billboard on the interstate with a sketch of the suspected killer—a white man. Cops announced what kinds of shoes the killer wore at two murder scenes, causing some veteran investigators to worry he would destroy the evidence.

Worse, police began to realize they might have more than one serial killer prowling Baton Rouge at the same time, a frightening if statistically unlikely possibility.

Mounting public hysteria was confusing matters even more. More than 27,000 tips flooded in from the public and swamped the task force. Many leads were simply ignored, even when they came from other police agencies. When Dianne Alexander's composite sketch was shared with Baton Rouge cops, they dismissed it because her

would-be rapist was black and drove a Mitsubishi. Their killer was a white man driving a white pickup. Moreover, Dianne was black—although very fair—and their killer favored white women.

On September 4, a woman called the task force to tell them that she knew the killer, a man named Derrick Todd Lee, her convicted stalker. But when investigators went to Lee's house and saw he was a slightly pudgy black man and didn't drive a white work truck, they dismissed him as a suspect.

Enter Detective David McDavid, a small-town cop from Zachary, 15 miles (24 kilometers) north of Baton Rouge. In 1992, he had worked on the disappearance and murder of Connie Warner, a forty-one-year-old mother abducted from her Zachary home with no signs of forced entry. Her badly decomposed body was found in a Baton Rouge ditch more than a week later.

A year later, he caught the case of two necking teenagers who were slashed by a machete-wielding Peeping Tom in a cemetery. The attacker ran away when a cop drove up to roust the kids. One of the victims later identified a local troublemaker well known to Zachary cops: Derrick Todd Lee, a petty burglar, stalker, and peeper with a long rap sheet.

Then in 1998, Detective McDavid pulled another missing-persons case. Twenty-eight-year-old single mom Randi Mebruer had disappeared from her Zachary home. A pool of blood congealed on the floor as her three-year-old son wandered in the front yard, but her body was never found. McDavid quickly noticed that Mebruer lived just around the corner from the house where Connie Warner had disappeared six years before—and in a neighborhood where Derrick Todd Lee was suspected of peeping for the past year or so.

Armed with the evidence in those three cases, McDavid went to the Baton Rouge task force. And the task force sent him away.

Meanwhile, women were disappearing and dying.

On November 21, 2002, twenty-three-year-old Marine recruit Trineisha Dene Colomb was visiting her mother's grave in Grand Coteau, Louisiana, when she vanished. Her car was found near the grave, and a hunter later found her body along a path in a wooded area in the Lafayette suburb of Scott. She'd been savagely beaten and raped, her head slammed against a tree trunk, and her dead body left to be eaten by vermin.

The task force didn't think Colomb's murder was related. It didn't happen in her home. Colomb was half-black. She wasn't stabbed.

But a key piece of evidence was left behind: DNA. Two days before Christmas 2002, the state crime lab confirmed that Trineisha Dene Colomb had been killed by the man they now called the South Louisiana Serial Killer, but his identity was no clearer.

On Christmas Eve, Mari Ann Fowler disappeared from the sidewalk in front of a Subway restaurant in Port Allen, just across the Mississippi River from Baton Rouge. Her body was never found.

And on March 3, 2003, Carrie Lynn Yoder, a twenty-six-year-old doctoral student at LSU, disappeared from her Baton Rouge apartment. Ten days later, a fisherman found her beaten, half-naked body in the water near the Whisky Bay Bridge, where Pam Kinamore's body had been discovered eight months before. Her killer had beaten her so severely that nine ribs had been snapped from her spinal column, puncturing her liver and lungs. Her face was so badly damaged that she had to be identified by dental records.

DNA evidence showed her to be the fifth official victim of the Baton Rouge serial killer. The task force was stunned by what came next: Sophisticated tests of the killer's DNA showed he was a black man. Specifically, his genetic makeup was 85 percent sub-Saharan African and 15 percent Native American.

Everything they thought they knew was crap.

ON THE TRAIL OF A SERIAL KILLER

Around the same time, former neighbors of Connie Warner and Randi Mebruer in Zachary started to report that their longtime Peeping Tom was back, and police found evidence that it was true.

That's when a veteran detective named Dannie Mixon began to look deeper into Derrick Todd Lee, a serial peeper who was now thirty-four years old and long a suspect in the Zachary crimes. He knew about Lee's abusive father and domineering mother. He knew Lee was learning disabled and had spent time in special classes, where he sucked his thumb and called the teacher "mama." He knew how Lee had tortured his dog and puppies as a kid. He knew Lee learned early in life how to talk his way out of trouble and cast blame on others.

He knew every car Lee had ever driven. He knew Lee's good days and bad days—and he saw that the killings often happened just after Lee lost a job, or money was low, or he got thumped by his probation officer. And he noticed that Lee, who had been in and out of jail on a variety of raps, was always out of jail when the five known victims were killed—and when Connie Warner and Randi Mebruer died or disappeared.

Armed with the added evidence that the Baton Rouge serial killer was an African American, Mixon convinced a judge to issue a search warrant to swab Lee for DNA.

On May 5, Mixon went to Lee's home and took the swab himself, but he didn't need science to tell him what his gut had already told him. They had the right guy.

The next day, while police waited for the results of his DNA test, Lee told his wife something was about "to blow up on us" and that police would try to pin a crime on him. He quickly packed a bag and took a bus to Chicago, but, oddly, he returned three days later. In another frantic rush, he and his wife abruptly pulled their two children out of school and cleaned out their little brick house in the small town of Starhill, north of Baton Rouge, giving some possessions to friends and family and throwing others—like their sofa—in a Dumpster behind a truck stop. They spent their last night in a motel before saying a final good-bye as Lee sent his family to Detroit.

Then he boarded another bus to Atlanta. There, he moved into a cheap motel, got a job on a construction crew, and used his first paycheck to pay for a barbecue for his new buddies. He didn't have a car, so he bummed rides to local pawnshops, where he hocked gold jewelry. He didn't waste time finding companionship: The smooth-talking Lee dated several women in Atlanta and promised them cognac if they would come to his room. Despite his flirtations, Lee even started a Bible study group among the motel's fifty or so tenants.

But on May 25, a Sunday, the Louisiana crime lab delivered the shocking news that Derrick Todd Lee was the Baton Rouge serial killer. His DNA matched trace evidence found on the five dead women.

Police rushed to his house and battered down the door, but found the home abandoned. Neighbors said he'd skipped town two weeks before. Cops had no idea where he or his family had gone. A serial killer was on the wind.

The task force named their killer in a press conference and distributed Lee's picture. The *Baton Rouge Advocate* trumpeted "WANTED" in war type over a front-page blowup of an old mug shot of Derrick Todd Lee, and the local TV station went wall-to-wall with coverage.

The news seeped all the way to Detroit, where Lee's wife was staying with her aunt and uncle. That night, her family called the FBI.

Lee's wife said he was in Atlanta, but she didn't know where. She said she knew nothing about any murders.

Back in Louisiana, cops were interrogating one of Lee's mistresses when her phone rang. It was him. Caller ID showed a number in the 404 area code—Atlanta. When cops called it back, a Pakistani motel manager answered. He confirmed Lee was staying at the motel in a $135-a-week efficiency.

The next morning, police, marshals, and FBI agents descended on the dowdy Lakewood Motor Lodge in Atlanta, but Lee had already checked out. They scoured the city without luck until, late on the night of May 27, an Atlanta patrol officer found a man resembling Lee wandering around a tire store in southwest Atlanta.

"Can I see some identification?" the cop asked.

The man calmly handed over his driver's license, and without so much as an unkind word, Derrick Todd Lee—possibly the worst serial killer in Louisiana's often bloody history—was arrested, three days after his own DNA betrayed him.

All the clues were soon to fall into place: the phone cord from Dianne Alexander's home found near Pam Kinamore's body, souvenirs taken from dead women, stolen phones, the bloody shoe prints found at crime scenes, the vehicles, the timeline . . . it would all come together like a million-piece puzzle.

Back at the police station, Lee had very little to say.

"Y'all might as well go ahead and give me the needle," he told his interrogators before he stopped talking altogether. "I'm closing the book."

He said nothing as he was booked for the murder of Carrie Lynn Yoder and for the attempted rape of Dianne Alexander, fingerprinted, and locked up. He waived extradition, and the next morning was flown home to Louisiana on an FBI jet to face his accusers.

And the star witness against him, besides his own DNA, would be the only woman who'd survived an attack by Derrick Todd Lee.

Dianne Alexander.

AFTER HIS CAPTURE IN ATLANTA, BATON ROUGE SUSPECTED SERIAL KILLER DERRICK TODD LEE WAIVED HIS EXTRADITION IN FULTON COUNTY SUPERIOR COURT ON MAY 28, 2003, AND RETURNED TO LOUISIANA TO FACE FIRST-DEGREE MURDER CHARGES.

Getty Images

"I DID NOT FORGET YOUR FACE"

Derrick Todd Lee stayed true to his promise to close the book on his crimes. He never spoke about any of them.

During police interrogations immediately after his arrest, he insisted repeatedly, "I got no story to tell." He told them he didn't understand DNA, said he'd made peace with God, and didn't care whether he was executed; he even flirted subtly with FBI profiler Mary Ellen O'Toole. But he had plenty to say about police harassment and all the women who looked down on him.

"I'm here to tell you I done walked around, man, with, uh, a lot on my mind, a lot in my heart, bro, a lot of sleepless nights because there was some things I got accused of I know I ain't had nothin' to do with it," he said.

"I done been in the wrong place at the wrong time, you know, dealin' with women. I been dealing with women or done slept with some women you, uh, you're probably sayin' I'm gonna tell you a lie about. I can bring some women name up, you know, right now, and you probably go and ask them. Say, 'You ever been with Derrick?' They'll tell you no. But I know and that person know, you know what I'm sayin'?

"I been with women where I didn't want to get seen, be seen with me in a date, but like, you know what I'm sayin', I done been there. I remember women, like they high society, and then when they was around they friends, they didn't want they friends to know they was dealin'. You know, everybody got they little skeletons in they closet. . . .

"I done been with some women, where some women tell me, say, 'Lord, if somebody see you here, they'll ask me what's wrong with me.' I done been through all that in my life."

But that was the closest Derrick Todd Lee ever came to explaining his crimes, with vague references to oversexed "high society" women who were too pretentious to be seen with him, and the torture it caused.

He had nothing to say about the dead women, nor the missing women linked to him, nor any victims whose names were still not known. He refused to offer anything that looked like a confession, except to say that it didn't bother him in the least if they "electrocuted me up" because he was right with God, and that's all that mattered.

On August 5, 2004, in Port Allen, Lee stood before a jury of six men and six women to answer for the second-degree murder of Geralyn DeSoto, the first of many trials he was to face. In this case, he faced a maximum of life in prison because prosecutors lacked the necessary aggravating elements for a death sentence—and still had better cases ahead.

DeSoto, only twenty-one, was found stabbed and beaten to death in her home in the small town of Addis, across the river from Baton Rouge, on the same day she registered for graduate school at LSU in January 2002. Evidence suggested that just before noon that day, someone broke into her mobile home, bludgeoned her with a telephone, and stabbed her three times. Still alive, she ran to her bedroom, where she grabbed a shotgun, but her attacker snatched it from her before cutting her throat from ear to ear—so deep that it scraped across her spinal column—and sadistically stomping her belly. He did not rape her.

Bloody boot prints matching Lee's shoes were found, and the knife he used to slice DeSoto's throat was found in his vehicle.

In her fight, DeSoto herself had collected the evidence that would eventually identify her attacker. It was beneath her fingernails. Ultimately, science proved it matched only four-tenths of 1 percent of all the males on Earth—and one of them was Derrick Todd Lee. Even more damning, Lee's DNA contained rare markers that raised the odds that somebody *else* killed Geralyn DeSoto to thirty trillion to one.

If modern science had built a solid case against Lee, prosecutors were counting on Dianne Alexander to put a human face to his atrocities. As his only known survivor, she would bear witness to Lee's murderous methods.

Tense and frightened, she came into the courtroom, swore to tell the truth, and sat facing Derrick Todd Lee for the first time since her attack two years before. But she didn't look at him. She didn't have to.

She answered questions clearly and without flourish as she recounted the summer day that Lee stood on her doorstep, appealing to her kindness as a way to get what he wanted. She told the jury how he had threatened to stab her in the eye, made her take off her panties, tried unsuccessfully to get an erection, choked her with the phone cord, beat her savagely, and then fled in frustration when her son arrived home.

"I have no idea how many times he hit me," she testified. "I only remember the first blow."

Asked if she saw the man who attacked her, Dianne pointed directly at Lee, who sat emotionless at the defense table, and seemed to speak directly to him.

"While my eyes were closed, I did not forget your face."

The defense asked her about the police sketch and the make of car her son had seen, arguing that Lee was not the man she described. But the cross-examination was brief.

As Dianne stepped off the witness stand, the prosecutor scanned the faces of jurors. They had been touched by her story. They liked her.

The next day, Lee interrupted the proceedings to ask the judge whether he could fire his court-appointed lawyer, whom he believed was not being aggressive enough.

"My life is on the line here," he argued at the bench. "He ain't representing me like he said. . . . He lied to me from go, from day one."

But the judge told him that he couldn't fire a public defender and that his only other choice was to represent himself. Lee relented and the trial continued as the evidence against him mounted. The primary defense was simple: The prosecution hadn't connected all the dots, they were exploiting the public's misdirected and white-hot anger, and DNA was unreliable.

After four days of testimony, the jury required just one hour and forty minutes to find Derrick Todd Lee guilt of second-degree murder in the death of Geralyn DeSoto. Six days later, the judge sentenced Lee to life in Louisiana State Penitentiary at Angola, without the possibility of parole.

As the prison van drove away, Lee banged his head against the inside wall.

But his trials, literally and figuratively, were not over.

Two months after his conviction in Geralyn DeSoto's killing, Lee faced a new trial for the murder of Charlotte Murray Pace, a twenty-two-year-old student slain just two months before the attack on Dianne Alexander, who would again be the star human witness against Lee.

This time, Lee (who had a new court-appointed defense team) faced the death penalty.

Of all the cases linked to Lee, Pace's had the grisliest crime scene. She had been raped and then had been stabbed eighty-three times with a knife and a 12-inch (30.5 centimeter) flat-blade screwdriver. One of the thrusts had gone through her eye into her brain. Her throat was cut, her skull fractured with a clothes iron, her face mutilated, and her hands terribly bruised, as though she'd fought her attacker to the death. Bloodstains were smeared and splattered throughout her townhouse, suggesting she'd struggled from room to room, even though she was gravely wounded. The killer had taken "trophies": a Louis Vuitton wallet containing a BMW key, a silver ring, her driver's license, and a cell phone.

This time, the judge allowed prosecutors to also introduce evidence in the murders of Pam Kinamore, Carrie Lynn Yoder, Trineisha Dene Colomb, and Gina Wilson Green—all connected by Derrick Todd Lee's DNA—as evidence of his methods and psychopathy.

And once again, DNA evidence was insurmountable. A forensic scientist testified that the unique markers in Lee's DNA were so rare that the probability of anyone else having the same genetic code was 1 in 3.6 quadrillion—or 500,000 times the Earth's current population.

A steady stream of witnesses told the grisly story of five women's horrific killings, describing the last time they saw their friends and loved ones alive and pointing to frightful crime scene photos while a subdued Lee sat and listened quietly.

RELIVING THE HORROR

The last witness to take the stand was Dianne Alexander. Inside she was nervous, but outwardly she was poised.

Again, she calmly recounted the sequence of her attack in vivid and succinct detail. She told how Lee had threatened to stab her in the eye—as Pace had been. She told how he had cut the phone cord to strangle her—the same cord fragment found near the body of Pam Kinamore. And how the bare-chested Lee had sweated on her during his frustrated rape attempt—sweat found on the collar of her dress that matched Lee's DNA.

BORN AGAIN IN THE 1980S, DIANNE ALEXANDER'S DEEP FAITH HAS BUOYED HER THROUGH THE DARKEST MOMENTS OF DERRICK TODD LEE'S ATTACK AND THE TURBULENT YEARS SINCE AS SHE TRIES TO MAKE SENSE OF IT.
Ron Franscell

Again, she relived the horror visited upon her.

Again, she was called to point to her attacker, sitting just a few feet away, watching her.

"Are you sure?" the prosecutor asked her.

"Positive. Without a shadow of a doubt. I'll never forget that face."

The desperate defense called her a liar. They said her testimony had changed over time. They said she was coached by prosecutors. They said she described a different man to the police artist. But Dianne held firm, and the jury was visibly angry at the hostile questioning.

The prosecution rested after that and, to everyone's surprise, so did the defense.

During closing arguments, some jurors wept openly as the prosecutor showed the smiling portraits of the dead women and begged the jury to find Lee guilty; the defense again railed against the fallibility of DNA testing and listed a dozen inconsistencies and holes in the prosecution's case. But the jury of six men and six women took only eighty minutes to find Lee guilty of Charlotte Murray Pace's first-degree murder.

During the penalty phase, Lee's lawyers argued that he was mentally retarded and, thus, under a recent U.S. Supreme Court ruling, could not be executed. Expert witnesses on both sides disagreed about Lee's mental capacities.

This time, the same jury took ninety-three minutes to deliver Derrick Todd Lee's sentence: death.

Afterward, they said it was the strength of the DNA evidence and Dianne Alexander's testimony that convinced them of Lee's guilt.

Today, Lee sits on Angola's death row, monitored twenty-four hours a day. He spends all but one hour a day in his cell.

To date, Derrick Todd Lee has been officially linked by his distinctive DNA to seven murders, and he is strongly believed to have committed four others.

In 2008, the Louisiana Supreme Court upheld his death sentence. A tangle of appeals is ongoing, and no execution date has been set.

Charges in Lee's other alleged murders were dropped once he was sentenced to die. The charges Lee faced in Dianne Alexander's 2002 attack were set aside after she told prosecutors she wanted "to end a difficult period of her life and move on."

To date, Derrick Todd Lee has been officially linked by his distinctive DNA to seven murders, and he is strongly believed to have committed four others. A dozen more South Louisiana slayings over the twenty years before his arrest bear frightening similarities to his known crimes, but they might never be solved.

"I GOTTA LET IT GO"

For Dianne Alexander, every day since Derrick Todd Lee invaded her home and her life, every morning has been a little like waking up and starting life over.

And not necessarily in a bad way.

She graduated from nursing school with honors. She is writing a book about her experience as Lee's sole survivor. She dreams of taking up painting. And she has fallen in love all over again with her husband, Oliver.

Not that life has been easy. The trauma churned up her whole family. Dianne's husband and son cleaned up her blood themselves. For months, Oliver spent his free moments driving around Lafayette and Baton Rouge looking in vain for that gold Mitsubishi Mirage. If he found it . . . well, he didn't know what he would do.

For a while, Dianne's hate for Lee was a wriggling maggot deep down inside, small but ultimately destructive. She couldn't go back to the house where she had once felt so comfortable, so safe, so she and Oliver lived with relatives until they could sell the place and get another.

Dianne's posttraumatic stress was very real. She drifted through periods of volatile anger and eviscerating depression. She would scream and lash out at those closest to her, who were also suffering in the turbulent wake of Derrick Todd Lee. Arguments always circled back around, sometimes viciously, to the attack.

Because their eyewitness testimony and evidence had been critical to Lee's capture, Dianne and her son, Herman, eventually sought $150,000 in reward money offered by Crime Stoppers of Baton Rouge and Lafayette, but they were refused. The organization said its policies prevented it from rewarding crime victims, even if they were the keys to arresting a serial killer. A 2006 lawsuit by the Alexanders against Crime Stoppers is still wending through the courts.

Dianne still doesn't know why Lee chose her. Maybe her creamy, coffee-colored skin and hazel eyes made her look white from a distance. Maybe she lived in a place where nobody would hear her scream. Or maybe she was simply the first person he saw when his compulsion kicked in. Nobody knows because Derrick Todd Lee has never spoken about any of the cases.

Dianne believes fervently that his inability to rape her was because of her compliance. He lusted for a struggle. But she didn't give it to him. Her submission to his attack, at least in her mind, neutralized his sado-sexual compulsion. But, again, nobody knows.

Eventually, Dianne and Oliver sought counseling, and for Dianne especially, the church was a comfort. A couple times a week, she faithfully attends an Evangelical church in a Lafayette strip mall, not far from where she and Oliver live now in a small town west of the city, and she can hardly speak of the attack without invoking God in some way.

"Let God deal with him," she says today.

That's why she no longer hates Lee. She takes God's word about forgiveness. A death-penalty opponent, she certainly doesn't await his pending execution with any particular eagerness. If anything, she says, she'll pray for his soul.

"I gotta let it go," she says now, "because if I don't, it'll destroy me before it destroys him."

CHAPTER 8

THE DEVIL YOU KNOW

ANTHONY MAJZER AND SERIAL KILLER DAVID MAUST

PONTIAC CORRECTIONAL FACILITY IS A HOLE where Illinois throws its trash. Founded as a reform school for "incorrigible boys" just after the Civil War, out on the edge of town, it devolved into a savage world apart. During the Depression, in the days before it became a maximum-security lockup, prisoners in solitary got only a daily slice of bread to eat.

Outside, its stone and red-brick buildings, encircled by miles of razor wire, are known as the Pontiac Correctional Center; inside, it is known as Thunderdome, a dark, deafening purgatory where no man, not even a monster, takes tomorrow for granted.

In a state where crime has always come easy, only the worst of the worst go to Pontiac. In the 1950s, an armed robber named James Earl Ray did time there, ten years before he killed Martin Luther King Jr. In 1978, a thousand rioting inmates killed three guards. By the 1990s, Chicago street gangs like the Latin Kings, the Black Gangster Disciples, and the Gaylords had more control over the place than the warden.

In Pontiac, getting shanked in the neck while you sleep or being sliced open with a razor blade just for wearing the wrong tattoo is considered fair play. By the time a guy gets to Pontiac, he damn well better know who to watch. Guards might look the other way; madmen might save your life.

Either way, friends and enemies aren't always what they seem.

A SIMPLE PLAN

Tony and Dave's plan was simple: After they did their time, these two jailbirds would blow Illinois for Wyoming, where they'd start a big marijuana farm, get rich, and live an untroubled life.

Dave owned 100 acres someplace out there in the Big Empty, where they would never be bothered by cops or squares or anybody else. He showed Tony pictures of the little farmhouse, and he had the deed in his cell. Dave had the money and Tony knew how to grow pot that they could then wholesale to his gang homeys in Chicago. It was a freakin' sweet business plan, man. Dave was getting out of the joint first, but as soon as Tony strolled out of Pontiac with his gate money, they'd pack up Dave's Mazda 929 and head to Wyoming, which Dave said was real beautiful, like fucking heaven. Miles and miles of nothing but your own law. Yeah, Wyoming would fill them up, these hollow guys in a hollow place with a hollow past. Tony believed him because his friend Dave was a smart guy. Damn straight. A generous guy who'd be a good partner.

Tony Majzer, already a career criminal at twenty-four, wanted it to be true in the worst way. He had never been to Wyoming, and he wasn't even sure where the hell it was. But it sure couldn't be as crappy as life had been for him so far.

A HISTORY OF VIOLENCE

Tony was born on July 1, 1976, in Chicago's Cook County Hospital to an unwed, seventeen-year-old junkie. Not long after giving birth, she hung a chain with an Italian horn charm around his little neck and abandoned her child in a public park.

The baby was shoved into the bowels of the foster care system, but by some miracle, he was adopted at age four by a couple in Schiller Park, a middle-class suburb west of downtown. His adoptive dad was a shipping clerk for a local company and was known around the neighborhood as Coach, and his new mom was a good-hearted but strict office manager who had once worked for the Secret Service and came from a family of cops. They couldn't have their own kids, so they fostered and adopted orphans and other discarded children like Tony.

Tony loved them both, especially Coach, as much as he hated the mother he never knew. His loathing for her festered in him. He blamed her for the worst parts of himself.

But Tony never really had a chance. Dyslexic, hyperactive, and angry, school was a death march. He despised anybody in authority. He started shoplifting before he could read, and the few times he got caught, he was let go.

Then at age six, he bashed another first grader in the head with a nail-studded two-by-four, just because the kid said something Tony didn't like. At seven, he punched his second-grade teacher in the face for locking him out of the classroom.

Soon, Tony was shipped off to a special school for kids with behavior problems, kids just like him—and worse. Everything went downhill from there.

At eleven, when most kids were still collecting Care Bears and Pound Puppies, he hooked up with the Gaylords, a violent Chicago street gang. One of the oldest street gangs in the city, the Gaylords started after World War II as a mostly white, North Side softball club, but in the 1950s it grew into a greaser gang with little interest in games. In the '60s, it evolved from a group of slicked-back-hair, bad-ass hot-rodders who rumbled over turf and girls into a full-fledged crime racket, selling drugs and guns while it protected its own invisible borders from encroaching black and Latino gangs—with murder, when necessary.

By the '80s, the Gaylords had more than six thousand members and controlled large chunks of Chicago's crime landscape. Kids like Tony Majzer were just what the gang needed to refresh the ranks and ensure their violent legacy. In return, they taught him to survive on the street.

At thirteen, Tony took up boxing, mostly because it was a free pass to hit somebody—or to be hit. He lost only one fight in sixteen bouts.

He was a good baseball player, too—so good, he dreamed of playing in college, or maybe even the Show, until he was shot in the knee during a drive-by.

He bounced around from one alternative school to another, almost never welcome for very long. Violence was a daily ritual for him. By the time school officials allowed him to go to a regular high school, he was a lost cause. Two months into the new school year, he pummeled a rival gang member in the hallway. He was sent to another tough alternative school that wasn't tough enough. Finally, he was warehoused in a school for the worst thugs in the district, where he felt right at home. No proms, no student councils, no pep rallies. Just survival.

Tony grew up thin, sinewy, and tough. By the time he was seventeen, he'd been shot by rival gangsters from the Simon City Royals five times. Rather than arouse cops' interest by going to a hospital, he plucked four bullets out of his own flesh. Six months later, when he saw his attackers on the street, he stalked them with two loaded .45s. He shot one in the head, one in the chest, and pumped three bullets into the third's belly. He didn't know if they died, and he didn't care. That was just the law of his jungle.

At twenty, a drug-addicted Tony pulled his first hard time. He got eighteen months for helping a friend who burglarized a neighbor's house. Tony looked a lot younger than he was, and, as a gangbanger, he certainly had plenty of enemies, so it wouldn't be a cakewalk. But with an army of Gaylords in the house, he felt as safe as a skinny, white, gangster man-child could feel on his first day in prison.

One day, sitting in the weight yard at the Illinois River Correctional Center with some of his

KILLER DAVID MAUST WANTED SO BADLY TO BE NEEDED THAT HE KILLED ANYONE WHO REJECTED HIM.

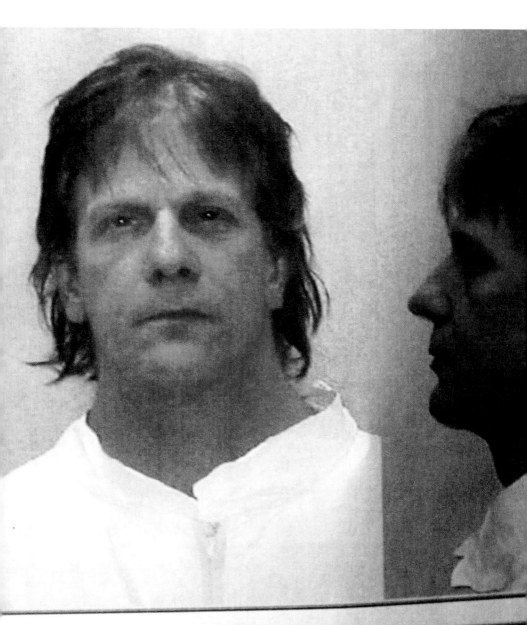

#: IN0450700   Name : MAUST, DAVID, EDWAR

: 357-48-1850   DOB: 04/05/1954

: MALE   HEIGHT: 5'10"

ENSE: M23016554098   STATE: ILLINOIS

homeboys, Tony noticed an older white con, maybe in his forties, watching him. Eventually, the long-haired guy walked over and started talking small, the usual stuff between inmates.

The guy said his name was David Maust. He said he was doing thirty-five years for murdering a trucker who had been screwing his wife. Killing his wife's secret boyfriend made him a stand-up guy to most cons, but to Tony, he came off as soft and didn't seem to know anything about the street. Dave was a big man, but Tony immediately pegged him as no threat. In fact, Tony presumed Dave needed his gang connections for protection.

A friendship sprouted. For the next year, Tony and Dave spent most days together. Dave was "a trusty," an inmate who gains wider privileges and more freedom to wander around the prison doing certain jobs. He happily got Tony whatever he needed—soap, shampoo, smokes—and Tony liked the company. It was never sexual; Tony suspected Dave might be bent that way, but it didn't come up. Dave just liked to fantasize out loud about resuming a normal life on the outside, or at least what passed for normal. He seemed to relish his role as the father figure to Tony and some of the other younger cons. He cast them all as players in his post-prison daydreams.

Like the Wyoming pot farm.

Eventually, Tony was paroled on his burglary beef but landed back in prison when he violated his parole. This time, they locked him up in Pontiac on another eighteen-month stretch while Dave finished his time at Illinois River and was paroled back to the world in the summer of 1999.

LAST HURRAH

Back in the world, Dave traded handyman chores for a studio apartment on South Kenilworth in the sedate Chicago suburb of Oak Park, Illinois, and took other odd jobs, occasionally sending money to Tony in prison. They stayed in touch, embellishing the dream they shared and making plans for their getaway.

Just before Christmas 2000, they decided the time had come. Tony, who was now living in a halfway program and wearing an ankle bracelet, packed his bags and boarded a slow bus to Chicago. He drank a fifth of vodka on the ride, and he made himself giggle imagining what it would be like to have all the pot and money he could ever want. He was smashed when Dave picked him up at the bus depot and took him to a little diner on the down side of town, where Tony was too drunk to eat. That night, he passed out on the sofa in Dave's tidy little apartment in Oak Park.

Because his strict mother refused to let him stay at her home, Tony stayed at Dave's apartment. For a couple weeks, they lived like two drunken college roommates who just happened to be ex-cons.

While Dave waited for his cash to be wired—there was apparently some small hang-up with the bank, nothing serious—they partied and drove around the city on shopping sprees. Dave, who always carried a wad of cash, lavished gifts on Tony—a computer, clothes, expensive new sneakers, a television, a DVD player, and more. They went to strip clubs and taverns. Dave draped his pet boa constrictor around the shoulders of a bare-chested Tony and photographed him naked like a couple of frat boys goofing around. And they talked constantly about Wyoming, an imaginary landscape whose myth loomed larger for Tony as every day passed. *As soon as Dave's cash came through . . .*

One night, Dave asked the veteran gangbanger Tony a macabre question: When gangsters wanted to get rid of a body, how did they do it? Tony was only too happy to share a little street secret: Paint the corpse to mask the stench of decomposition.

> **One night, Dave asked the veteran gangbanger Tony a macabre question: When gangsters wanted to get rid of a body, how did they do it?**

Otherwise, Dave was usually easygoing, although he grew testy when Tony talked about his girlfriends. Once, when Tony brought an old flame with him to Dave's apartment, Dave kicked them out. It almost seemed like he was jealous.

Finally, the grand getaway was at hand. Dave announced his money had finally arrived and decided they would leave early Sunday morning, January 7, for Wyoming.

Saturday would be the last they would see of Chicago, of the law, of their shitty old lives. Saturday would be their last hurrah.

They rose early that morning and went to breakfast at a Denny's in Franklin Park. Over eggs and pancakes they made travel plans. Tony was ready to hit the road. No, Tony was *past* ready.

"Hey, we gotta do the contest before we go," Dave told Tony.

"What contest?" Tony wondered.

Didn't matter much. He liked a challenge.

"I promised to give $450,000 to the kid who can drink the most shots of hundred-proof booze in fifteen minutes without puking or passing out."

"Bullshit."

"No, man, I'm serious. Three kids tried it already. It's your turn now."

"Yeah? What'd they do?"

"The record stands at fourteen right now," Dave said.

"Fourteen shots? Fifteen minutes?"

"And no puking or passing out."

"I just have to drink more than fourteen shots and I get, what, about a half-mill?"

Maust smiled and nodded. "Hundred proof. Your choice."

Tony didn't have to think very long.

"I'm in," he said.

HOMICIDAL URGES

David Edward Maust was nobody's friend.

Not because he was unfriendly, diffident, or disagreeable—although he was, at times, all those things.

But because he always tried to kill them.

> **David Edward Maust was nobody's friend.**
> **Not because he was unfriendly, diffident,**
> **or disagreeable—although he was,**
> **at times, all those things.**
> **But because he always tried to kill them.**

He was born April 5, 1954, in the small town of Connellsville, Pennsylvania, to feuding, dysfunctional parents. His abusive father came and went from the household with every blustery fight. His mother was committed to a psychiatric hospital for a time. And David, one of four children, was never quite right, even before a horrible fall that many believe left him brain-damaged as a toddler.

Growing up, he was often forced to stay outside the house until suppertime—and would be brutally punished if he was five minutes late. He once tried to set fire to the sheets in his little brother's crib and later tried to drown him in a pond.

As a young boy, his mother often called him into her bed, where she stroked his body, French-kissed him, and forced him into weird sex. Days after divorcing in 1963, David's mother tried to send him away with his father, who refused his skinny, blond son. So she packed up her kids and moved to Chicago.

A few months later, she committed her nine-year-old son to the Chicago State Hospital, a dreary children's asylum for violent, disturbed, and retarded kids. She told him she would return when there was enough food for him—but told doctors he was a murderous freak. For the next four years, she visited David only when the courts forced her, although he often sat day after day at the window during visiting hours, watching for her to come up the long walk to the asylum's front door. When asked, he would make excuses for her—for himself—such as "her back is bothering her" or "she is sick today."

He tried to escape several times, but he was always captured. The asylum's staff described David as a reliable, sensitive, and appealing child with a profound fear of abandonment and rejection.

But the manias, delusions, and compulsions that would mark him for the rest of his life had already begun to harden inside him.

At thirteen, with barely two years of schooling, David was transferred to a children's home not far from his mother's house—and she promptly moved without giving a forwarding address. At fifteen, he used an electrical cord to nearly choke a friend at the home to death when the boy wouldn't play a drinking game with him.

David was immediately sent back to the asylum, where a psychiatrist diagnosed him with a dangerous schizoid personality, but he didn't stay long. A few weeks later, David escaped and never looked back.

He tracked down his mother, who wielded a knife and threatened to kill him if he didn't leave her house. He drifted among odd jobs and lived with different relatives for a year until his mother convinced him to enlist in the U.S. Army at age seventeen—and made him promise to send her all his pay. *Why not?* he figured. *I owe her for . . . well, she needs the money.*

David got out of basic training on November 19, 1971, and shipped out to Fort Ord in California, to be trained as a cook's helper. He hadn't been there but a couple weeks when he saw two young brothers near the front gate, trying to make a buck by shining soldiers' shiny black shoes. Promising them twenty dollars to help him deliver a message, he took them to a vacant field nearby and started to choke them. One escaped, screaming bloody murder, and David fled. For whatever reason, he was never questioned about the attack and a year later was shipped to an American base in Germany.

But the change of scenery didn't lessen David's homicidal urges. They worsened. In once incident, he stabbed a seventeen-year-old boy, who never reported the attack. David had dodged yet another bullet, but his luck wouldn't hold much longer.

In 1974, twenty-year-old David met Jimmy McClister, the thirteen-year-old stepson of a U.S. Army sergeant on his base, at a bowling alley. They became fast friends, but for reasons David could never explain, four months later he tied the boy to a tree in a forest, beat him to death with a piece of lumber, and buried the body under some leaves and branches.

Police found the poorly hidden body. After witnesses linked David to Jimmy, he was court-martialed for murder. His defense? David claimed he had unintentionally caused Jimmy to wreck while riding a moped they had stolen. The resulting injuries killed him, and David panicked, burying his friend under some woodland debris.

If David's story seemed preposterous, the witnesses against him—those familiar with the relationship—were even worse. He was convicted of involuntary manslaughter and larceny and sentenced to four years in Fort Leavenworth.

"I WOULD LIKE TO HAVE THE DEATH SENTENCE"

In prison, David suddenly had to face some dark truths about himself, particularly his twisted sexuality. He didn't consider himself gay, although deep down, he felt sex with a woman would make him unfaithful to his mother. David had dated women, but never had sex with them; he never initiated sexual contacts with men, although he'd sometimes been forced into sex with other inmates. Voices inside his head thrashed it out endlessly.

He was attracted to another inmate, Bert, and they grew close. David was paroled in 1977 after less than three years, and while he waited for Bert to get out, he visited his mother to get his Army pay. She had spent all but twenty-five bucks on herself. She enraged him all over again.

Bert eventually joined David on the outside, but the old demons came along. Before they parted ways forever, David tried to stab Bert—rushing him, nearly eviscerated, to the hospital afterward—and later attempted to shoot him with a misfiring gun. Both incidents went unreported, but even after Bert fled for his life, David tried in vain to win him back.

By 1979, David found he could make good money and satisfy his perverse jones in kiddie porn. He paid kids to pose nude or have sex with other boys, then sold the pictures. One night, David stabbed a companion in a frenzied sexual rush and was arrested for attempted murder. Although the man testified vividly against him, David was acquitted. Incredibly, after at least a half-dozen near-fatal attacks and a murder, he had paid almost nothing for his sins.

But his compulsions were catching up to him.

In 1981, while prowling the streets of Wood Dale, Illinois, in his Blazer, David spied a kid he knew, fifteen-year-old Donald Jones. He called Jones over to his truck and offered him a hundred and fifty bucks to sell some pot. Jones agreed.

As part of the ruse, David drove Donald to an abandoned quarry near Elgin, where the two took some beer down to a secluded spot on the water's edge. There, David punched the kid several times, tied his wrists and ankles with shoelaces, and forced him to drink several beers. As it began to rain, David stripped Donald naked and stabbed him hard in the belly.

"I'm only fifteen years old," Donald whimpered. "Please don't kill me!"

He threw the bloodied boy into the water, still alive but unconscious. Donald thrashed around for a few moments before he drowned. David pushed his floating body out into deeper water, buried the knife, and went back to his Blazer, where he calmly loaded his gear under the curious eye of a local cop.

Two days later, Donald Jones's corpse was fished out of the murky water at the bottom of the quarry. David was questioned, but investigators found no reason to hold him.

The heat was on, so David packed his bags and headed for Texas in December 1981.

He'd barely been on the island of Galveston a week when he picked up a teenager outside a 7-11 by promising him an oil-rig job. Instead, David took the boy back to his hotel, where he tied him up and blindfolded him with his own T-shirt.

But David was unable to subdue the kid, so he cracked his skull three times with a hefty steel pipe.

The boy wasn't dead, but David left him tied up on the bed, puking and bleeding for almost three hours. A trickle of blood from the boy's right ear scared David, who inexplicably decided to release the kid. He drove the boy to a local park, gave him five bucks, and drove away.

But David wouldn't be able to dodge this bullet.

Police arrested him. After a year in jail awaiting trial, he was convicted of assault on a child and sentenced to five years in prison, but he had barely settled into his cell at the prison in Huntsville when his whole twisted world turned upside down: David Maust, now twenty-nine years old, was indicted for the murder of Donald Jones, the fifteen-year-old boy he had stabbed and drowned in an Illinois quarry.

David was extradited to Chicago in 1983, but there was found to be mentally unfit to stand trial. For eleven years, David was bounced through several different Illinois mental hospitals before he was finally judged competent to be put on trail.

"I have been thinking about Donald Jones a lot," David wrote in a jailhouse diary. "And I have been thinking about the bad things I did in my life, and now I would like to have the death sentence. . . .

> "I sometimes would think there was still hope for me; that I could have a family of my own to love. But now my hope is just about gone, and these things I cannot have. But I would still like to have had my own family, and if I would have had my own son I would never have put him in a State Mental Hospital. I would keep my son with me, and I would love him with all my heart, and I would help my son with his life, and I would be there when he needed me. . . .
>
> "So on May 13, a Friday, in the year 1983, I thought it would be best if I told the truth for the first time in my life. For the murder of Donald Jones, I want the death penalty."

Thus, it was easy for David Edward Maust to plead guilty to Jones's murder. He didn't get his death wish, though: He was sent to Illinois River Correctional Center to serve thirty-five years for a killing he readily admitted.

AN UNSUSPECTING WORLD

David's demons were bigger than he was. Soon, he was pining for companionship, playing the father figure, best buddy, and surrogate dreamer with the troubled boys all around him. They became the family he never had . . . and could never keep alive.

He didn't tell anybody the truth about murdering Donald Jones. It was too dangerous to admit to killing a child in the joint. Instead, he made himself a hero, a cuckolded husband who merely defended his marital property against an interloper. Yeah, that was better. He wrote in his journal:

> "It's true; I did play games in my mind—just lies I would tell younger inmates so that I could get to know them and have someone I could do things with and share my days with. . . .
>
> "It's true, I did like being around the younger inmates because I liked lis-tening to the words they used and listening to what was important to them, like how they talked about their love for their families and the exciting cool things they did with their friends while growing up at home because I missed out on a lot of that and so it was cool to listen to.
>
> "I enjoyed my days of caring about them, being there for them and helping them make it through prison with nobody causing them a bad time."

One of those boys was Anthony Majzer, who quickly became David's next best friend.

Worse, David—a man who'd already killed two young men and attacked several others—would only serve five of his thirty-five years before he was unleashed again on an unsuspecting world.

And he wasn't finished.

After breakfast, Tony and Dave went back to the apartment where Dave peeled a hundred dollar bill off the roll in his pocket and gave it to Tony.

"Go get the stuff and bring it back," he said.

Tony drove Dave's Mazda to a package store in nearby Schiller Park and bought a fifth of Smirnoff and a case of Budweiser. He even drove past a building where he thought he might like to open a nightclub with the money he was going to win. He picked up an old flame and fucked her before he returned to the apartment, thinking the whole time how much he was going to love being rich.

Dave was watching football on TV when he got back. The Oakland Raiders were playing the Miami Dolphins. Tony put the vodka in the freezer and popped a couple cold beers while they watched the game.

There, on the couch during the game, Dave leaned over and tried to kiss Tony on the cheek. Tony pushed him away and told him in blunt terms he wasn't gay.

"If you do it again," Tony said gravely, "I'll kill ya."

Dave apologized and swore it would never happen again.

After the game, Dave stood up.

"Okay, let's get this contest going," he said.

Tony sat at the kitchen table. Dave handed him a personal check for $450,000, with Tony's name already typed in. Only the signature line was blank.

"It could be yours, man, if you beat the record," he teased.

"If this check doesn't clear," Tony joked, "I'm coming back here to kill you."

Dave started to pour the chilled vodka into a shot glass, but Tony waved him off.

"Not that way," he said. "Put it all in one glass."

Dave smiled. "One glass? You sure?"

"Fuck yeah."

Dave measured fifteen shots into a water glass and slid it across the table to Tony. They both glanced at the cheap clock on the kitchen wall as Tony took a big swallow. He didn't need fifteen minutes. He gulped the entire glass in less than three minutes.

"Okay, now no puking or passing out for another fifteen minutes," Maust said ominously, rising from the table and going back to the sofa behind Tony, who kept his eyes on the ticking clock. His mind, not yet clouded by the vodka, was all tangled up in his dream nightclub, the passing seconds, Wyoming, the money . . .

Six minutes passed, then seven. Tony exhaled a sweet metal tang, and his belly started to burn. Eight minutes. He looked at the check and tried to envision his club in the dark, all decked out in neon and women and music . . . nine minutes . . . and he just wanted to be gone already, on the way to Wyoming, where he could live high and rich and be a kid again . . .

Tony really didn't feel the first blow to the back of his head.

Nor the second.

But before a third vicious jolt cracked his head, he pivoted to see David land one across his forehead with a foot-long steel rod, possibly a weight-lifting bar.

"What the fuck?" Tony hollered as he crumpled to the floor. Blood dribbled down his face, drenching his white cardigan and seeping into the carpet. He was dazed but conscious.

Looking insane, Dave continued to whale on Tony, who curled into a ball to try to fend off the blows and screamed, "Wait, we're friends! We're friends!"

Suddenly, Dave stopped his fierce assault as if he'd snapped out of a brutal trance. He threw the bar on the kitchen table and slumped into a chair.

But Tony wasn't waiting for whatever came next. Woozy from the beating and the booze, he summoned the focus to kick Dave's chair, sending him sprawling on the floor. In a second, he pounced on Dave and whipped a knife from his pocket—a knife Dave had just bought him.

"Motherfucker, I'm gonna kill you!" he seethed, pressing his blade against Dave's throat. He had lost too much blood and wobbled on his feet.

Dave admitted there was no money, no farm, no house . . . no Wyoming. It was all a lie.

No money? Tony felt faint and cold.

"I need to warm up," Tony said, still holding the knife on Dave. "Put some hot water in the tub."

Dave drew a hot bath and Tony locked himself in the steamy bathroom with his knife and the telephone. His blood trickled into the water as he slipped into the tub, trying to warm up from the shock. He dipped his index finger in his seeping wounds and wrote his name and address on the tub's tile, then rinsed it away. *If I die and they search for old blood stains,* he thought, *they'll find it.*

Then he dialed the phone. His father answered. Tony told him he'd been jumped by some gangbangers and was in bad shape.

"I don't know if I'll make it," he said, comforted by his father's voice. "But I love you."

He dried off, dressed, and then went back out to the living room. Dave was waiting, scared. He had no place to run. In a flicker of clarity, Tony realized he needed to get to a hospital, and Dave would have to take him.

"You're taking me to the hospital," Tony said, holding the knife on Dave again.

"Please don't tell anybody what happened," Dave begged. "Please."

Tony prodded Dave to get going, forcing him into the car through the passenger side and holding the knife against his neck all the way to Gottlieb Memorial on North Avenue.

In the emergency room, Tony underwent several CT scans and X-rays of his skull. The tight skin across his skull was shredded, exposing the bone beneath. He was suddenly half-deaf in one ear and would soon develop a lazy eye and migraines. While doctors sewed up his gashes with forty-eight staples and twenty-eight stitches, Dave went to coffee with Tony's distraught parents, playing the role of hero and embellishing the cover story even more.

The medical staff wanted Tony to spend the night for observation, but he refused. He didn't trust hospitals or cops, and he was due back at his Wisconsin halfway house in the morning; the Wyoming trip was clearly not the escape plan he had hoped. Still unwelcome at his parents' home—even after a ruthless bludgeoning—Tony made a decision that cast some doubt on his survival instincts: He went home with David Maust.

Not to a hotel.

Not to a homeless shelter.

Not to a real friend's house.

Not to a bench at the bus terminal.

Not even to the secluded back booth of an all-night diner.

He was returning to his would-be killer's turf to spend the rest of the night. His only hope was to make the morning bus going back to the halfway house.

They left the hospital sometime after midnight. Dave drove while a woozy, aching Tony held the knife. Dave apologized profusely on the way home, and Tony wasn't sure what to think. Confusion was already screwing with his damaged head. Dave was his friend, he thought. *Maybe it was a brain tumor or a flashback*, Tony thought. *Maybe he just snapped. Maybe it was temporary insanity. Maybe . . .* Tony wanted desperately to believe something went terribly haywire with his friend and that whatever it was had passed as abruptly as it had surfaced. He didn't want to think he had been so totally duped by a friend.

Back at the apartment, a still-wary Tony helped clean up his own blood, which had pooled in a great circle on the floor and was spattered on everything.

Even more baffling than his decision to go home with Dave was his decision to share his bed that night, but he wanted to keep a close eye on the man who tried to kill him. That night, he didn't sleep more than a few minutes at a time, aware of Dave's slightest movement.

> **Even more baffling than Tony's decision to go home with Dave was his decision to share his bed that night, but he wanted to keep a close eye on the man who tried to kill him.**

The next morning, Dave dropped him off at his parents' home in Schiller Park, and they never saw each other again. Coach drove Tony to Wisconsin. On the way, the son told the father what had really happened.

"You're not making this up?" Coach asked, incredulous.

"No."

"Why didn't you tell me last night?"

"He was right there."

Embarrassed, confused, and afraid, Tony begged his dad to stay away from David Maust and not tell the cops anything. Dave was dangerous and unpredictable, he warned. Besides, in Tony's world, you stayed away from cops and took care of your own business in your own way. More than once, he thought about sending some old gang buddies to pay a visit to the Oak Park apartment.

In the coming weeks, when Tony called to try to convince Dave to pay his $8,000 hospital bill, Dave always hung up. One time when he called Dave's apartment, a kid answered.

"Get away from David," Tony warned him. "He will kill you."

The boy scoffed. Dave was a good guy and would never hurt him, he said. He wouldn't listen. He, too, thought he knew the real Dave.

Two months after the attack, Tony finally reported it to the Oak Park Police Department, but Dave denied everything. With no other witnesses or evidence, the cops chalked it up to a gay lover's quarrel between two worthless ex-cons and walked away.

Once again, astoundingly, David Maust had eluded any responsibility for his crimes.

And once again, a world of new friends lay before him.

PAYING FOR HIS SINS

David Maust stayed in his Oak Park apartment for a couple more years. A neighbor once asked him about a strange blood trail leading from one of his broken windows and a foul odor outside his apartment, but David had a ready explanation about a fistfight with his son—who didn't exist.

In February 2003, Maust moved to a rented house on Ash Street in Hammond, Indiana, a gray and gritty steel town just across the state line from Chicago. He went straight to his grisly work.

On May 2, 2003, Maust killed nineteen-year-old Nicholas James, a coworker he had befriended at the trophy shop where he worked.

"I just went after him," Maust wrote in his journal later. "I don't know why, I just did. I planned to kill him three times but talked myself out of it.

"I came up behind him. I hit him in the head. I hit him with a baseball bat. Not a real bat. It was a souvenir. It had lead in it. I hit him once. After the first blow he was out of it, but he was still moving, so I hit him again. He was still moving. I hit him again and again."

Maust tore up a concrete floor in the rented house's dank basement. He covered Nicholas James's naked corpse with blue house paint, wrapped him in plastic, and buried him in the hole, which he covered in concrete.

Later that summer, Maust met thirteen-year-old Michael Dennis and sixteen-year-old James Raganyi, a couple of runaways. He gave them pot, money, and booze. He took them bike riding and to ballgames. He wanted badly to be their father and their friend.

On September 10, both boys came to Maust's house for liquor, which he supplied happily. And when the two boys passed out on David Maust's couch, he strangled them both, duct-taped their naked bodies in black plastic sheeting and buried them in a basement hole he had dug five days earlier beside Nicholas James's hidden tomb. And, again, he concealed their graves with a new concrete slab.

"They didn't feel nothing," he wrote in his journal.

When the boys were reported missing, their trail led cops to Maust's Ash Street house, where they had been seen hanging around. When questioned,

Maust was friendly and cooperative. He let investigators wander around the place, but they found nothing.

But Detective Ron Johnson, a missing-persons investigator for the Hammond police, got a cold feeling from Maust. The ex-con's odd smile haunted the veteran cop, but more important cases demanded his attention.

Months later, Maust's landlord mentioned some new concrete work in the basement, and Johnson had a bad feeling. With the owner's permission, Johnson and two cops drilled a hole in the floor.

Coffin flies flew out.

Almost thirty years after he killed Jimmy McClister in Germany, more than twenty years after he killed Donald Jones in Elgin, Illinois, and more than three years since he tried to kill Anthony Majzer, David Maust's luck finally ran out.

His case never went to trial. In a November 2005 plea bargain, Maust avoided the death penalty by pleading guilty to three counts of first-degree murder. He received three consecutive life sentences without the possibility of parole.

Maust was extraordinarily candid about his life and crimes, as if by finally saying things out loud, he might unburden himself.

SERIAL KILLER DAVID MAUST'S PIPE-WIELDING SURPRISE ATTACK ON TONY MAJZER LEFT A WEB OF UGLY SCARS—AND A DEEPER MISTRUST OF FRIENDS AND STRANGERS ALIKE.

Ron Franscell

He told investigators that he had planned to hide Anthony Majzer's body in the wall of a closet in the Oak Park apartment. He'd even bought hundreds of pounds of cement to do the job in Oak Park, but when he couldn't kill Anthony, he ended up hauling the cement to the new house in Hammond—and used it instead to bury the three boys he killed there.

And in neat, meticulous script, he started handwriting a voluminous journal about his childhood, his sins, his demons, and his perverse psychology. It eventually spanned more than 1,200 pages.

At Maust's sentencing, his own brother told the judge that David had tried to kill him twice.

"I think anyone who does such crimes should pay with their life," David's brother said.

A clinical and forensic psychologist who examined Maust found him to be a unique specimen. "In fact, one would be hard-pressed to design a developmental sequence more likely to produce a profoundly disturbed, relationship-ambivalent, and aggression-vulnerable individual than the childhood experienced by David Maust," he told the court.

Later, David's defense lawyer added his own perspective.

"There is a stereotypical vision of serial killers—a person without a shred of conscience," he told a reporter. "David had one. He was capable of horrific violence, obviously, but he was also capable of genuine contrition. He was genuinely sorry right up until the time he did it again."

This son of a psychotic, narcissistic mother and an abusive, often absent father, this child who had been dumped in a "snake pit" asylum at age nine, this pathetic man who desperately wanted to mean something to someone was certainly going to pay for his sins.

But on his own terms.

In county jail while awaiting transfer to the prison system, he twice tried suicide by stabbing himself with a pencil, although he recovered both times.

On January 19, 2006—the day he was to be transferred to prison—he finally succeeded. Barely two months after his sentencing, David Edward Maust was found hanging in his Lake County Jail cell. He had braided a bed sheet into a noose. He died at fifty-one.

Maust left a seven-page suicide note that again expressed his deep remorse for killing five young men and said he had considered writing a letter to his latest victims' parents, telling them where to find the bodies, but decided against it.

"Dying is not my first choice," the note said, "but it is the right thing to do. For when I look in the eyes of the mother's [sic], I can feel the pain of their sorrow and I'm so very sorry for the pain they feel."

He also longed, as always, for his mother.

"I wish my mother would come and get me," he said. "But I know she won't. I wish she would come and take me home."

His self-loathing was on full display when his thick journal became public.

"I am the evilest person to live on this earth and to save the taxpayer's money, I should've been destroyed long ago," he wrote.

If there were other dead boys out there, Maust didn't say. When police searched the Oak Park apartment, they saw no evidence of any burials, even though some people remain convinced Maust likely killed more than the five boys he admitted to.

But among Maust's many handwritten admissions was this:

> "On January 6, 2001 (Saturday—late in the afternoon), I tried to kill Anthony Majzer, a 25-year-old I met in prison.
>
> "I wanted to build a life with Anthony as his friend and be there for him and hope he would be there for me but Anthony was not going to let that happen because he was never going to change his ways. You see, I wanted to care about him and help him in life because he had all kinds of problems and so I was hoping he would come live with me so I would also have someone to do things with but he only wanted to use me for what he could get and go away.
>
> "An [sic] it's true that I only met Anthony because I lied to him and told him 'I had lots of money from selling drugs.' I was hoping in time I could turn that lie into the truth as we became better friends but Anthony wanted me to support him. So that Saturday night or should I say late afternoon I tried to get him drunk and then I beat his head in with a pipe but then I diced [sic] not to kill him and took him to the hospital.
>
> "That night when we got back I told him the truth about how there was no money. After that he started blackmailing me for money or he tried to, but I changed my phone number so he would think I moved and I never heard from him again.
>
> "That night we came back from the hospital we slept together with are [sic] clothes on, but I did have naked pictures of both him and Kenneth [another of Maust's earlier infatuations]. I had about 20 pictures each of Anthony and Kenneth, but only half were naked pictures and I wanted the pictures because they were friends of mine and every once in a great while I would look at them. . . .
>
> "I was a very lonely person at times and would pray that God would send someone to be my friend and live with me. . . ."

FLEETING FORGIVENESS

Today, Anthony Majzer blames himself for three dead boys, maybe more. He's convinced the young kid he warned on David Maust's phone is dead, too.

He wonders why he didn't kill David Maust when he had the chance.

Tony was watching television in a federal prison in Minnesota when the news of Maust's arrest first broke. He felt ill, then he cried.

AFTER A LIFETIME OF
ABANDONMENT, CRIME, AND
VIOLENCE, EX-CHICAGO GANG-
BANGER TONY MAJZER SAYS
HIS GREATEST MOTIVATION
FOR STAYING STRAIGHT IS
HIS SON ETHAN AND
SOON-TO-BE-WIFE CARA.

Ron Franscell

After Maust was sentenced, Tony even plotted how he might be able to commit a crime and be sent to the same prison, where he would kill his tormenter. He tried to tell the cops about Maust again, but he was a convict, and they simply didn't trust anything he had to say, so he gave up.

Then the nightmares about those faceless dead boys started. Tony began to fantasize about how Maust's corpse might have looked.

Tony and Dave had been too similar for Tony's comfort. Abandoned children with profoundly flawed mothers and absent fathers. An unbearable yearning for a real family. Violence. Poor education. Emotional issues galore. Prison experience. Contentment on the far edge of society.

In 2005, on parole for his federal charge of being a felon in possession of guns, Tony met his current girlfriend. They had a son, Ethan, two years later and are making plans to marry someday soon. He finally has his family, and they have become his sole reason for staying straight.

Tony's been clean for two years, and for the sake of his son, he works hard to keep his criminal past—and his demons—from coming back. He got into a trade school for cabinet-making and now lives in a tidy apartment in La Crosse, Wisconsin.

David Maust still haunts him, but the dreams aren't as frequent now. Tony's shaved head bears a web of grotesque scars where Maust beat him nearly to death. And some nights, fewer than before, he allows himself to sink into bouts of self-blame.

He is agonizingly aware that his own choices in life make him a less sympathetic victim, and he can live with that.

While victims often sort through their anger and guilt by forgiving their attackers, Tony hasn't forgiven David Maust. He hasn't even forgiven himself. He's now locked in a prison of his own making.

"It's just hard now to know what's true," Tony says. "David Maust was the only guy who ever pulled the wool over my eyes. That's what I live with every single day. My life sucked, but I have to believe these kids . . . these kids had a better shot than I ever did. It's so unfair. I feel like I let them down, and they know it."

CHAPTER 9

A PRAYER BEFORE DYING

MISSY JENKINS AND THE WEST PADUCAH HIGH SCHOOL SHOOTING

THE SUN HADN'T YET RISEN on a cold, melancholy Kentucky morning, and Missy Jenkins was already running late. What fifteen-year-old girl would be in a hurry to roll out of a warm bed into a chilled and gloomy world for the first day of school after the four-day Thanksgiving break?

When she couldn't suspend time any longer, Missy yanked on a pair of black sweatpants, a white blouse borrowed from a friend, and a black sweatshirt, quickly pulled her hair back into a ponytail, grabbed her tennis shoes and a Pop-Tart, and hit the front door with her twin sister Mandy in tow. No time for hugs and kisses good-bye.

"We're leaving!" she hollered to her parents. She didn't wait for a reply as the door slammed behind her.

Missy and Mandy caught a ride to school, as usual, with a friend whose sister was a senior and had a car.

The tight-knit Heath community wasn't big, and the rural Heath High School was only fifteen minutes from Missy and Mandy's house. With about six hundred students, the high school was the center of community life, typical of many small towns. The biggest discipline problems were tardiness, unexcused absences, and minor classroom disruptions.

The girls were cutting it close if they wanted to join the prayer circle, where a few dozen students gathered in the school lobby every day before class to join

hands and pray. Worse, Missy wasn't feeling well, she needed to go to the bathroom, and she had a first-period test in World Civilizations.

Missy glanced at her watch. Time was suddenly speeding out of her control.

They hurried into the school foyer to find the prayer circle already coming together. Missy quickly spied a friend, Kelly Hard, whom she asked to come to the bathroom with her.

"Let's just do the prayer circle," Kelly said, "and we'll go to the bathroom after." No big deal, Missy thought. The ceremony was often short and sweet, and she could make it through, no problem. So they put down their books and joined the circle of a few dozen students that curled around the entire foyer. She held hands with Kelly on her left and with sister Mandy on her right.

The girls bowed their heads and closed their eyes to pray for any of the students who offered prayer requests. Missy put a lot of stock in prayer. She trusted it. It comforted her.

When they finished, the circle's organizer and prayer leader, a senior football player and son of a preacher named Ben Strong, said a simple "Amen."

Then all hell broke loose.

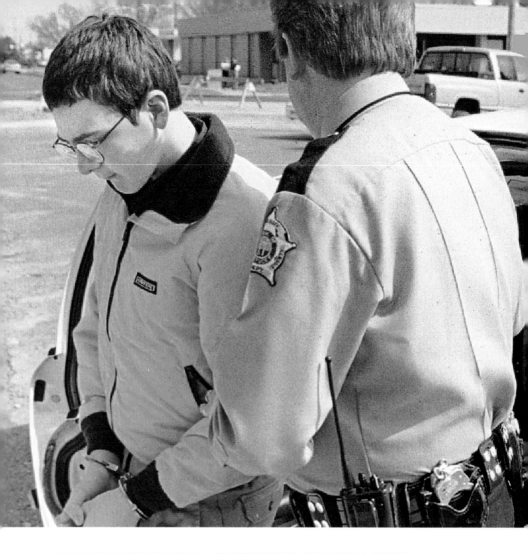

ALIENATED AND ISOLATED

Michael Carneal, a fourteen-year-old freshman, rose before dawn, too. He showered and dried himself, as he usually did, with six separate towels. He dressed in dark clothes and reached under his bed for a hidden bundle.

Today was going to be a big day at school for him. He was a B student and played in the school band. He came from a good family and attended church. His popular older sister was a Heath valedictorian. He was bright and compliant with his teachers but also forgetful and nervous. And although he had friends in passing at Heath, no one was close, and he existed on the fringe of several cliques, truly belonging to none.

Five-foot-two (1.5 meters) and considered a little dorky, Michael suffered teasing and some bullying, ranging from being called "four eyes" to being noo-gied until his scalp bled. On a band trip, he was rolled up in a blanket and hit with sock balls by upperclassmen before a chaperone broke it up. In eighth grade, some kids called him "gay" and a "faggot" after a student newsletter's gossip column reported that he liked another boy.

One day, a classmate came up to Michael and asked for one of the doughnuts he was eating. Michael shared the package with the kid, who spit on one of the doughnuts and threw it back.

But Michael was also a jokester who gave as good as he got, craving attention and friends alike. He could be just as harsh with his own remarks and childish pranks on his classmates. Once he showed the band kids a homemade button with Missy's picture on it and teased her for being "fat."

He had made the kind of trouble freshman boys at country schools make, but he wasn't a troublemaker. He set off a stink bomb in eighth grade and once sold a baggie of parsley to a friend, claiming it was marijuana. In his first two months at Heath High School, he racked up five relatively minor infractions, including using a library computer to visit the *Playboy* website, marking a classmate's neck with a ballpoint pen, and stealing a can of food from his life-skills class.

In many ways, Michael Carneal was just a cloying, awkward misfit wrestling with puberty and desperately seeking his peers' approval. In other words, he was a lot like millions of kids.

But there was a darker side to Michael that most never saw. Self-conscious and insecure, he felt picked on and pushed around. His alienation from other kids made him think about suicide. The summer before school started, he sliced his own forearm, but told adults he was injured in a bicycle accident.

Weird, secret delusions were cropping up, too. He was afraid to sleep in his own bed because he feared monsters were coming to get him, so he often slept in the family room. He was afraid falling trees would crash through his house. He hid kitchen knives under his mattress. He laid towels over all the bathroom vents because he believed he'd seen glowing eyes watching him. He sometimes walked on furniture because he imagined slashers with chainsaws were hiding near the floor to cut off his feet. He often announced when entering his bed-room, "I know you are in here."

Into the wee hours of the dark night, he sat at his computer, playing violent video games, visiting chat rooms, and sending out hundreds of e-mails, safely distant from all the perils of personal contact. But he was also surfing porn sites that he shared with schoolmates, reading about bomb- and weapon-making at *The Anarchist's Cookbook* site, and studying war gamers' attack plans. Even his school essays began to take on a more violent, suicidal tone, but not enough to send up red flags.

GOTHS AND GUNS

In an effort to fit in, he often gave stolen CDs as gifts to other students—or sometimes gave away his own possessions and said they were stolen—because he believed low-grade crime made him cool. Not long before this dark, cold morning, he stole some hundred dollar bills from his dad's wallet and gave them to the goth kids he was now trying to impress.

Michael wanted badly to be so cool that his imaginary enemies could be belittled. He wanted to be a goth, to belong to a group of kids who didn't belong. He even wore mocking homemade buttons that said "Preps Suck" and had written a short story he called "Halloween Surprise," in which all those popular kids were attacked with grenades and a shotgun by the brother of a boy named Mike, who gave the corpses of the slaughtered classmates to his mother as a gift.

The scruffy, cynical goth kids purposely didn't fit in. They dressed in black, cut their hair in macabre ways, wore dog collars, painted their fingernails black, listened to death metal, and didn't care what other people thought of them.

The goths derided the Bible thumpers of the prayer circle as hypocrites, no better than the well-scrubbed preppies who thought they were better than everyone. The goth kids were openly derisive, talking loudly and laughing intentionally during prayer time.

Although a lifelong churchgoer, Michael adopted the goths' misanthropic sneering at religion. He began to call himself an atheist, but it was all for show, mostly just to fit in. He considered freshman Nicole Hadley, a prayer-circle regular who had recently moved to West Paducah from Nebraska, to be one of his best friends. She had walked with him at their eighth-grade graduation ceremony, a local custom of some significance between friends. Nicole often visited Michael at his house and openly nudged him to be more religious. It wasn't unusual that he had called her on the phone almost every night in November 1997, ostensibly about science homework, but mostly just to hear her voice.

And secretly, he had a crush on sophomore Kayce Steger, another prayer-circle girl and a devout Christian whom he asked on a date about a month before. She had politely rebuffed him.

Nevertheless, the diminutive Michael thrived on the illusion that he was a tough-guy nonconformist. The day before Thanksgiving, Michael boldly told one of the goth kids that "the hypocrites in prayer group were going to go down, 'cause I am going to bring 'em down."

Indeed, Michael told several people, including prayer-circle leader Ben Strong, "something big" was going to happen in the school lobby soon. But ever since he'd logged on to a website called "101 Ways to Annoy People" and began a deliberate campaign to nettle his classmates, his grandiose threats rang hollow. He even warned some to stay away from the prayer circle after Thanksgiving, but most thought it was going to be another stink bomb. He mused in the cafeteria about taking over the school in an armed assault, and kids laughed. When he pulled a handgun on students in the band room the day before Thanksgiving, the kids chalked it up as just another of his infantile pranks. Nobody tattled because nobody took Michael Carneal seriously.

That first Monday after Thanksgiving, he stowed his secret, duct-taped bundle and his olive-drab backpack in the trunk of his sister's Mazda before she drove him to school. He told her they were props for a skit he was performing in English class that day.

But they weren't. Michael Carneal's awkward kit contained two antique shotguns and two .22 rifles wrapped in an old blanket, all stolen from a neighbor's gun cabinet. In his backpack were a .22 Ruger semiautomatic pistol he also filched from a neighbor's garage, earplugs, three spare eleven-bullet clips, and more than a thousand rounds of stolen ammunition.

When he arrived at school with his considerable arsenal, Michael entered through a back door into the band room (where a band teacher asked what he was carrying and was satisfied by the same English-skit response), wandered up through the empty auditorium, through back hallways, past the main office, and into the crowded lobby, where the prayer circle was gathering. He walked past his goth friends and put the blanketed bundle on the floor beneath the school's trophy case.

Somebody asked him what he was carrying and again, he said it was for a class play. Satisfied, the other student turned away, and nobody else talked to him. Michael was again alone in a roomful of people as he pulled out his gun.

Nobody noticed. It angered him that, yet again, nobody noticed.

You've got to do this for yourself, said the voice in his head. *For yourself.*

He slung his backpack off his shoulder and set it on the floor. He unzipped it and reached in. He fumbled with his earplugs and dropped one.

Stupid kid, he thought to himself. *Can't even get the earplugs right.*

He racked a clip into his chrome pistol just as Ben Strong said his final "Amen."

"PLEASE KILL ME"

When the prayers finished, Missy Jenkins felt better. She hugged her friend Kelly and headed toward her book bag. She had only taken a few steps when she heard a *pop* that sounded like a firecracker.

She pivoted toward the sound, her ears ringing. She saw Nicole Hadley fall limply to the tile floor with what appeared to be blood on her head. *She's faking this*, Missy thought. *This is some kind of a joke.*

The two more random pops rang out, then a rapid-fire series of seven more. The only gunshots she'd ever heard were on TV, and these pops sounded nothing like that. She was wondering who might pull such a frightening prank when her body suddenly went numb and she crumpled to the floor. To her, it felt as if she floated down. She never felt herself hit the floor, never felt any pain. She lay on the cold floor, unable to move, wondering what was happening.

Screaming students were running all around her. Mandy was crouched over her, making sure she was alive and covering Missy's body with her own.

"What's going on?" Missy asked her sister.

"There's a gun," she said. Her voice was panicky, her eyes wide.

"A gun? Who's got a gun?"

"Michael."

"Michael? Michael who?"

"Michael Carneal."

It didn't make sense to Missy. Nothing made sense. She didn't know what was happening, didn't know why she couldn't feel her belly. She knew she must have been shot, but there was no telltale blood on her to mark a wound.

For twelve seconds, Michael fired in steady succession, until his clip had only one bullet left. He never reached for extra bullets, even though he had hundreds at his feet.

Kelly Hard had been hit in the shoulder. Nearby, Kayce Steger lay face-down and not moving. Jessica James, a senior in the band with Missy, had been shot beneath the shoulder and was wracked with violent convulsions as her life bled away.

Principal Bill Bond rushed out into the chaos and took cover with Ben Strong behind a pillar near the shooter. But before they could jump him, Michael dropped his gun and slumped in tears. Bond and Strong rushed in.

"What are you shooting people for?" Strong yelled at the whimpering little boy who had just shot into a crowd of forty teenagers.

"Shooting people," Michael heard himself say.

"What for?" Ben asked, coming closer.

Michael was in shock. "I don't know."

Principal Bond grabbed the gun and trundled Michael into a nearby office.

"Kill me," Michael cried as he was hustled away. "Please kill me."

Missy's algebra teacher, Diane Beckman, knelt by her side, trying to keep her awake. All she could do was pray.

"Am I going to die?" Missy asked her.

"No, you're not going to die," she said. "You're going to be fine."

"But I'm paralyzed. I can't feel anything."

"No, you're not paralyzed. You're just in shock," she insisted. "You're not paralyzed."

"But I know I am because I can't feel my legs or my stomach," Missy said.

Suddenly, Missy felt like vomiting, and Beckman helped her turn to one side to throw up without choking herself.

Before the ambulances arrived, Missy lapsed into a dream: She was walking and laughing with a stranger when a bicyclist aimed right at her. She jumped out of harm's way, then resumed her walk. Then she was awake again, staring at the ceiling of Heath High School. That's all she remembered about the dream, but while she had feared dying before, she was inexplicably at peace now.

Paramedics, delayed by morning rush hour in the city and the two-lane back roads, finally arrived and quickly focused on the three girls most seriously injured—Nicole Hadley, Kayce Steger, and Jessica James. In a few moments, they gingerly slid Missy onto a backboard and wheeled her to a waiting ambulance for the 12-mile (19-kilometer) journey toward the hospital and the rest of her life.

Michael Carneal, an awkward misfit who only wanted to be liked, had fired ten bullets into a crowd of fellow students, none more than 50 feet (15 meters) from him. Three were dead or dying, and five were wounded.

And in less time that it takes to say "Amen," Missy Jenkins's life was changed forever.

WAKING UP FROM A NIGHTMARE

As Missy was wheeled into the emergency room, many of the doctors and nurses were weeping. They, too, had children at Heath High School, and they didn't know who would be wheeled next through the ER doors.

Doctors began to work on Missy, hooking her up to a chest tube and IVs. They asked her to move her legs, and although it felt to her like she was, she wasn't. Using a needle, they prodded her body to find out where she could feel and where she couldn't.

They also found the entrance wound, a small hole in her upper left chest, just below her collarbone, but they would need X-rays to know more.

Missy's distraught family began to arrive at the hospital, and the doctor allowed them to visit her for just a few minutes before she went to radiology. She read the sadness and fear in their faces. Some cried.

Ironically, Missy comforted *them*. She had tried to make herself cry but couldn't. She was at a strange peace with what had happened to her less than an hour before. She told them they shouldn't cry because she was alive.

The X-rays revealed a more sobering truth. A single bullet had entered Missy's chest, punctured her left lung, and crashed into the T_4 vertebra, splattering shards of lead and bone into her spinal cord before it exited just between her shoulder blades. While the spinal cord itself was not hit by the bullet, the fragments had paralyzed Missy below the chest and doctors believed that trying to remove them would only do more damage.

She had a long rehabilitative road ahead, they said, but she would probably never walk again.

Missy didn't understand all the medical talk, but she heard what she needed to hear. She couldn't fathom being confined to a wheelchair for the rest of her life, which had hardly begun. She wondered whether the paralysis might go away sometime.

She also learned that Mandy had narrowly missed serious wounding—or worse. At the hospital, somebody noticed an angry red scrape across Mandy's neck where a bullet had grazed her. Suddenly, the twin sisters realized that they had both escaped death in miracles measured by millimeters.

That night, before her family left the hospital at the end of a horrifying day, Missy asked to speak privately with her mother.

Missy told her that she had forgiven Michael Carneal, who had paralyzed her for life just hours before.

It stunned her mother, but she understood the strength of Missy's faith, if not her willingness to forgive her would-be killer so quickly. Later, Missy's mother shared her decision with the rest of the family who, in their own time, came to agree with her.

"It was like I was in a dream . . . and I woke up," Michael Carneal told a teacher while he sat in the principal's conference room waiting for police to arrive.

"I looked at him and he just had this glazed look in his eyes," Principal Bond said later. "When I got the gun, I told him to go to the office and sit down. He didn't react any more than if I had caught him smoking in the boys' room."

When asked by investigators why he shot his fellow classmates, Michael's first response was that he was tired of being teased and bullied, but he admitted that none of his vaguely described tormenters was in the lobby that day.

Less than two hours after the rampage, Michael was sitting in the police station. When asked by investigators why he shot his fellow classmates, Michael's first response was that he was tired of being teased and bullied, but he admitted that none of his vaguely described tormenters was in the lobby that day.

"Was you mad at somebody?" McCracken County Sheriff's Detective Carl Baker asked him.

"Not anybody in particular."

"Wasn't mad at your mom and dad?"

Michael shook his head. "Uh-uh."

"Mad at the teachers?"

"Not really."

"You mad at the principal?"

"Uh-uh," Michael said. "I guess I just got mad 'cause everybody kept making fun of me."

The kids at school called him "freak" and "nerd" and "crack baby," he said as he began to cry.

He described in some detail how he had broken into a neighbor's garage on Thanksgiving to steal guns and ammo from a locked cabinet. He had stashed them in an Army duffel bag one night and carried them home, where he crawled through his bedroom window and hid them in his closet. Shortly before the shooting, he said, he took some of the guns to a friend's house for safekeeping. The rest he wrapped in a blanket, secured them with duct tape, and shoved them under his bed.

When police searched his room, they found more than two dozen empty cartridge boxes, a typewritten note titled "The Secret" on his nightstand, the handwritten lyrics to a song called "Paralyzed Monkey," and "Mist-Erie," a short story Michael had written about atomic bomb testing.

Detective Baker walked Michael through the actual shooting—or what little he remembered.

"I was just sitting there and I reached in my backpack and pulled out a handgun," Michael recounted calmly.

"What kind of handgun was it?" Baker asked.

Michael would describe himself as being in a transfixed hypnotic state while he was firing the pistol, shooting more at movement and shadows than at specific people.

"It was a .22 Ruger, and I put in a clip and turned off the safety and cocked it and then just started firing."

"Who all was standing in that group, do you know?"

"Uh-uh."

"Did you know any of the kids in that group?"

"I knew Ben."

Oddly, Michael didn't mention his dear friend Nicole Hadley, whom he had shot in the forehead and who was, at that very moment, on life support.

Or Kayce Steger, the girl he had asked on a date and who was already dead. Or Missy Jenkins, his friend from marching band, now paralyzed. Or any of the other students whom he had lived and gone to school with all his life in his small town.

"What was going through your mind while you was firing the gun?" Baker pressed.

"I don't know, it was all, like, blurry and foggy. I just didn't know what was going on. I think I closed my eyes for a minute."

In later interviews, Michael would describe himself in a transfixed hypnotic state while he was firing the pistol, shooting more at movement and shadows than at specific people. Strangely, his waking dream was shattered when he saw one of his bullets chip a plaster wall and it snapped him back to reality.

Michael looked around at the carnage. He saw kids bleeding on the floor, others screaming and running helter-skelter. He was not entirely certain what had just happened, or why.

"Then I stopped and I realized what was going on and I just sat down and Ben popped up from behind a column and told me to calm down. So I set the gun down and he, he came over there and he, he was telling me to calm down and not to worry about it."

"Is he kinda, sort of a friend or just somebody you know?" Baker asked.

"He's nice to me," Michael said. "Then Mr. Bond came out there and grabbed me and jerked me away and we, and then he pulled me down the hall, and Ben kept yelling, 'I need to talk to him for a minute!' And Mr. Bond just said, 'Get away.'"

Under further questioning, Michael talked about how he and a friend had fantasized about shooting up the school or the mall for more than a year after they had seen *The Basketball Diaries*, a 1995 movie in which the main character (played by Leonardo DiCaprio) dreams about storming his classroom and systematically shooting a teacher and five classmates to death while other students cheer.

"When you pulled the trigger for the first time, did you realize people could get hurt?"

"I, I don't know," Michael replied. "I really wasn't thinking until, until I stopped shooting."

"Okay, when you took the guns to school, had you thought about the fact that somebody was probably gonna get hurt?"

"No, uh-uh."

As the first of many police interviews ended, Michael's lawyer asked him whether there was any message he could deliver to his family.

"Tell 'em I'm sorry," he said, crying again. "I've ruined their lives."

A SYMBOL OF SURVIVAL

Five days after the shooting, an overflow crowd in the two-thousand-seat Bible Baptist Heartland Worship Center wept over three white caskets, each lined in blue crepe and scrawled with messages from grieving classmates, like "I loved you" and "I will miss you in English."

Some mourners tucked stuffed animals inside the casket of Nicole Hadley, whose head rested on her favorite Winnie the Pooh pillowcase. Beside each casket stood a framed display of casual photos, and the biers displayed their favorite possessions: Jessica James's French horn, Kayce Steger's clarinet, Nicole's Pooh bear.

In the devoutly religious community, the emotion reached its crescendo when the Heath High School choir sang "The Prayer of Saint Francis." Among the singers was Kelly Carneal, Michael's sister.

Snapshots of the three girls in life flashed across a large screen over the three caskets. Mourners included Kentucky governor Paul Patton, former Kentucky governor Julian Carroll, and popular Christian singer Steven Curtis Chapman, a 1981 Heath graduate, who sang two songs.

Nicole Hadley was a tall, fourteen-year-old freshman who played clarinet in the school marching band and was on the freshman basketball team. A few weeks before the shooting, she told her parents she wanted to donate her organs when she died. So two hours after a bullet pierced her brain, doctors transplanted her lungs into a forty-two-year-old man with emphysema, while her heart, kidneys, liver, and pancreas went to other needy patients. She had dreamed of being a doctor.

Honor student Kayce Steger, a fifteen-year-old sophomore, also played in the school band and on the softball team, even though she worked after school at a Subway sandwich shop. She wanted to become a police officer after high school. She was buried in her favorite dress, a green satin homecoming gown.

Senior Jessica James was seventeen, quiet, and studious. Deeply religious, she taught Bible school and worked one summer with inner-city kids in North Carolina. She, too, played in the school band and wanted to study psychology in college.

After the service, as mourners stood silently in the bitter December cold, three white hearses took the girls to three different cemeteries to be buried.

But Missy Jenkins couldn't attend. Unable to raise her head from her bed in intensive care, she watched the service on television through special reflective glasses.

She cried because she couldn't be there, and because their deaths were still not real to her. She couldn't see her three friends lying in their caskets. The news of their deaths came to her through a morphine haze, and she still didn't truly comprehend it. One day they said a prayer together and the next day they were all dead. And for an innocent fifteen-year-old girl, the concept of death is less transparent than the promise of laughter or the thrill of a first kiss.

But Missy wasn't dead. In fact, she had become a symbol of survival. Cards and letters began to pour in, as many as six hundred a day, from all over the world. So many of them contained money that her parents quickly opened a trust fund to pay for a lifetime of Missy's considerable expenses.

Visitors came, too. Among them were Michael's parents. Missy tried to be sunny, but the Carneals were crying and shaken. They told her they were sorry for what happened, but the shooting was never mentioned again. The visit, though it only lasted a few minutes, was uncomfortable because nobody could find the right words.

Missy knew they blamed themselves, and some angry people blamed them, too. But she also knew they were good parents who cared very much for their children, and who volunteered at the school. In the end, Missy felt sorry for *them*.

Five months after being shot, Missy was released from the rehabilitation hospital in Lexington. She arrived home to celebrating friends, balloons, signs, and a newly built wheelchair ramp. Among the kids who came to welcome her home was a goth friend of Michael's, and it pleased Missy to see him there.

She started school again at Heath High School toward the end of the 1998 spring semester. Arriving on the first day in a special van donated to her family by a local car dealer, she found the entire school decorated for her. After a joyous greeting, students gathered in the prayer circle, as they had every day since the shooting.

Missy wheeled herself to the exact spot where she'd stood the day she was shot and reached out to hold hands. But today, the prayer circle was bigger than it had ever been. Even some of the goth kids joined.

When the prayer ended and students had left for class, Missy asked Mandy to show her exactly where she'd lain wounded that morning, to tell her what she had seen. It didn't bother her to be there. She just wanted to know that her memory was right.

AFTERMATH

In October 1998, Michael Carneal pleaded "guilty but mentally ill" for killing three fellow students and wounding five others. The judge agreed to accept the pleas on condition that the maximum penalty—life in prison without possibility of parole for twenty-five years—would be imposed.

Two months later—slightly more than a year after the shootings—Michael faced his victims and their families at an emotional sentencing. But he looked at the floor throughout most of the hearing.

"As a mother, my life has forever been changed," said Gwen Hadley, Nicole's mother. "My family is no longer whole."

Joe James, Jessica's father, said he sometimes forgets, even after a year, that his daughter is dead.

"Though my mind says she is gone, my heart still misses her enough to sometimes include her in my plans," he said.

Sabrina Steger, Kayce's mother, couldn't contain her tears.

"Dinner is usually sitting in the family room [because] the empty chair at the dining room table is too painful of a reminder," she said. "Even answering the simple question of 'How many children do you have?' has become very complicated."

USING STATE-OF-THE-ART TECHNOLOGY TO HELP HER WALK AGAIN, PARAPLEGIC MISSY JENKINS WAS ABLE TO DANCE WITH NEW HUSBAND JOSH SMITH AT THEIR WEDDING IN 2006.

Courtesy of Missy Jenkins

Missy went last. She wheeled herself to face Michael and demanded that he look at her. He raised his face, and she looked directly into the empty eyes of a little boy.

"I want to tell you that I am paralyzed. I'm paralyzed from my chest right here down. And I spent five months in the hospital and I still struggle. I feel really helpless that I can't do things I used to do. I can't go to the bathroom like regular people. It's hard to get dressed. I see people running around doing stuff like everybody else, and I can't really do it because I am stuck to my chair.

"They tell me that I'll never walk again. I think I will, though. But if God doesn't want me to walk, that's okay. And I just wanted you to know because I have to live with it every day now.

"I don't know why you did this to me and everybody else, but I know that I'm never going to forget it because I see it every day in my mind. But I don't have any hard feelings toward you. I'm just upset that this happened and I'm upset that everything had to go this way, but I can live this way. It's going to be hard, but I can do it."

Shortly after Michael's sentencing, Missy got a call. The *Ladies' Home Journal* had chosen her among its most fascinating women of 1998, among such notables as the Duchess of York, comedian Whoopi Goldberg, singer Trisha Yearwood, and Congresswoman Mary Bono.

And soon after that, she was invited to talk about forgiveness to a nation-wide audience on *The Oprah Winfrey Show* and other TV talk shows.

"Walking in general is just something I miss," she said in one interview. "You never really, you know, really think about what you have until it's gone. So I really want to walk again. And that's what I wish for. I guess I kind of miss my childhood, too."

That spring of 1999, eager to share her story, Missy was just beginning to see how she might turn her affliction into an inspiring asset when a new horror thrust her—willingly or not—back into the media's unblinking glare.

Columbine.

> Missy was just beginning to see how she might turn her affliction into an inspiring asset when a new horror thrust her back into the media's unblinking glare. Columbine.

Two years after Heath, Columbine gave a ghastly new face to school violence. Two alienated Colorado teens killed twelve students and one teacher, and wounded twenty-four others, becoming the second-worst American school shooting to that time. Only Charles Whitman's Texas Tower rampage was worse (see chapter 6).

One of the few differences between Columbine and Heath was that the shooters, Dylan Klebold and Eric Harris, killed themselves rather than be arrested.

The media flocked to Missy, hoping she could offer the unique perspective of a student in the line of fire. She embraced the chance to talk about the pain, the aftermath, and the forgiveness, even though she spent her prom night dodging a dogged *People* magazine photographer.

A few weeks later, with President Bill Clinton and First Lady Hillary Rodham Clinton, she participated in a discussion about guns and violence televised by *Good Morning America* from the White House.

The media exposure paid an unexpected bonus when a company, Dynamics Walk-Again Rehabilitation Center in Los Angeles, contacted Missy. Dynamics executives had seen her on TV and offered to fit her with a new high-tech brace they had invented to help paraplegics walk. In three months, they could literally put her back on her feet.

In March 2000, fitted with Dynamics's leg braces and electrodes, Missy shuffled a quarter-mile (half a kilometer) in the Los Angeles Marathon in a drenching rain to prove something to herself and the world. Although still mostly confined to her wheelchair, Missy spoke briefly at the first Million Mom March against gun violence in Washington, D.C., and attended her own senior prom in a dress donated by a Hollywood fashion designer.

In June, to a thunderous standing ovation, Missy Jenkins walked slowly across the stage to accept her Heath High School diploma. And later that summer, having never cast a single vote in her life, Missy walked onto the stage of the Democratic National Convention in Los Angeles to share her story, again to deafening applause.

Throughout her college years at Murray State University in nearby Murray, Kentucky, the media came calling, but Missy was dealing with more private worries. She began to wonder whether she could ever be loved by a man, whether she could have a baby, how she would lift that crying baby from its crib, how she could shop for groceries . . . how she could be the woman, wife, and mother she wanted to be. In her junior year, she was named Ms. Wheelchair Kentucky, but she wondered how to tell her dates all the humiliating truths about her damaged body. She wondered whether she would ever dance again.

Then she met Josh Smith, a former high school football star who had grown up on a tobacco farm and wanted to be a physical education teacher. They dated for two years before he finally proposed.

Missy graduated in 2004 with a degree in social work and a desire to work with troubled teens like Michael Carneal. In time, she got her dream job as a counselor at an alternative school where she works closely with defiant and marginalized kids who have run into trouble with grades, behavior, and social expectations.

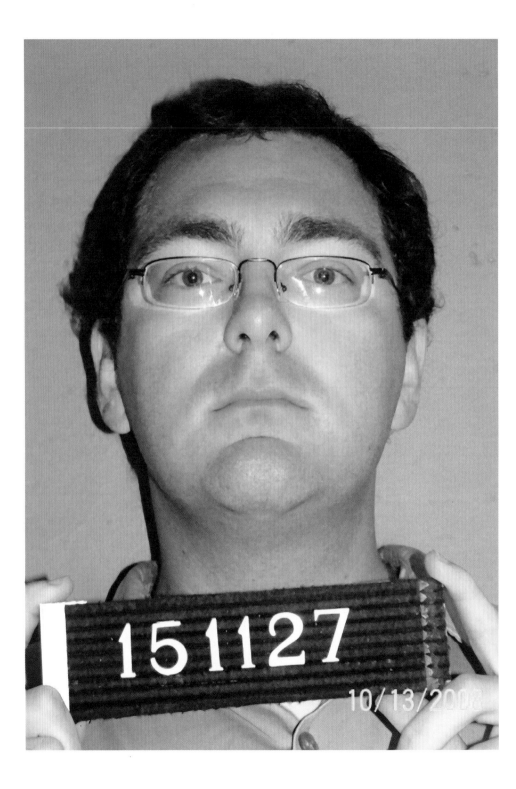

In 2006, she and Josh married. With the help of her brace and a walker, she was able to stand for the ceremony, and later danced her first dance. To stand up on this special day meant everything to her.

She also became a mother in 2007, when her son Logan was born. Her dreams were coming true. A second son, Carter, was born in April 2010.

And she began to think she should tell her story in a book.

AN ALTERNATE IDENTITY

Questions have been asked a thousand ways. Answers have never been satisfying.

Michael Carneal's enigmatic massacre was the second in a series of American school shootings that happened within months of one another. Two months before Heath, two students were killed in Pearl, Mississippi. Less than four months after, four students and a teacher died in a middle-school shooting in Jonesboro, Arkansas. After that, a teacher was shot dead at a school dance in Edinboro, Pennsylvania, and two students were shot to death at a school in Springfield, Oregon.

Most forensic psychiatrists who have studied Michael Carneal believe he understood the consequences of his actions, but it's not clear whether he was mentally ill when he opened fire. After the fact—because Michael had never been diagnosed with any mental illness before the attack—they all note his strange behaviors, odd paranoias, and difficulty interpreting social situations correctly.

> **Michael went on to develop full-blown schizophrenia in prison and has been heavily medicated, but psychiatrists still aren't sure whether his paranoid tendencies played a role in the shooting.**

Michael went on to develop full-blown schizophrenia in prison and has been heavily medicated, but psychiatrists still aren't sure whether his paranoid tendencies played a role in the shooting.

As evidence, they offer the fact that Michael did not shoot at the "preps," the clique he identified as his nemesis. Few preps participated in the prayer circle. And nobody—not even Michael himself—has claimed he was teased by the kids who were in the prayer circle that fated morning, many of whom were people he considered friends. When he was told that he had killed his close friend Nicole Hadley, Michael said the news made him feel "crappy."

MASS MURDERER MICHAEL CARNEAL REMAINS IN A KENTUCKY PRISON FOR KILLING THREE TEENAGE GIRLS IN HIS 1997 RAMPAGE AT HEATH HIGH SCHOOL IN WEST PADUCAH, KENTUCKY, ALTHOUGH HE IS ELIGIBLE FOR PAROLE IN 2023.

Associated Press

If he was unleashing pent-up rage at his bullies, would he not have attacked his bullies instead of friends and innocent bystanders?

Instead, they see a child at a fragile moment in the development of his identity, an immature boy who believed he was not the student his sister was, not his parents' favorite, not important to anyone or any particular group—not noticed.

So psychiatrists believe he might have developed an alternate identity, one very different from the boy Michael Carneal saw in the mirror. "Everybody talked how I was not like my sister," he told a psychologist after the attack, "so I figured if I was the exact opposite, people would pay attention to me more."

Most school shooters are children who are especially socially isolated; they have few or no friends and have trouble making friends of the opposite sex. Michael was more complex: Many of his classmates considered him a friend, but he believed he was widely disliked and had no friends. His social insecurities were not unlike those of most adolescents, but they blinded him to the fact that he was not as isolated as he felt. In short, he isolated himself more than he was isolated by his classmates.

Thus, some say, the shooting provided him a very public way of asserting his power and winning respect from all the people who saw him as only a fringe figure and a marginal clown.

After the Columbine shootings, Michael fell into deep psychosis and twice attempted suicide because he blamed himself for those shootings.

After the Columbine shootings, Michael fell into deep psychosis and twice attempted suicide because he blamed himself for those shootings.

A year after the December 1, 1997, shooting spree that left three girls dead at Heath High School, their grieving families filed wrongful-death lawsuits against more than fifty defendants, including Michael's parents, the school, video game makers, websites, and the makers of the movie *The Basketball Diaries*, arguing that they all could have predicted Michael's deadly violence and should have taken steps to prevent it. But they didn't stop there: The families also sued seven Heath High School students—including Ben Strong—whom they claimed knew "something big" was about to happen and could have prevented the slaughter.

The Jenkins family was asked to be part of the legal case, but declined.

In 2000, a federal judge dismissed all defendants except Michael from the lawsuit. The court ruled that none of them, especially the video game, movie, and website makers, could possibly have known what Michael would do. Despite subtly disturbing signs, Michael had flown under the radar.

"This was a tragic situation, but tragedies such as this simply defy rational explanation and the courts should not pretend otherwise," the judge wrote in a thirty-nine-page opinion.

So the girls' families quickly agreed to a $42 million settlement offer from Michael's lawyers—a mostly symbolic victory because Michael faces the rest of his life in prison with no assets.

A CHANCE FOR HEALING

Missy Jenkins sought answers in a different way.

Starting just two years after the shooting, Michael had called and written several letters to Missy, sometimes creepy but always apologetic. After the sixth letter and the second phone call to her house, Missy asked the prosecutor to stop any contact. It scared her. She simply wasn't ready to deal with the boy who was both a friend and a killer in her mind. She had forgiven him, but that didn't mean she wanted to be pen pals.

But then she saw a new chance for healing. Hers, not his.

At her request, the prison system allowed her and Mandy to speak to Michael Carneal privately for two hours at the Kentucky State Reformatory, where Inmate #151127 lived in the psychiatric ward.

They met in a conference room, Missy in her wheelchair and Michael in a tan jumpsuit, unshackled. Here before her was the little freshman boy she had known so long ago, 6 feet (1.8 meters) tall now and filled out, but still a little shy and meek behind his big glasses. The meeting started nervously for both of them, with Michael looking at the floor, just as he had at his sentencing.

But as they spoke, he warmed to Missy and made eye contact. The sisters told him how much they had liked him in school. Michael talked about the day of the shooting, the long-ago letters, what prompted the attack. Missy asked him whether he thought he belonged in prison, and he skirted the issue except to say he believed he should be punished but that he could also benefit from treatment.

She told him she forgave him, not to make him feel better but so that she could move on. She told him she would certainly miss out on a lot, but she refused to miss out on life.

And she told him that she regretted that she could not feel the kicking of a baby that was growing inside her at that very moment.

Michael apologized profusely to Missy and Mandy, and they accepted his contrition as sincere. Toward the end of the meeting, Missy asked Michael if there was anything he'd like for her to share in her many speeches and a book she planned to write about her experience.

Yes, he told her. Two things. First, tell kids to talk to someone, anyone, if they are having problems. And second, say nice things to people and understand how it can make a difference in a life.

Missy didn't leave with all the answers she sought, but she left satisfied about many things. That Michael was damaged by bullying. That he had fired blindly, targeting nobody in particular. That he never considered the consequences until it was too late. And that he was truly sorry.

She felt some of her anger peel away. Being angry at Michael was giving him too much power over her.

"I've always said that there will never be closure for me," Missy wrote later. "But I think that visit was the closest I'll ever come."

In 2007, Michael Carneal's lawyers filed an appeal, saying he was insane at the time of the shooting and should not have been able to enter a guilty plea. In 2009, the Kentucky Supreme Court rejected his request for a new competency hearing and a retrial, so Michael must continue to serve out his sentence. He won't be eligible for parole until 2023, when he will be forty years old.

"I can't change anything that happened, by dying or anything else," Carneal once told a reporter. "I wish I could change things but I can't."

Missy Jenkins almost never says "can't."

She still refers to herself as being *possibly* paralyzed for life, because she genuinely believes there might be a day when she is not.

In her dreams, she always walks.

She never thinks she should have died that day. The dead fulfilled a purpose in life, and so is she.

She doesn't believe she was in the wrong place at the wrong time, but rather in the right place at the right time.

"Before this happened to me, I really didn't feel like I had a direction in my life," she said in one of her many interviews. "I was a fifteen-year-old kid who thought nothing would ever happen to me like that. After this happened to me, it gave me direction."

She didn't want to carry any dark things around inside her, things that would weigh her down and embitter her.

"I could've died that morning, so I wanted to finish out life being happy, not being angry."

She put everything down in the book she dreamed of writing. Teaming up with William Croyle, a newspaperman who followed much of her journey, she wrote *I Choose to Be Happy* (Langmarc Publishing, 2008). With a foreword written by gun-control crusader Sarah Brady—wife of Jim Brady, the presidential press secretary shot in the head during an assassination attempt on President Reagan in 1981—and endorsements by ABC News's Diane Sawyer and one-handed, former Major League pitcher Jim Abbott, *I Choose to Be Happy* is a clear-eyed, candid account of her near-death and resurrection as "a visual against violence."

Steeped in Missy's abiding faith, it is a remarkable summary of survival, not sorrow.

"I will never forget what Michael did to me. How can I?" she writes in her book. "I'm reminded of it every day when I can't jump out of bed in the morning, reach the cabinets in our kitchen, or stand face to face with my husband. There will never be closure.

"But . . . I forgave him and my future was enlarged. It helped me discover a Missy Jenkins I never knew existed."

CHAPTER 10

ALONE IN A DARK SEA

TERRY JO DUPERRAULT AND THE *BLUEBELLE* MURDERS

THE WIND WAS IN THE SOUTHEAST, although in the blackness of the night sea, it mattered little. Storm clouds hid the pale crescent moon and stars. A child, alone and adrift, couldn't see her hand in front of her sunburned face. Now it was beginning to rain.

But as the drops hit the black water, it glowed.

She didn't know the sea. She didn't know about the tiny creatures that emit sudden, ephemeral flashes of light when disturbed by a swimmer's hand, a boat's oar, a zephyr, the slicing prow of a ship, or a drop of rain. She didn't know their magical light had evolved over eons as a warning against danger and death from predators.

She only knew the surface of the sea all around her flimsy cork raft was suddenly luminous, as if the stars had disintegrated into blue-green dust and fallen into the opaque sea, like she, too, had fallen into the sea. It had happened so fast—the waking, the blood, the rising water, the gun, the sudden silence after the boat disappeared with a sigh beneath the swirling waves, taking her mother and brother with it.

It all felt like a dream.

Arthur Duperrault dreamed big.

He'd grown up in Green Bay, Wisconsin, a little port and paper city on the shores of Lake Michigan that epitomized Midwestern wholesomeness. And

Arthur epitomized Green Bay: Studious, sober, and decent, he was president of Green Bay West High School's Class of 1939 and a champion debater.

After graduation, he enrolled at Lawrence College in Appleton, Wisconsin. But during his freshman year in 1940, when the Nazi blitzkrieg in Europe and Japanese aggressions in the Pacific threatened to draw America into war, the muscular, red-haired Arthur dropped out of college and enlisted in the Navy.

The Navy trained him as a medical corpsman and sent him to the Burma Road, a rugged mountain route used by Britain to supply the Chinese in their war against Japan. But it was on the transport to the Far East that Arthur fell in love with warm, tropical seas.

In almost two years with Allied troops in the jungles of Burma, Arthur won the admiration of his officers as he tended to men with jungle fevers and battle wounds, often in the harshest conditions. After the United States entered the war, the Navy shipped Arthur home to Washington, D.C., but it was too far from the action to suit the adventurous Midwesterner, so he volunteered to go back to China as a medic for another year.

In 1943, at the height of the war, he was assigned to the Pentagon. In Washington, he met the spirited, dark-haired Jean Brosh, a small-town Nebraska girl who worked as a secretary at the FBI headquarters. They married in late 1944, and when Arthur was honorably discharged in November 1945, they returned to Wisconsin to start a family and a new life.

For Arthur, that meant returning to college. He enrolled in Chicago's Northern Illinois College of Optometry on the GI Bill, boarding at the school during the week and returning home on weekends for four years. For Jean, it meant raising their young son Brian and being patient.

As Arthur opened his optometry practice in Green Bay, Jean gave birth to a daughter, Terry Jo. As Arther's practice grew, so did his family. Another daughter, Rene, was born in 1954. The Duperraults were living the idyllic postwar life, with all the professional honors, personal achievements, and profits that came with it.

Brian, the eldest, was his father's shadow. He went everywhere Arthur went and did everything his father did. Like his father, he grew up short but athletic.

The middle daughter, Terry Jo, was a tomboy who preferred the rough and tumble life. She grew up tall and pretty, and by the time she was ten, she was already taller than her older brother. She often played alone in the woods, inventing her own adventures, scarring her knees, and, at least once, suffering a gash that her mother—always the farm girl—stitched up herself. Terry Jo even hated summer camp because the other girls were such . . . girls. She was always happy to accompany her beloved father to the lake, where he taught her to fish and swim. He was her one and only hero.

Rene, the youngest, was the dainty one. Petite and blonde, she refused to wear "boy clothes" like her sister and preferred dolls and tea parties to roughhousing.

"Doc" Duperrault, as he became known, was as innovative and adventurous in his practice as in his life. He became a respected leader among his peers, largely through his early embrace of contact lenses, decades before they became popular.

But Arthur was never satisfied with sitting back or procrastinating. He stayed unusually fit and involved. He became a state handball champion, a tireless volunteer at the local YMCA, and a passionate golfer. He also won national attention when he dug frantically in a collapsed trench for hours to rescue the family dog and in another heroic act, leaped fully clothed into the frigid water of Green Bay to rescue a child who was drowning.

MAIDEN VOYAGE

Arthur also became a skilled sailor, and he dreamed of a great shipboard adventure with his family in the tropics. Family weekends in Wisconsin were often spent on the water, but Arthur fantasized about living a year at sea, sailing port to port, educating their three children—Brian, now fourteen; Terry Jo, eleven; and Rene, seven—under sail in both academics and life, following the wind on a once-in-a-lifetime odyssey.

Nearing forty in 1960, he feared the ideal moment might soon pass. But even if his passion for a life at sea was doubtless, Arthur wasn't certain whether his family shared his dream. So he planned a kind of "shakedown" cruise—one season at sea, maybe a year if it worked out. He hired an optometrist to run his practice, and in the fall of 1961, Arthur and Jean took their children out of school and headed to Fort Lauderdale, Florida, where a 60-foot (18.3 meter) chartered ketch named the *Bluebelle* waited for them.

The *Bluebelle*, a sleek, two-masted sailboat, was a former racing yacht, and its lines recalled an elegant past. A 60-foot (18.3 meter) tall mainmast and 45-foot (13.7 meter) tall mizzen mast towered over the graceful, snow-white hull. The boat's white wooden dinghy and black rubber life raft were stowed to the port side of the cabin; an oval cork life float—essentially a white, canvas-covered life ring with rope netting—was lashed starboard.

With a 13-foot (3.9 meter) main cabin that contained two sleeping areas, a kitchenette, and a head, plus an aft sleeping berth, the *Bluebelle* would be perfect for the five Duperraults and their hired skipper.

In early November, Arthur chartered the *Bluebelle* for the Duperraults' first cruise, a week's journey to the Bahamas and back. It was to be the first test of the family's seaworthiness, the first hint

JOHN GALANAKIS, A SEAMAN ABOARD THE GREEK FREIGHTER *CAPTAIN THEO*, SNAPPED THIS PHOTO OF 11-YEAR-OLD TERRY JO DUPERRAULT ON HER LONELY CORK RAFT JUST MOMENTS BEFORE HIS SHIPMATES PLUCKED HER FROM THE SEA.

John Galanakis

of whether life on the water for long periods would be smooth sailing—or a shipwreck. Either way, Arthur would know quickly within a few days at sea.

On November 8, 1961, the *Bluebelle* was ready to sail. Early that balmy Wednesday morning, the Duperraults arrived at Bahia Mar Marina in Fort Lauderdale with food, clothing, and all the provisions they would need for the week. The children played on deck while everything was made ready.

The *Bluebelle*'s owner, a swimming-pool contractor named Harold Pegg, met them at the slip with a load of ice and introduced them to their captain and his "crew," who happened to be the skipper's wife.

The captain was a strapping man, muscular, tanned, and movie-star handsome. His wavy hair gave him a hero's air. He didn't make small talk, and when he spoke, he spoke in a dignified, proper way—except for a slight stammer and a bit of a lazy eye. His blonde wife, who was very pretty, slender, and more expressive, would be his first mate and cook. She said her name was Dene, and she, too, was originally from Wisconsin, a former airline stewardess who had married the captain only three months before. This voyage was to be a kind of honeymoon for them, too.

So the time had come for Arthur Duperrault and his family. While Brian helped throw off the lines that tethered them to land, the skipper powered up the *Bluebelle*'s 115-horsepower Chrysler engine, and they motored toward open water. Soon, they were under sail into an 18-knot southeasterly wind, slicing through the warm waves toward their first stop: Bimini.

If Arthur had any lingering doubts about his children's sea legs, they were dashed as he watched Terry Jo and Brian scramble out on the bowsprit like old shellbacks to feel the sea-spray in the face and to watch the razor-sharp bow carve through the chop. They were laughing and happy. It's how he had always pictured it. His fantasy mariner's life was under way.

But in his dreams, Arthur had never imagined someone else at the helm. And this captain, a man named Julian Harvey, was plotting a nightmare course.

CHARMING DEVIL

By all outward appearances, Julian Harvey led a charmed life.

Born in New York City in 1917, he was five when his parents divorced. While his mother became a chorus girl at Shubert's Winter Garden, a Midtown Manhattan theater where some of the biggest names on Broadway played, Julian and his younger sister were raised by a wealthy aunt and uncle on Long Island.

Young Julian—he hated his name because he thought it was unmanly—grew up extraordinarily handsome, funny, and bright. He dressed impeccably, was outgoing, and became a graceful gymnast. Athletic and popular with the girls, he led a privileged childhood, even as a teenager during the Depression.

In high school, he fell in love with boats. He built several boats of his own and sailed them in Long Island Sound.

He also fell in love with women, with more complicated results. A brief high school marriage had been made necessary by such romantic abandon—the first of many in Julian Harvey's future.

After graduation in 1937, Harvey worked for a time as a door-to-door salesman, but cold-calling often set off a nervous stammer and caused his lazy eye to roll uncontrollably, so he quit. For about a year, he modeled for New York's prestigious John Robert Powers Agency, where his portfolio noted his "magnificent build."

He briefly attended the University of North Carolina in 1939, then transferred to Purdue, majoring in engineering. But like Arthur Duperrault, he saw war clouds gathering on the horizon in 1940, and rather than wait to be drafted as a grunt, Harvey enlisted in August 1941—four months before Pearl Harbor—as an air cadet in the U.S. Army Air Corps, which was the precursor of the Air Force.

"That's where the glory is," he told friends.

While training to fly, war broke out. Twenty-four-year-old Harvey—already an "old" man among the patriotic kids streaming into the service after the bombing of Pearl Harbor—was commissioned as a second lieutenant and assigned to fly B-24 bombers. At first, he flew sub-hunting missions along the eastern seaboard, in which he found no U-boats but played the role of the dashing aviator superbly: He met his second wife, a wealthy seventeen-year-old debutante, at a social function for officers and married her a few months later.

In the fall of 1942, Harvey was sent overseas, where he flew thirty bombing missions from England and Libya. He racked up an impressive file of commendations and an equally impressive number of crashes. But even as his crews and commanders increasingly saw him as accident-prone, his heroic looks and manner always carried him through any turbulence he might have created for himself.

> **How odd it was, the passersby said later, that this extraordinarily fit young man had made no effort to rescue his wife and mother-in-law who were trapped below him, even when other Samaritans tried.**

While Harvey was bombing Nazis in Europe, his wife bore him a son, Julian Jr. Shortly after being sent back stateside in 1944, Harvey told his young wife that he wanted a divorce. She kept the child and he kept his freedom.

Even before the war had ended, Harvey became a test pilot, adopting a jaunty, unconventional uniform of "a special-cut Eisenhower jacket, pearl-pink chino trousers, and a yellow scarf"—an outfit nobody challenged because he was a war hero and he virtually oozed the gallant aura that endeared him to women and generals alike.

After the war, Harvey became a jet fighter pilot, which only enhanced his legend. Now thirty-one, he met and married another young socialite, twenty-one-year-old Joann Boylen. In 1948, they had

ARTHUR AND JEAN DUPERRAULT OF GREEN BAY, WISCONSIN, DREAMED OF A RETIREMENT AT SEA IN THE TROPICS, SO IN OCTOBER 1961, THEY LOADED UP THEIR THREE CHILDREN FOR A "TRIAL RUN."

Courtesy of Tere Fassbender

a son, Lance, but Harvey knew he was too smart, too handsome, and too damn charming for one woman. He continued his affairs with abandon. And Joann was enraged by them.

On a rainy night in April 1949, Harvey, Joann, and her mother were driving on a rain-slicked highway near Valparaiso, Florida. Their car skidded, crashed through a bridge guardrail, and plunged into a dark, deep bayou.

A few minutes after the wreck, passersby found Harvey looking down into the water from the old wooden bridge, unhurt and strangely unemotional. He explained in vivid detail how he had seen the accident unfolding, and, even as the car was tumbling through the air, he opened his driver's side door and leaped to safety. How odd it was, the passersby said later, that this extraordinarily fit young man had made no effort to rescue his wife and mother-in-law who were trapped below him, even when other Samaritans tried.

A rescue diver and the highway patrolman who investigated the crash were equally suspicious. Harvey's story just didn't sound right to them, but they had little hard evidence to prove their belief that Harvey had staged the accident.

Joann's father demanded a military investigation of the young flier's story, but there was nothing to be done. Nobody looked further into the curious case, and no charges were ever filed. But a base doctor—not a psychiatrist—took a personal curiosity in Julian Harvey, and after a few informal visits, he concluded that the outwardly glib, charming, and suave Harvey was, in fact, a sociopath who was incapable of love, addicted to danger, a promiscuous liar, and a grandiose narcissist. His assessment was never a part of Harvey's file.

So Julian Harvey collected his wife's life insurance payout, and within a few weeks, he was living with another woman.

He collected women at an equally astonishing rate. In 1950, he married his fourth wife, a Texas businesswoman whom he divorced three years later. And in 1954, he married his fifth wife, a bright young woman he met in Washington, where he was again billeted as an Air Force staff officer.

Still fascinated with sailing, Harvey bought a 68-foot (21 meter) yacht called the *Torbatross*. One day, he set sail with friends on the Chesapeake Bay and rammed into the submerged wreckage of the famed battleship *Texas*, a Spanish War hulk that had been bombed by air ace Billy Mitchell in 1921 to flaunt American air power. Harvey and his crew escaped safely, but the *Torbatross* went down, and Harvey collected a $14,258 claim against the U.S. government. One of his passengers, however, found it strange that Harvey had deliberately circled the dangerous *Texas* wreck twice before ramming it directly.

Harvey's Air Force career continued, apparently impervious to his behavior. He flew 114 combat missions in Korea, and over the course of nineteen heroic years, earned the Distinguished Flying Cross with cluster, an Air Medal with eight oak leaf clusters, and fifteen more decorations.

But he'd also crashed three airplanes and built a reputation for having an unusual number of in-flight mishaps. His renowned unluckiness was credited with an inordinate number of dead-stick landings, midair flameouts, and engine trouble—some of which got him out of dangerous dogfights and flak-filled bombing runs. But never did anyone suspect that the dashing, dauntless Harvey could possibly be shirking his duty. He was just unlucky, that's all.

Major Julian Harvey retired in 1958 with a medical discharge, but because he had served briefly as a temporary lieutenant colonel, he kept the superior title.

Around that same time, his fifth wife filed for divorce, claiming Harvey's infidelities and secret anger were intolerable. Escaping the messy business of another split, he sailed his new 80-foot (24 meter) luxury yawl, the *Valiant*, to Havana—but 10 miles (16 kilometers) off the Cuban coast, the *Valiant* caught fire and sank. Harvey and a crewman both escaped unhurt, but again, he collected a $40,000 insurance settlement.

"Julian told the Coast Guard a beautiful story," one of Harvey's sailing friends said years later. "He was a real expert at storytelling because he had had so much experience talking himself out of trouble. He told me he set the fire himself because he was in a financial jam and needed the insurance money."

For the next few years, Harvey drifted through South Florida's sometimes shady sailing underworld, where gun running, drug smuggling, and insurance scams were common. When investigators went calling, Harvey's name often came up. Increasingly, his good looks and charisma were no longer enough to float him above suspicion.

In 1960, in Miami, he spied a shapely woman sunning herself on the beach and boldly introduced himself. She was Mary Dene Jordan Smith, an attractive blond TWA stewardess and aspiring writer. Harvey led her to think he was rich, but he was, in fact, flat broke. They married in late July 1961, but their relationship was stormy from the beginning, and their arguments were usually about money. One such fight erupted after Dene had promised to send $25 a month to her ailing father back home in Wisconsin, just to help him pay his medical bills, but Harvey refused to let her.

That fall, Harold Pegg hired Harvey and Dene to crew his ketch, the *Bluebelle*, where they could live and earn $300 a month by taking on Pegg's paying customers. The first charter would be the Duperraults, a nice little Wisconsin family who paid $515 to sail for an idyllic week in the Bahamas.

But they had enough money that on September 8, Harvey was able to take out a $20,000 double-indemnity life insurance policy on his sixth wife, Mary Dene.

After all, a man with his prodigious record of accidents couldn't be too careful.

LITTLE GIRL ALONE

Terry Jo Duperrault was in heaven.

For five days, the *Bluebelle* traversed endless, open tropical seas. Her father traded off with Harvey at the helm while the children played on deck. Rene played with her dolls and Brian fished while their mother read books and absorbed the pure sunlight.

CAPTAIN JULIAN HARVEY, THE
DASHING SKIPPER OF THE
CHARTERED KETCH *BLUEBELLE*,
WAS A WAR HERO AND FORMER
MODEL WHOSE CHARM HAD
GOTTEN HIM OUT OF MANY TIGHT
SQUEEZES.
Courtesy of Associated Press

They could swim in the mesmerizingly clear blue water around the boat or row the dinghy ashore to explore beaches and jungles. They swam, snorkeled, and fished for lobster. Every night, they anchored off serene island beaches from Great Isaac Cay to Gorda Cay, away from people and light and the cares they left behind.

Terry Jo, an eleven-year-old girl who'd never known a dark day in her life, couldn't believe life could be so carefree. The turquoise water, the striped fish, the lonely beaches piled with perfect conch shells, the azure sky, and the billowing clouds—she absorbed it all and never wanted to give it back. She even wrote a letter home to her school classmates that said she never wanted to come back.

She was becoming a young woman, too. Her breasts were just beginning to develop, and she felt awkward in her new swimsuit, especially around the handsome Harvey, who seemed to watch her more than the rest. They'd spoken very little, except when they met, and she thought he was nice enough, although his odd eye bothered her.

Her mother, who dabbled in art, fell in love with the colors of the islands, and she imagined coming back. So did Arthur, who told a Bahamian bureaucrat that he intended to build a winter home on Great Abaco Island someday.

On Sunday, they spent their last day at Sandy Point. Arthur met a seventeen-year-old fisherman named Jimmy Wells on the beach and invited him to dinner aboard the *Bluebelle*, where Dene had prepared chicken cacciatore and salad in the galley. The meal was pleasant enough, and everyone was happy.

Afterward, Jimmy left the boat, and as the sun set, Harvey headed for open water, toward home 200 miles (322 kilometers) away. Arthur and Harvey planned to anchor for a few hours in the lee of Great Stirrup Cay, get three or four hours of sleep, then push on to Great Isaac, where they'd again anchor in the lee for a little more sleep, then reach Fort Lauderdale Tuesday night or Wednesday morning.

The Duperraults and the Harveys sat in the *Bluebelle*'s cockpit past dark, reliving the adventure and enjoying the night air. Around 9 p.m., Terry Jo, always the first to bed, went to her main cabin bunk beside the stairs from the deck above, while everyone else stayed up talking. She fell asleep in her clothes, an embroidered white cotton blouse and pink corduroy pedal pushers.

Sometime in the night, she was startled awake by her brother's screams and loud stomping.

"Help, Daddy, help!" Brian shrieked. Then silence.

Terry Jo laid in her bunk, paralyzed with fear. She heard loud thumping noises outside. When she finally summoned the nerve, she opened a little door into the center cabin. To her horror, she saw the bodies of her mother and brother lying on their backs in pools of blood. There was no doubt they were dead. She quickly climbed the stairs to the empty main deck, where she saw more bloodstains.

Then she saw Harvey. He was carrying a bucket. When he saw her, he shouted at her to go back to her bunk.

"What happened?" she cried out.

"Get down there!" Harvey growled as he shoved her back down the companionway. His crazy eye seemed to be swirling in his skull.

Waves were breaking over the deck now. The *Bluebelle* was sinking fast.

Terrified, Terry Jo hid in her bunk, where she waited for maybe fifteen minutes, shaking with fear. She wanted to keep her cool. She felt as if she were outside her body, looking down on herself. Rene wasn't in the bunk they shared, and she hadn't seen her father. She could hear water splashing on the deck above.

Suddenly, Harvey threw open her door and stood watching her, a silhouette against the dwindling lights. He was holding a rifle in his hand, but he didn't speak. His evil shadow just stared at her, then left.

Terry smelled the acrid, oily smell of diesel fumes. Then to her horror, she saw water sloshing on the floor of her cabin. It was slowly rising.

When it had risen high enough to float her mattress, she waded out of the cabin in knee-deep water, fearing she'd bump into her mother and brother's corpses, and back to the top deck. Harvey appeared out of the dark.

"Are we sinking?" a frightened Terry Jo asked him.

"Yes," he said. "Here, hold this."

Harvey threw her a rope as he rushed forward, but she missed the rope and it fell into the dark water.

Harvey looked around in a panic. "The dinghy's gone!"

Terry Jo saw the dinghy drifting away off the port side. Harvey leaped into the water and swam toward the dinghy until Terry Jo could not see him anymore. He wasn't coming back.

Waves were breaking over the deck now. The *Bluebelle* was sinking fast. Terry Jo remembered the cork life ring on the starboard side and unlashed it just as the boat sunk out of sight, a ghost ship that would never be found.

Terry Jo was alone in the deafening blackness of the sea. She held tight to the canvas-covered float, afraid of being sucked down by the sinking *Bluebelle*. She lay low on the rotting ropes that formed the bottom of her life raft and stifled her crying, afraid of being heard by Harvey, who she now believed was a killer.

Worse, she had no food, no water, no protection against the elements or predators, no way to signal for help.

There was only darkness.

Until the rain came later that night and the sea lit up for a little girl alone.

"SOMETHING IS KIND OF WRONG HERE"

A little past noon the next morning, Seaman Dennis Gochenour was sitting watch in the poop deck of the tanker SS *Gulf Lion* when he spotted a life raft and dinghy 4 miles (6 kilometers) out. There was a man aboard, waving his shirt.

When the *Gulf Lion* came alongside to rescue the barefooted man wearing khaki pants and a flower-printed shirt, they made a gruesome discovery hidden beneath a small sail: the corpse of a little blond girl, wearing red shorts and a greenish short-sleeved shirt. The raft also contained a survival bag full of flares, food, and water-purifying equipment.

Once safely aboard, the man identified himself as Captain Julian Harvey, master of the ketch *Bluebelle*.

The boat, he told his rescuers, had been caught in a freak squall around midnight. Everyone—the five Duperraults, his wife, and Harvey—was on deck when a rogue, 40-mile (64 kilometer)-per-hour gust snapped the main mast, which pierced the deck and ruptured a fuel line below. It also pulled down the mizzen mast in a snarl of wires and rope, wounding some of the passengers.

A fire erupted and spread so quickly that he couldn't quell it with extinguishers. Soon, he was cut off from the others, who had taken refuge on the stern, were tangled in ruined rigging, or had already jumped overboard.

The *Bluebelle* was quickly consumed by flames and went down before Harvey could rescue anyone. He said he circled the area of the wreckage for several hours, looking for survivors, but found nobody, except the drowned body of a little girl in a life vest—he thought her name was Terry Jo—floating facedown in the sea. He claimed he tried to resuscitate her but couldn't.

Harvey, who bore no wounds of any kind, seemed unusually cool to the sailors who listened. They thought he might just be in shock. Neither Harvey nor the little girl smelled of smoke; their clothing wasn't scorched; the raft and dinghy showed no signs of fire.

His best guess was that everyone drowned as the boat sank, even though the children all wore life jackets in Harvey's account.

He even cast some of the blame on the Duperraults themselves.

"I don't have any use for city folks," he said. "They're not my kind of people anyhow. They get panicky. I run regular in the winter months—I'm about the only boat that runs between Miami and Nassau. I get them out in the boat and it gets rough and I've even had to lash them down to the deck."

The old sailors on the *Gulf Lion* had plenty of questions for Harvey, none answered. They couldn't imagine how a broken mast might pierce the deck and hull the way Harvey said, or why the lighthouse just 14 miles (23 kilometers) away never saw any fire on a dark night, or even why Harvey never asked about survivors.

Seaman Gochenour, the man who first saw Harvey's raft, had an unsettling feeling about the *Bluebelle*'s skipper.

"I looked at him back in the mess hall," Gochenour said a few days later. "You know, there are people you can look into their eyes, and you might look right down into the depth of them, and I looked at him just about like that. It looked like I could see clean down into his body and soul, you know. He shook his head and he turned and looked away. And I just thought to myself, 'Something is kind of wrong here.'"

> Harvey answered every question,
> although his answers seemed pat and
> unemotional. He expressed no remorse
> about the accident, even though his beloved
> new bride had likely perished.

Back in Miami, the news of the *Bluebelle*'s sinking was already hitting the papers. The death of six people and the survival of one in a squall was national news. So by the time Harvey returned to Miami, the Coast Guard, reporters, insurance men, and *Bluebelle* owner Harold Pegg were waiting with questions of their own.

On the morning of November 16, 1961, Coast Guard Lieutenant Ernest Murdock convened the official Coast Guard hearing into the *Bluebelle* wreck. He and Captain Robert Barber had been assigned to investigate the tragedy, which seemed to them to be much deeper than Julian Harvey's account. No debris, victims, or survivors had yet turned up almost four days later.

A smiling, cordial Harvey took the stand as the first witness. As the questioning began, so did his stammer and rolling eye, but Murdock attributed it to the ordeal he had survived, nothing more.

Harvey retold the story about the squall, the broken masts, the fire, and the sinking. He explained how he had searched two hours for survivors but found none. He claimed the radio was broken before he could radio an SOS, and he hadn't thought to send up emergency flares.

The more Harvey talked, the more incredulous Murdock became.

"Was everyone awake at the time of the accident?" the lieutenant asked.

"Everyone was awake," Harvey said. "The little eleven-year-old girl was screaming. I tried to keep her quiet. She probably had a nightmare or something. She didn't know what was going on. She woke up and wasn't wildly hysterical but with a little bit of shock."

Harvey answered every question, although his answers seemed pat and unemotional. He had a glib answer for every question, even when the answers were inconceivable for any experienced sailor. He expressed no remorse about the accident, even though his beloved new bride had likely perished.

But his story differed slightly from the tale he told after swearing a friend to secrecy the night before. In that version, Harvey claimed the masts fell on Arthur Duperrault and Dene, cutting them horribly.

"I lost my nerve when I saw their blood and guts on the deck," Harvey told his friend tearfully, "and I jumped overboard. The next thing I knew, I was pulling the little girl into a boat with me."

Murdock excused Harvey from the stand and called Harold Pegg, the *Bluebelle*'s owner. Harvey took a seat at the back of the room to listen to his boss's testimony.

Pegg hadn't been on the stand long when Captain Barber burst into the room. "They've found a survivor!" he announced. "A little girl is alive."

Harvey looked stunned. "Oh, my God!" he blurted out. "Isn't that wonderful?"

A few moments later, Harvey asked to be excused so he could make arrangements to explain the tragedy to his missing wife's family. He agreed to meet with Murdock and Barber the next morning to answer any further questions.

Harvey didn't go far. Using the name John Monroe of Tampa, he checked into the Sandman Motel, about 2 miles (3 kilometers) up Biscayne Boulevard from the Coast Guard offices, a little before 11 a.m. He went straight to his room and never came out.

In the room, Harvey unpacked photographs of his son, Lance, and of his wife, Dene. He propped them on top of the toilet tank and sat down naked on the cold tile with his back against the bathroom door.

Around noon the next day, a maid stumbled into a bloody mess. Harvey had slashed his left thigh and wrists with a double-edged razor blade, smeared his warm blood on the bathroom walls in grotesque scrawls, then slashed his own carotid artery. He was forty-four.

His two-page suicide note asked a friend to care for his son, Lance, then a fourteen-year-old student at Miami Military Academy.

"I'm going out now," Harvey wrote. "I'm a nervous wreck and just can't continue."

The *Bluebelle* was never mentioned. Investigators found a pile of unpaid bills and dunning letters among Harvey's papers, along with the insurance policy on Mary Dene's life, but no more solid answers about the *Bluebelle*. Whatever secrets Harvey kept were as lost as the *Bluebelle* itself.

Except that now there was another survivor and one more story to be told.

SOLE SURVIVOR

For three cold nights and blistering days, Terry Jo floated. She didn't sleep at all the night of the killing, afraid she'd bump into Captain Harvey somewhere in the dark. She forced herself to stay awake until dawn, keeping quiet and small.

She was adrift in the Northwest Providence Channel, a 1-mile (1.6 kilometer) deep underwater canyon threaded among the islands and dumping into the Gulf Stream between the Bahamas and Florida. If she wasn't found, her raft would be carried north and east, farther out to sea, deeper into the North Atlantic. The likelihood of her delicate raft surviving Atlantic seas was as infinitesimal as a little girl on a great ocean.

Her first morning adrift was sunny. Parrot fish nibbled at her buttocks and legs through the float's rope mesh, which was slowly disintegrating after years of being exposed to sun and saltwater. So she tried to balance as much as she could on the edges of the canvas-covered ring itself to keep from breaking through the ropes entirely.

When she saw distant islands on the horizon, she paddled with her little hands toward them. *That's where my dad is*, she thought. She imagined finding him and drinking wine, which she had never tasted, but because her parents drank it, it must be a comforting thing. But wind and currents made it difficult, and she drifted farther, not closer.

> Sleep was difficult and erratic. Terry Jo could see ships' distant lights at night, but she had neither enough strength nor hope to try to paddle toward them in the dark.

That night she slept for the first time. She dreamed of an airfield with blue lights, and as she ran toward it, she realized she had abandoned her life ring and was flailing about in the dark water. She feared sleeping after that and prayed for the morning to hurry.

When daylight finally came, the sky was overcast, and the water was rough. Ships and planes passed close, but they never saw her. She saw what she thought were sharks nearby, and she was barely able to cling to her fragile little raft as wave after wave crashed against her.

Sleep was difficult and erratic. She could see ships' distant lights at night, but she had neither enough strength nor hope to try to paddle toward them in the dark. And when she fell asleep, she dreamed of crashing into rocks or falling off her float into shark-infested water.

By the third morning, her salty skin was badly burned by the sun, which blinded her as it reflected off the surface of the sea. Her legs were cramping, and she felt as if every part of her was on fire. She hadn't eaten or drunk any fluid since before the *Bluebelle* disappeared, and her tongue and throat were drying out, her saliva thickening. Great clusters of sargassum floated all around her, but the idea of putting the salty weeds and their berries in her mouth sickened her.

The sea grew more dangerous, too. Winds picked up, and whitecaps crashed over the float. It was everything she could do to balance herself on it and not be thrown into the deep. She felt feverish and weak, but she clung to the ring with everything she had left.

Terry Jo had been adrift for eighty hours when the Coast Guard cut its search-and-rescue operations back. The chance of finding survivors was too slim to justify the costs of the planes and ships they had been sending out since Julian Harvey was found.

They were wrong.

A sailor aboard a Greek freighter, the *Captain Theo*, bound for Houston saw a white raft bobbing in the channel, a mile (1.6 kilometers) out. It had been all but invisible among the whitecaps. And the girl sitting in it, her legs dangling over the side, wore a white blouse. If he hadn't been looking directly at the raft, he might have missed it in the endless camouflage of white waves.

The crew of the *Captain Theo* plucked the dazed little girl from the sea. They carried her up a rope ladder to the deck and asked who she was and what had happened. She could muster only a hand sign—a thumb's down—before she fell unconscious.

When Terry Jo regained her wits thirty minutes later, she answered only a few crucial questions before lapsing into a deep sleep. The *Captain Theo* quickly telegraphed the Coast Guard in Miami:

"Picked up blonde girl, brown eyes, from small white raft, suffering exposure and shock. Name Terry Jo Duperrault. Was on Bluebelle.*"*

A Coast Guard helicopter was immediately dispatched to the *Captain Theo* to bring Terry Jo to Miami's Mercy Hospital, where a throng of reporters waited for their first glimpse of the "sea waif."

She was comatose. Her skin was badly burned and her delicate lips had swollen and split open, but those were the least of her problems. She had survived about as long as any human could go without water, and the dehydration had damaged her kidneys. Her heart was beating erratically and could barely push her thickened blood through her little body.

Her doctor said one more day adrift would certainly have killed her.

If she had been exposed to the broiling sun for the entire time—nearly four days—she would likely have died, her doctors said. Periods of overcast skies and rain may have delayed her death long enough for the *Captain Theo* to find her.

Intravenous lines were replenishing Terry Jo's lost fluids and electrolytes, but her body temperature was too high and her heartbeat too weak. Her doctor feared she might suffer a heart attack, massive organ failure, or pneumonia. Only time would tell.

In the meantime, police guards were posted outside her hospital room. Too many unanswered questions swirled around Julian Harvey's accounts to leave the only other *Bluebelle* witness unprotected.

Terry Jo emerged from her coma on the second day in the hospital but remained in critical condition. She couldn't speak, but she ate a little, and her vital signs were improving.

The world was waiting to hear from Terry Jo, but her doctor wouldn't let her speak to anyone—nor anyone speak to her. Her physical state was too precarious to endure the news that her entire family was likely murdered and that Captain Harvey had survived the sinking, and that he had just been found dead a few hours before in a gory suicide.

But she knew. Even before anyone told her the gruesome details, Terry Jo sensed she was alone in the world. She began to fret about how she would get home to Wisconsin on her own, how she would live without a family or money, and how she could possibly pay for her hospital care.

When someone finally told her that Rene's body had been found, Terry Jo did the macabre math. She'd seen her mother and brother dead on the *Bluebelle*, so only her father was unaccounted for. She began to imagine all the scenarios in which her father might have survived, swam to a nearby island, and was waiting to be rescued, too. It obsessed her because now more than ever, she needed her father.

By her third day in the hospital, letters and gifts began trickling in from a world that had been touched by the rescue of "brave little Terry Jo." Headlines began to call her the "sea waif" and "sea orphan." The crew of the *Captain Theo* sent a life-sized doll—much like one she had lost when the *Bluebelle* sank. Others sent money and offers to adopt her. One day, a rosary from Pope John arrived.

DARK DETAILS

On the same day Harvey's corpse was found, Coast Guard investigators Murdock and Barber were allowed to interview Terry Jo.

Speaking with a calm detachment into a tape recorder, she recounted everything she had seen and heard that night—the stomping, her brother's cries, her mother's bloodied body, the permeating smell of diesel, Captain Harvey with the rifle, the rising water, Harvey jumping overboard, her scramble for the cork float—the dark silence.

"Terry Jo, did you see a broken mast or fallen sails?" Captain Barber asked.

"The main sail was all wrinkled and going all over, and the mast was leaning," she said. "I wasn't sure if the mizzen was up, but I think it was."

"You mean that the masts were up but the sails were all slack, is that correct?"

"The masts were up, yes."

"You didn't see any damage or broken part on the mast, did you?"

"No."

In a word, a little girl had unwittingly shot down Harvey's wild story about a snapped mast and a tangle of wires. And she wasn't finished.

"You say you saw nobody on deck except the captain, but you saw the blood," Barber said. "Could you have seen others if they had been there?"

"I suppose I could, because there was a lot of light," Terry said. "It was coming from lights on top of the sail."

THE SEA HAS ALWAYS INSPIRED A SWEET MELANCHOLY FOR TERE DUPERRAULT FASSBENDER, WHO BARELY SURVIVED FOUR DAYS ADRIFT AFTER HER FAMILY WAS MASSACRED ON A CHARTERED YACHT NEAR THE BAHAMAS IN 1961.

Ron Franscell

A light at the top of the main mast was always burning at night, and a pair of lower floodlights would have illuminated the deck. Barber and Murdock knew immediately that if the main mast had really collapsed, there would have been no lights.

"Did you see any fire at any time?" Barber continued.

"No, but I smelled oil."

"But you did not see any fire at any time, is that correct?"

"That's correct."

"And you did not smell any smoke? You recognize the smell of smoke and fire, don't you? You did not smell anything like a fire?"

"No."

Terry Jo had no idea that the story she was telling differed significantly from Harvey's. The interviews continued over the next several days, and Barber and Murdock became more convinced that they were dealing not with a tragic accident at sea, but with a mass murder.

Terry Jo remained in the hospital for two weeks. During that time, she learned that her family was lost, that Harvey had survived and told a vastly different tale, and that Rene had been buried in Green Bay, alone.

The newspapers reported that Harvey, according to his last wishes, was buried at sea in a red velvet shroud because he wanted to be with his dead wife. Dark details of his enigmatic life began to surface, including the numerous boat disasters and the suspicious 1949 car accident that killed his third wife and mother-in-law.

A few months after Terry Jo's rescue, the Coast Guard issued its three-hundred-page official report on the *Bluebelle* sinking. Its conclusion: A destitute Harvey had likely killed his wife and most of the Duperrault family before scuttling the *Bluebelle* to collect $40,000 on his wife's double-indemnity life insurance policy. The report said the boat might lie as deep as 780 fathoms—almost a mile deep—making salvage operations available in 1962 nearly impossible and leaving many forensic questions unanswered.

The report also suggested a literal sea change that was soon adopted: All boats' life-saving equipment should be colored bright orange to make them easier for rescuers to see.

Ironically, when Barber and Murdock finally told Terry Jo that Harvey had killed himself, she felt bad for the man. She hadn't seen him hurt anyone, so for many years she didn't see him for the monster he was.

But none of her feelings ran deep. Terry Jo floated along the surface of her emotions as she had floated at sea, overexposed and barely clinging only to the things that would save her life.

At eleven, one life had ended, and another one began.

She never got angry, never grieved.

And she never cried.

HEALING

Terry Jo went home to Green Bay to live with an aunt and uncle who shielded her from any reminders of the tragedy. She existed within a kind of protective bubble, where nobody was allowed to talk about "the accident." No sadness, grief, or anger was tolerated, as if it were a sign of weakness.

Once, while attending a funeral, Terry Jo began to cry uncontrollably. She fled to a restroom where she could weep privately, but a relative came in and snapped, "Terry Jo, that's enough."

Her aunt and uncle deflected any intrusions that might conjure grief. Reporters often asked to talk to her, but they were always refused, except for one photo shoot in which nobody was allowed to speak, only snap pictures of a happy Terry Jo at play.

Depression crept up on her. She saved clippings from the letters strangers sent and read them when she could be alone. At parties, she heard other children complaining about their mothers and fathers, and she wished so badly she could say the words *mother* and *father*.

Only a couple of years after her rescue, "brave little Terry Jo" began calling herself "Tere" (pronounced the same as "Terry") in hopes of becoming somebody other than the child who must always portray a happy face to the world. As Tere, she could cry if she wanted to cry, and nobody would care.

Using money from her parents' life insurance and a $50,000 settlement from *Bluebelle* owner Harold Pegg, Tere enrolled herself in a swanky, all-girl private school in Illinois. When it became too lonesome, she went home and suffered a nervous breakdown.

She became obsessed with the notion that her father was still out there someplace. Maybe he had hit his head and lost his memory. Maybe he was stranded on a deserted island. Maybe he was looking for her, too.

She grew up—though in many ways, she never stopped being 11-year-old Terry Jo. After high school, she enrolled at the University of Wisconsin-Stevens Point, spent a summer session alone in Spain, and then abruptly dropped out.

Tere became a rootless vagabond. She followed a ski-bum boyfriend to Colorado for a year. She tried a little more college but quit. She first married in 1971 and had a daughter, Brooke. After divorcing, she and Brooke lived in a tent at Jungle Larry's African Safari in Florida. She married again in 1976 and moved with her Army husband to West Berlin, where she had two more children, Blaire and Brian—named after her dead brother.

That marriage, too, dissolved. So did a disastrous third.

In 1981, twenty years after the tragedy, Tere gave her first newspaper interview to the *Green Bay Press-Gazette*. She spoke candidly about how she never went back to the family home, how she desperately missed her father, how she retreated to her scrapbooks when she got too sad, and how she had lost a huge chunk of her childhood. She also pondered how her consuming fantasy about her father's survival colored her search for a true companion.

Tere married again in 1995 to Ron Fassbender, whom she met while working for the Wisconsin Department of Natural Resources' water management division. They moved to Kewaunee, Wisconsin, on the shore of Lake

Michigan—ironically, just 3o miles (48 kilometers) from where, in 1927, the *Bluebelle* was the first yacht ever built by the Sturgeon Bay Boat Works.

In 1999, at the urging of a psychologist, Tere agreed to be injected with sodium amytal, a "truth serum," in hopes of recalling more details about the *Bluebelle* tragedy. But she also wanted to know with more certainty if she had told the truth back in 1961, too.

"I never felt afraid to confront the possibility that there might have been something I didn't remember because it was too terrible, but I knew I had already remembered some pretty terrible things," she wrote in her 2010 memoir, *Alone*. "When the psychiatrist decided that I hadn't repressed anything, and assured me that I had told the truth, I felt a new level of peace in my life, another step in healing."

But Tere has never stopped believing her beloved father is still alive, just lost. Her head, her family, and her lawyer have all told her it is impossible and that she should move on. But somewhere deep down in the heart of her heart, she has always hoped she will see him again.

Despite the ordeal that has defined her, Tere is drawn to the water. The sound of waves and the smell of the salty breeze take her back to happier times. And even in her late fifties, she holds out the faint possibility that she might look up one day and see her father walking down the beach toward her.

"I love being near the water and take as many walks along the shoreline as I can," she wrote in *Alone*. "It is a wonderful feeling but, at times, melancholy . . . I can hear the waves that sometimes remind me of my time on the ocean and of my family from so long ago. I feel closer to them there. While there is a melancholy feeling, it is also soothing; all in all, a sweet sadness. It is a place where my loyal little dog, Angel, and I can just be free and think."

Tonight, she walks along the jetty out to the Kewaunee lighthouse. A storm is rising in the west, but she doesn't want to go home.

Again, Tere is waiting on the rain.

SELECTED BIBLIOGRAPHY

The author conducted personal interviews with the survivors, their families, police, and others, and amassed thousands of pages of documents, clippings, videos, and photographs. This bibliography provides an overview of his most substantial print references.

"THEY'RE ALL DEAD": CHARLES COHEN AND THE INSANE SPREE KILLER HOWARD UNRUH

Abstract of Psychological Evaluation of Howard B. Unruh (Case No. 47,077), Trenton State Hospital, Trenton, New Jersey. September 12, 1949.

Berger, Meyer, "Veteran Kills 12 in Mad Rampage on Camden Street," *New York Times*, September 7, 1949.

Boyer, Barbara, "Sixty Years Ago Today, a Camden Gunman Killed 13," *Philadelphia Inquirer*, September 6, 2009.

"Crazed Veteran Slays 12 Persons in Camden," *Philadelphia Inquirer*, September 6, 1949.

Norman, Michael, "Criminal and Crazy," *New Jersey Monthly*, April 1979.

Norman, Michael, "A Portrait of the Jersey Mass Killer as an Old Man," *New York Times*, March 8, 1982.

"The Quiet One," *Time*, September 19, 1949.

Shubin, Seymour, "Camden's One-Man Massacre," Triangle Publications, December 1949.

"Tear Gas Ends Mass Murder," *Philadelphia Inquirer*, September 7, 1949.

Transcript of Camden Police Interview of Howard Barton Unruh, City Detective Bureau, Camden Police Department, Camden, New Jersey. September 6, 1949.

"Veteran Runs Amok for 12 Murderous Minutes," *Life*, September 19, 1949.

"TODAY IS GONNA BE VISUAL": BRENT DOONAN AND THE ATLANTA DAY-TRADER SPREE

Cohen, Adam, "A Portrait of the Killer," *Time*, August 9, 1999.

Doonan, Brent. *Murder at the Office*. Far Hills, NJ: New Horizons Press, 2006.

Dugan, Ianthe Jeanne, Ellen Nakashima, and Marc Fisher, "Barton Suffered Heavy Losses Before Shooting Rampage," *Washington Post*, July 31, 1999.

Goldstein, Amy, "Gunman's First Wife, Mother-in-law Slain in '93," *Washington Post*, July 30, 1999.

Hill, Shelley, "Atlanta Shooting Victims Remembered in Services,"
Associated Press, August 2, 1999.

Sack, Kevin, "Killer Confessed in Letter Spiked with Rage," *New York Times*,
July 31, 1999.

Torpy, Bill, "Ten Years Later, Buckhead Massacre Resounds," *Atlanta
Journal-Constitution*, July 25, 2009.

SEVENTY-SEVEN MINUTES IN HELL: KEITH THOMAS AND THE MCDONALD'S MASSACRE

Brown, Gary, "The Monday After: Mass Murderer James O. Huberty Was Born
in Canton," *Canton Repository*, July 19, 2009.

Flynn, Georg, and Ed Jahn, "A Quiet Upbringing But a Rage to Kill,"
San Diego Union, July 20, 1984.

Golden, Arthur, "21 Die in San Ysidro Massacre," *San Diego Union*, July 19,
1984.

Gomez, Linda, "Ninety Minutes at McDonald's," *Life*, January 1985.

Granberry, Michael, "A 77-Minute Moment in History That Will Never Be
Forgotten," *Los Angeles Times*, July 16, 1989.

Gresko, Jessica, "20 Years Later, San Ysidro McDonald's Massacre
Remembered," Associated Press, July 18, 2004.

Kreidler, Mark J., "San Ysidro Site is Barren, but the Agony Lives On,"
Los Angeles Times, January 6, 1985.

"When Rage Turns Into Mass Murder," *U.S. News & World Report*, July 30, 1984.

NIGHTMARE AT NOON: SUZANNA GRATIA HUPP AND THE LUBY'S MASSACRE

Chin, Paula, "A Texas Massacre," *Time*, November 4, 1991.

Hayes, Thomas C., "Gunman Kills 22 and Himself in Texas Cafeteria,"
New York Times, October 17, 1991.

Hupp, Suzanna Gratia. *From Luby's to the Legislature: One Woman's Fight Against
Gun Control.* Privateer Publications, 2009.

Karpf, Jason and Elinor Karpf. *Anatomy of a Massacre.* WRS Publishing, 1994.

Kelley, Robert L., "EMS Response to Mass Shootings," *EMS*, October 2008.

Killeen (Texas) Police Department, Complete Police File on the Luby's
Cafeteria Massacre.

"Luby's Cafeteria, Shut Since Killings, Reopens," *Washington Post*, March 13,
1992.

"Luby's Tragedy: 15 Years Later," *Killeen Daily Herald*, October 15, 2006.

Merchant Mariner's Service Record of Georges Pierre Hennard, National Maritime Center, United States Coast Guard, Martinsburg, West Virginia.

Morello, Carol, "A Daughter's Regret," *Washington Post*, May 13, 2000.

Woodbury, Richard, "Ten Minutes in Hell," *Time*, October 28, 1991.

DEATH FROM ABOVE: TIM URSIN AND THE HOWARD JOHNSON SNIPER

"Death in New Orleans," *Time*, January 22, 1973.

Hernon, Peter. *A Terrible Thunder: The Story of the New Orleans Sniper*. Doubleday, 1978.

Hustmyre, Chuck, "Mark Essex," TruTV Crime Library, 2007.

Moody, Sid, "Essex 'Saw the World,' Began Hating Whites," Associated Press, January 13, 1973.

New Orleans (Louisiana) Police Department, Complete Police File on the Howard Johnson Sniper Mark Essex.

New Orleans Times-Picayune archives, January 7–20, 1973.

Persica, Dennis, "A City Under Siege," *New Orleans Times-Picayune*, January 7, 1998.

Smith, Phil, "Mark Essex—A New Hero in an Old Struggle," *Chicago Metro News*, January 20, 1973.

"Sniper Buried in Kansas," United Press International, January 13, 1973.

THE DARKEST TOWER: ROLAND EHLKE AND THE TEXAS TOWER SNIPER

Austin American and *Austin Statesman* archives, August 1–8, 1966.

Ehlke, Roland, "Reflections of Violence," *Concordian Magazine*, Fall 2006.

Helmer, William J., "The Madman in the Tower," *Texas Monthly*, August 1986.

Lavergne, Gary. *A Sniper in the Tower: The Charles Whitman Murders*. Denton, TX: University of North Texas Press, 1997.

"The Madman in the Tower," *Time*, August 12, 1966.

"Milwaukeean Heard Shot, Was Hit," *Milwaukee Sentinel*, August 2, 1966.

Rohde, Marie, "High Callings," *Northwestern Lutheran Magazine*, September 15, 1986.

"Texas Sniper's Murder Rampage," *Life*, August 12, 1966.

EVIL ON THE FRONT PORCH: DIANNE ALEXANDER AND THE SERIAL KILLER DERRICK TODD LEE

Mustafa, Susan, Tony Clayton, and Sue Israel. *Bloodbath*. New York: Pinnacle Books, 2009.

Naanes, Marlene, "The Two Sides of Derrick Todd Lee," *Baton Rouge Advocate*, June 22, 2003.

O'Toole, Mary Ellen, "Profile of the Baton Rouge Serial Killer," Federal Bureau of Investigation Behavioral Analysis Unit, Quantico, Virginia. Fall 2003.

Stanley, Stephanie A. *An Invisible Man: The Hunt for a Serial Killer Who Got Away With a Decade of Murder*. New York: The Berkeley Publishing Group, 2006.

"Suspected Killer Was Trailed for a Decade," *Washington Post*, May 29, 2003.

THE DEVIL YOU KNOW: ANTHONY MAJZER AND SERIAL KILLER DAVID MAUST

Dolan, Bill and Mark Kiesling, "Maust's History Filled with Violence, Instability," *Northwest Indiana Times*, January 4, 2004.

Kiesling, Mark, "Maust's Last Words," *Northwest Indiana Times*, January 20, 2006.

Maust, Dori. *Bloodstained: When No One Comes Looking*. Outskirts Press, 2009.

Robinson, Ruthann, "Maust Recalls Death Details," *Northwest Indiana Times*, December 18, 2005.

Robinson, Ruthann, "Maust's Troubled Childhood Led to Murders, Experts Say," *Northwest Indiana Times*, November 1, 2005.

A PRAYER BEFORE DYING: MISSY JENKINS AND THE WEST PADUCAH HIGH SCHOOL SHOOTING

Jenkins, Missy and William Croyle. *I Choose to Be Happy*. LangMarc Publishing, 2008.

"The Kid No One Noticed: Guns, He Concluded, Would Get His Classmates' Attention," *U.S. News & World Report*, October 12, 1998.

"Media Companies are Sued in Kentucky Shooting," *New York Times*, April 13, 1999.

Moore, Mark H., Carol V. Petrie, Anthony A. Braga, and Brenda L. McLaughlin, editors. *Deadly Lessons: Understanding Lethal School Violence*. National Academies Press: 2003.

"The Only Sense is of Loss," *Los Angeles Times*, December 2, 2002.

Samples-Gutierrez, Karen, "Torment of a Teen Killer," *Cincinnati Enquirer*, September 14, 2002.

ALONE IN A DARK SEA: TERRY JO DUPERRAULT AND THE BLUEBELLE MURDERS

Autopsy Report on Julian A. Harvey (Case No. 2646A), Metropolitan Dade County Medical Examiner's Office, Miami, Florida. November 18, 1961.

Fassbender, Tere Duperrault and Richard Long. *Alone*. Green Bay, WI: TitleTown Publishing, 2010.

"The Bluebelle's Last Voyage," *Time*, December 1, 1961.

"The Bluebelle Mystery," *Life*, December 1, 1961.

"Bluebelle Scuttled, Coast Guard Rules," Associated Press, April 25, 1962.

"Of Bloody Decks, Death and a Bluebelle," United Press International, December 11, 1962.

Transcript of U.S. Coast Guard Hearing Regarding the Sinking of Ketch Bluebelle, U.S. Coast Guard Investigative Section. November–December, 1961.

ACKNOWLEDGMENTS

Like anyone who plows these fields, I owe the greatest debt to the people who shared their stories at the risk of reliving them. Their memories are the beating heart of this book, and they deserve my deepest thanks: Dianne Alexander, Charles Cohen, Brent Doonan, Roland Ehlke, Tere Jo Fassbender, Suzanna Gratia Hupp, Missy Jenkins Smith, Anthony Majzer, Keith Martens, and Tim Ursin. They inspire me.

This book would not have been as authoritative without the insights and aid of many professionals who loaned their skills to it. Many thanks to former FBI profiler Mary Ellen O'Toole; Dr. Katherine Ramsland, Dr. Richard Noll, and Dr. Amy Saborsky; Captain Heather Kouts, New Orleans Police Department; Dr. Shawn Cowper, Yale University; Coast Guard Capt. Ernest Murdock (Ret.); Dr. Kathleen Nader; Barbara Boyer; Michael C. Lewis, U.S. Coast Guard National Maritime Center; Caitlin Rother; Nancy Renick; Robert Kelley; Paul Schopp; Jason Laughlin; Chester Cedars; Michelle McKee; and Reverend Carl Petering.

You would not be reading this except for the investment and wisdom of Will Kiester, Jill Alexander, and Cara Connors of Fair Winds Press, and my agent Gina Panettieri.

And most of all, I give thanks to (and for) my wife Mary, the one who always saw me off and always greeted me at the end of every journey. She makes me want to live forever.

ABOUT THE AUTHOR

Ron Franscell is a best-selling author and journalist whose atmospheric true crime/memoir *The Darkest Night* was hailed as a direct descendant of Truman Capote's *In Cold Blood* and established him as one of the most provocative new voices in narrative nonfiction. His work has appeared in the *Washington Post*, *Chicago Sun-Times*, *San Francisco Chronicle*, *Denver Post*, *San Jose Mercury-News*, *St. Louis Post-Dispatch*, and *Milwaukee Journal-Sentinel*. *Delivered from Evil* is his fifth book. Ron grew up in Wyoming and now lives in Texas.

INDEX

OTHER BOOKS
BY RON FRANSCELL

FICTION

Angel Fire (1998)

The Deadline (1999)

The Obituary (2010)

NONFICTION

Fall / The Darkest Night (2008)

A Crime Buff's Guide to Outlaw Texas (2010)